"*Emerging Perspectives in Art Therapy* is a unique, forward thinking ... work exploring future considerations for art therapy clinicians, educators, and students. A plethora of topics provide a substantive examination of arising, future landscapes; a progressive book that is rich in both breadth and depth of topics and content. A definite must read contribution to the profession."

**Janice Hoshino, Ph.D, ATR-BC, LMFT, ATCS**, Director, Creative Arts Therapy Institute, Antioche University Seattle

"Grounded in philosophy and theory with the intention of advancing the science of art therapy, Dr's. Carolan and Backos have gathered talented authors who do just that. These author/art therapists place the practice of art therapy in context while not forgetting process. As a feminist therapist, I appreciate how the authors promote culture, race, gender, and sexual orientation in the service of social justice. After 25 years as a clinician, I learned from this book."

**Susan Radbourne, Ph.D.**, Psychologist, Cleveland, Ohio

"An important and needed contribution to the field of art therapy, *Emerging Perspectives in Art Therapy* is based in theory and translates theory to practice. It explores influences from novel disciplines, including neuropsychology and technology, to art therapy. Carolan and Backos, who are board certified art therapists as well as psychologists and researchers, apply these multifaceted lenses to the study and practice of art therapy."

**Kristin Samuelson, Ph.D.**, Assistant Professor of Psychology at University of Colorado Colorado Springs

"As society wades through propaganda on the quest for truth, Carolan and Backos gift us with an essential compendium that critically examines contemporary art therapy theory and practice in the early 21st century. Written with competency and inclusion, this timely book respects the history of art therapy while simultaneously clarifying the present and informing the future. This text is a valuable and necessary contribution as the profession evolves through research and towards a unified definition of best practices."

**Juliet King, MA, ATR-BC, LPC, LMHC**, Director of Art Therapy and Assistant Professor, Herron School of Art and Design, IUPUI, Adjunct Assistant Professor, Department of Neurology, Indiana University School of Medicine

"Carolan and Backos have employed thoughtful and articulate individuals to provide current and contemporary writings in the field of art therapy. This comprehensive book covers both theory and practice issues. The book begins with philosophy, theory, and research, but it does not stop there. An array of timely and substantive topics is also covered including pedagogic concerns, neuroscience, issues of diversity and social change, and global perspectives. All this in a slim, but mighty volume."

**Marcia L. Rosal**, Professor Emerita, Florida State University

# Emerging Perspectives in Art Therapy

Art therapy is in a transitional phase where new paradigms of thinking, research methods, and ways of knowing are emerging. *Emerging Perspectives in Art Therapy* explores the knowledge base of art therapy by examining old assumptions and developing new knowledge. Dr. Carolan and Dr. Backos guide the reader through a multifaceted understanding of art therapy's core assumptions, philosophies, and theories. The second part of the book entrenches the reader in emergent knowledge in art therapy practices through a cultural lens. This book provides opportunities to explore art therapists' relationships with technology, ethics, education and neuroscience and challenges the reader to think about education, social justice, and community wisdom in novel ways. *Emerging Perspectives in Art Therapy* offers a unique contribution to the dialogue about pedagogy and philosophy in art therapy and offers insights for art therapists and other allied professionals regarding the use of art in a therapeutic and community context.

**Richard Carolan, Ed.D., ATR-BC,** is a Board-Certified Art Therapist and a Licensed Psychologist. He designed, developed, and currently serves as the director of the Ph.D. in Art Therapy at Notre Dame de Namur University. He has over 25 years of experience as an educator in Art Therapy Psychology and 35 years of clinical experience in working primarily with adolescents, adults, and families. Dr. Carolan has a private practice in Northern California and is the training director for Art Therapy/MFT interns in the San Mateo School District in Northern California. He is the 2014 recipient of the Educator of the Year Award from AATA and the Keller Teaching Award from Notre Dame de Namur University. His areas of professional interest and inquiry include addiction, psychological recovery, and intentional living.

**Amy Backos, Ph.D., ATR-BC,** is a Board Certified Art Therapist, Licensed Psychologist, and Chair of Graduate Art Therapy Psychology at Notre Dame de Namur University located in the San Francisco Bay Area. She serves as a member of the AATA Research Committee and of the Editorial Board of *Art Therapy: Journal of the American Art Therapy Association*. In addition to teaching in the MA and Ph.D. Art Therapy programs, she is Chair of the Internal Review Board at Notre Dame. She teaches art therapy in Nicaragua, works as a consultant to international businesses, and provides art therapy at a residential substance abuse treatment facility. Her clinical work includes 20 years with children, teens, and adults who experienced sexual assault and intimate partner violence, combat trauma, and substance abuse disorders. Additionally, Dr. Backos has six years of experience with the Veteran's Affairs Hospital providing evidence-based treatments and art therapy for veterans with PTSD, as well as working as a research associate conducting research on PTSD with Vietnam and Iraq veterans.

# Emerging Perspectives in Art Therapy
Trends, Movements, and Developments

Edited by Richard Carolan
and Amy Backos

NEW YORK AND LONDON

First published 2018
by Routledge
711 Third Avenue, New York, NY 10017

and by Routledge
2 Park Square, Milton Park, Abingdon, Oxon, OX14 4RN

*Routledge is an imprint of the Taylor & Francis Group, an informa business*

© 2018 Taylor & Francis

The right of Richard Carolan and Amy Backos to be identified as the authors of the editorial material, and of the authors for their individual chapters, has been asserted in accordance with sections 77 and 78 of the Copyright, Designs and Patents Act 1988.

All rights reserved. No part of this book may be reprinted or reproduced or utilized in any form or by any electronic, mechanical, or other means, now known or hereafter invented, including photocopying and recording, or in any information storage or retrieval system, without permission in writing from the publishers.

*Trademark notice*: Product or corporate names may be trademarks or registered trademarks, and are used only for identification and explanation without intent to infringe.

*Library of Congress Cataloging-in-Publication Data*
Names: Carolan, Richard, editor.
Title: Emerging perspectives in art therapy : trends, movements, and developments / edited by Richard Carolan and Amy Backos.
Description: New York, NY : Routledge, 2018. | Includes bibliographical references.
Identifiers: LCCN 2017047229 (print) | LCCN 2017048336 (ebook) | ISBN 9781315624310 (ebk) | ISBN 9781138652347 (hbk) | ISBN 9781138652354 (pbk)
Subjects: LCSH: Art therapy. | Art therapy—Methdology.
Classification: LCC RC489.A7 (ebook) | LCC RC489.A7 E46 2018 (print) | DDC 616.89/1656—dc23
LC record available at https://lccn.loc.gov/2017047229

ISBN: 978-1-138-65234-7 (hbk)
ISBN: 978-1-138-65235-4 (pbk)
ISBN: 978-1-315-62431-0 (ebk)

Typeset in Sabon
by Apex CoVantage, LLC

We dedicate this book to the next generation of art therapists—the harbingers of new ways of knowing art and the human experience; to Dr. Doris Arrington, from whom we have both learned so much; and to our loved ones who held the ground and allowed us to know ourselves.

For Charlie who says *Yes!* to adventure & believes in my dreams. And for our son Oliver, who inspires new dreams with his grace and humor. AB

For Julie, Maggie, Theeus and Taram–my co-artists in life. RC

# Contents

| | |
|---|---|
| *Contributing Authors* | xi |
| *List of Figures* | xv |
| *List of Plates* | xvi |
| *Introduction* | xvii |
| RICHARD CAROLAN AND AMY BACKOS | |

**PART I**
## Theory          1

1 **Philosophical Foundations of Art Therapy**    3
AMY BACKOS

2 **Theory and Art Therapy**    17
RICHARD CAROLAN AND KARRIE STAFFORD

3 **Art Therapy and Neuropsychology**    33
RICHARD CAROLAN AND AMY HILL

4 **Art Therapy Pedagogy**    48
AMY BACKOS AND RICHARD CAROLAN

5 **The Road Ahead: Preparing for the Future of Art
Therapy Research**    58
GIRIJA KAIMAL

6 **Transcending Media: Tangible to Digital and Their
Mixed Reality**    74
NATALIE CARLTON WITH TERESA SIT AND DUSTIN RYAN YU

x   *Contents*

**PART II**
**Practice**                                                                    91

7  **Ethics in Art Therapy**                                                     93
   LISA MANTHE AND RICHARD CAROLAN

8  **Wisdom Through Diversity in Art Therapy**                                  105
   LOUVENIA JACKSON, CLAUDIA MEZZERA,
   AND MELISSA SATTERBERG

9  **Art Therapy and Social Change**                                            123
   BY JENNIFER HARRISON

10 **Global Art Therapy**                                                       134
   ARNELL ETHERINGTON READER

11 **Emerging Paradigms in Art Therapy Supervision: The
   Use of Response Art**                                                        155
   GWEN SANDERS

   *Index*                                                                      169

# Contributing Authors

**Natalie Carlton, Ph.D., LPCC, ATR-BC,** is an associate professor and director of Drexel University's Art Therapy and Counseling program, which is an integral part of the larger Creative Arts Therapies Department. She has a devoted interest in media use and has engaged in reflective art therapy practices with diverse materials, including fabric crafts, clay and sculpture, drawing and painting, as well as sand play, photography, sound recording, and printmaking in her previous studio practice for children, youth, adults, and families in Northern New Mexico. Social justice art and movements, as well as power, privilege, and oppression frameworks are additional foci for her clinical and teaching approaches, research, and applied skill development. She is widely published on the topic of digital art therapy.

**Arnell Etherington Reader, Ph.D., MFT, ATR-BC,** is Professor Emeritus in the Graduate Art Therapy Psychology Department, Notre Dame de Namur University in California; she has been lecturing for 26 years. She continues teaching NDNU's International Art Therapy class in the UK, as well as Ph.D. and Masters classes. Having moved to the UK six years ago, she now lectures at Art Therapy Northern Programme, has a small private practice in Wokingham, and offers Living Art weeklong painting workshops. She is a licensed art psychotherapist and clinical psychologist in both the US and UK.

**Jennifer Harrison, Psy.D., ABPP, ATR-BC,** is a Board Certified Licensed Psychologist and a Board Certified Registered Art Therapist. She holds standing as a Diplomat for the American Academy of Experts in Traumatic Stress. She holds a Doctor of Psychology in Clinical Psychology from Adler University. She serves as assistant professor in the Graduate Art Therapy Psychology Department at Notre Dame de Namur University. Over the last 15 years, Dr. Harrison has worked in a variety of settings, including hospitals, community mental health clinics, school-based settings, and private practice with children, families, and individuals with complex presenting problems.

xii *Contributing Authors*

**Amy Hill, Ph.D., LMFT, ATR-BC,** completed her Ph.D. in Art Therapy at NDNU in 2016. Dr. Hill has facilitated individual, group, and family art therapy in an integrated trauma-informed education and specialty mental health treatment program for adolescents and families that have experienced complex trauma, which was the focus of her dissertation research. Additionally, she has facilitated art therapy groups for adults in a psychiatric hospital setting, for adolescents in residential treatment, for small communities in Nicaragua, and for adults suffering from chronic pain. Dr. Hill also serves as adjunct faculty in the Graduate Art Therapy Psychology Program at Notre Dame de Namur University, where she teaches courses in art therapy research.

**Louvenia Jackson, Ph.D., LMFT, ATR-BC,** is an assistant professor at Loyola Marymount University in the Marital Family Therapy/Art Therapy Department. She received her Ph.D. from Notre Dame de Namur University. Dr. Jackson's emphases are cultural humility, acquiring new knowledge, and self-exploration in art therapy. Her current motivation is on reciprocal community engagement and transformative learning in art therapy education. Dr. Jackson's work in art therapy pedagogy, cultural humility, and her dissertation research earned her the May 2016 Outstanding Service Award in the Art Therapy Psychology Department Ph.D. Program from Notre Dame de Namur University as well as the American Art Therapy Association 2016 Pearlie Roberson Scholarship.

**Girija Kaimal, Ed.D., MA,** is an assistant professor in the Department of Creative Arts Therapies at Drexel University. Her research examines physiological and psychological outcomes of creative visual self-expression. Dr. Kaimal currently leads two federally funded studies examining arts-based approaches to health, including working with family caregivers of patients with terminal illnesses and art therapy for military service members. She has led longitudinal evaluation research studies examining arts-based approaches to leadership development and teacher incentives and won national awards for her research. Dr. Kaimal is the Chair of the Research Committee for the American Art Therapy Association, an Assessment Fellow for Drexel University, serves on the editorial boards of four journals and the advisory boards of two educational foundations, and is a practicing visual artist. Dr. Kaimal has a Doctorate in Education from Harvard University, a Master's degree in Art Therapy from Drexel University, and a Bachelor's degree in design from the National Institute of Design in India.

**Lisa A. Manthe, Ph.D. Candidate, ATR-BC, LMFT,** focuses on developing and providing intensive clinical services to SED adolescents within New Directions School, known for its integrated and innovative approaches within art therapy. Ms. Manthe's current research focuses on the impact of nature-based trauma. Andy Goldsworthy inspired her art therapy groups on adolescence diagnosed with PTSD. In 2016, NorCATA awarded her with an HLM for her contributions to the field of art therapy. She is an adjunct professor in the Graduate Art Therapy Psychology department at Notre Dame de Namur University, and she is also a practicing artist who exhibits regularly. She believes that art is a way of creating community, vision, and voice.

**Claudia Mezzera, Ph.D., LMFT, ATR,** is a practicing marriage and family therapist and art therapist, and she is passionate about art therapy humanitarian work. Dr. Mezzera has worked with Ethiopian sex trafficking victims and piloted a multicultural self-care program for mental health care providers serving in Nicaragua. Dr. Mezzera is an adjunct faculty member in the Graduate Art Therapy Psychology department at Notre Dame de Namur University, and her recent research used imagery to evaluate self-esteem in Latinas. Her vision is to create curricula that enables service providers to offer culturally competent holistic art therapy programs in orphanages around the world.

**Gwen Sanders, Ph.D., LMFT, ATR-BC,** has been teaching in graduate art therapy programs for 20 years. She is HLM, Past President of NorCATA and a CAMFT and ATCS supervisor. Dr. Sanders is Practicum Director in Notre Dame de Namur University's Art Therapy Psychology department, where she received the George M. Keller Award for teaching excellence and her Ph.D. in Art Therapy in 2016. She and Dr. Amy Backos are the recipients of multiple research grants to take art therapists on service-learning community projects to Nicaragua since 2013. Dr. Sanders has had a private practice since 1996; worked as a clinical supervisor, EAP counselor and military family life consultant in Europe; and she has presented nationally.

**Melissa Satterberg, Ph.D., LMFT, ATR-BC,** has been working as a psychotherapist within the Greater Bay Area of California since 2005. Her works includes residential and outpatient day treatment for adults, foster care/adoption services, community and school-based treatment, and adult and adolescent intensive outpatient programs in a medical setting. Ms. Satterberg serves as adjunct professor in the Graduate Art Therapy Psychology Department at Notre Dame de Namur University. As a doctoral candidate, she focuses on the LGBT community, specifically with lesbian-identified women and using art therapy to increase understanding of sexual identity formation.

**Karrie Stafford, Ph.D., LMFT, ATR-BC,** holds a doctorate in art therapy, is a board certified and registered art therapist, and is a licensed marriage and family therapist. Dr. Stafford has a community-based private practice where she provides individual, couple, and family therapy as well as case consultation, training, and supervision. Her trainings

xiv *Contributing Authors*

focus on art therapy theory and practice. Dr. Stafford also specializes in dialectical behavioral therapy. Her work is rooted in mindfulness practices, while she maintains a humanistic perspective. Dr. Stafford teaches part time for the Graduate Art Therapy Psychology Department at Notre Dame de Namur University. Her teaching and research interests involve the relationship between artists and their art and the therapeutic potential therein.

# Figures

| | | |
|---|---|---|
| 1.1 | The role of the psychotherapist: Ashley Leonard. | 12 |
| 5.1 | Future clinical trends and related opportunities for researchers. | 63 |
| 6.1 | "Untitled." Photograph by Patrick Mooney, April 13, 2015. | 80 |
| 6.2 | "Confidence." Photograph by T. Sit, April 21, 2015. | 80 |
| 6.3 | Stills from "Cultura Ego." Video by Dustin Ryan Yu. | 82 |
| 6.4 | The HTC Vive headset and hand controls (left) and a Tilt Brush drawing in virtual space, as seen on the computer monitor (right). | 84 |
| 7.1 | "Inter-intra." Representing the evolving ethical frameworks we are in dialogue with as we encounter ethical challenges. | 94 |
| 8.1 | Transition. | 114 |
| 8.2 | A journal page from the collective journal research (Collaborator, Tervalon). | 116 |
| 9.1 | Darkness matters. | 126 |
| 9.2 | Outside myself. | 128 |
| 9.3 | Ambiguity. | 131 |
| 10.1 | Mentor doll. | 139 |
| 10.2 | Grounded feet but wandering heart. | 150 |
| 11.1 | Emerging transcendence. | 163 |
| 11.2 | Are words art? From the heart or the head? | 166 |

# Plates

1   The role of the healer by Erin Partridge.
2   The role of the artist: Response art by Joelle Fregeau.
3   *Grace.*
4   *Woman in water.*
5   *Eight Steps of Women* (re: Erickson) by Doris Arrington.
6   *Muñecas quitapenas* (worry dolls).
7   Nicaragua.
8   Recycled waste from my life.

# Introduction

*Emerging Perspectives in Art Therapy* grew from the challenge and the joy we found in exploring curriculum needs for the Ph.D. Art Therapy Psychology Department at Notre Dame de Namur University (NDNU). With the Carnegie Standards for higher education in mind, we created a growth-promoting climate for the Ph.D. students where our students were tasked with "generating new knowledge" in the field of art therapy. Years in the incubator under the vision and direction of the art therapy academic community at NDNU, the program opened its doors to the first cohort in 2013. Passion for the project and the ability to navigate the bureaucratic waters of both the university systems and the identified needs of the profession allowed the project to grow into a WASC approved program with enthusiastic students who were clearly ready to create new ways of knowing about art and art therapy.

We wanted to create a text that conveyed our passion and optimism for the future work of art therapists in a global society. This book adds to the chorus of literature that documents the creativity, clinical work, and research in the field of art therapy. This work offers a unique contribution by including discussion on how current phenomena in the literature, social life, and global politics informs our work. Furthermore, ideas from a host of experts offer suggestions for future directions in each of their areas of expertise. From these ideas, students and researchers can glean ideas for areas of future inquiry and research projects.

*Emerging Perspectives in Art Therapy* is divided into two sections to inform our work as we move into new areas of growth in art therapy: Theory and Practice. The theory section grew from the mission and responsibility for developing doctoral level students into leaders, visionaries, and even revolutionaries in the field of art therapy. It is based on writing and art from art therapists, philosophers, psychologists, neurologists, anthropologists, spiritual leaders, artists, musicians, and educators. The chapters in this section explore the influences from many disciplines that inform the transdisciplinary profession of art therapy (Talwar, 2016), including neuropsychology and technology. Additionally, we revisit areas in our professional domain such as philosophical

xviii *Introduction*

foundations, theory, research, and pedagogy, with fresh perspectives. We propose novel approaches that combine the work of our foremothers with prominent theories in art therapy and related disciplines. In selecting topics for the book, we share our vision for areas of growth in the profession and within each of us. In this work, we invite our readers to develop their own creative vision for the future of our profession.

Practice, the second section in *Emerging Perspectives in Art Therapy*, offers insight into clinical work as it relates to living in a global society and the ethical and social responsibilities we have as art therapists. Social justice and celebrating diversity are hallmarks of our university, and the American Art Therapy Association has taken an uplifting stand to support social justice for the disenfranchised and underserved. It is the underserved, poor, and overlooked who are generally the clients our students serve—we are obligated to move with grace and respect of our clients upon whose backs each generation of students are learning.

Attending to social justice and social change makes up important aspects of our ongoing work as clinicians, and we hope these chapters convey our continual striving for cultural humility and self-reflection (Tervalon & Murray-Garcia, 1998). Through these chapters on global art therapy, diversity, and social change, the authors contribute to the identity of art therapists as social change agents. The topic of ethics explores the collective wisdom of the field. Willingness to embrace the unknown is explored in the chapter on supervision and training. This curiosity and psychological mindedness fostered as students serves us throughout our professional lives in continuing to strive towards growth and self-actualization.

So, in the spirit of our global community, we share with you our collection of edited works by practitioners and leaders in the field who are embracing change in art therapy, promoting growth for those with whom they work and serve, and fully embodying cultural humility. We invite you, the reader, to first honor the wisdom of the elders in art therapy and then embrace the collective wisdom of the profession and the uncertainty of creative thinking brought forth in these chapters about emerging trends in art therapy.

## References

Talwar, S. (2016). Is there a need to redefine art therapy? *Art Therapy: Journal of the American Art Therapy Association, 33*(3), 116–118.

Tervalon, M., & Murray-Garcia, J. (1998). Cultural humility versus cultural competence: A critical distinction in defining physician training outcomes in multicultural education. *Journal of Health Care for the Poor and Underserved, 9*(2), 117–125.

# Part I
# Theory

# 1 Philosophical Foundations of Art Therapy

*Amy Backos*

## Foundational Pillars of Art Therapy

In order to forge ahead into emerging trends and new ways of thinking about art therapy, we are required to review some of the most relevant foundations of our work. To both remain true to the origins of art therapy, while simultaneously developing new paths, it is necessary to review the philosophical foundations on which art therapy rests. Talwar (2016) noted that the art therapy profession must continually and critically examine "the socially constructed definition of art therapy" (p. 117); doing so calls for continual self-reflection of our work with respect to the people we serve as art therapists. The philosophical foundations of art therapy intermingle to create the basis of its assumptions, practices, and research. This chapter describes three of the foundations that are critical to understanding the profession of art therapy and the role art therapists assume in communities, institutions, and agencies.

The primary foundational pillar is the role of healer. The role of modern-day healer rests on the assumption that individuals and communities can be healed and made better. This is coupled with the belief that we, as art therapists, have much to offer in healing individuals and improving the state of the world. The second foundational pillar is our role and identity as artists. We stand in the tradition of creators, makers, and provocateurs by constructing beauty and function, guiding and mentoring others, and challenging the status quo by nature of what we attend to in our art. We rely on art itself—the philosophy of art and its honored role across cultures—for its ability to document, soothe, provide catharsis as well as calm during times of chaos, and engage and challenge the viewer. The third philosophical foundation of art therapy is that of psychotherapist. Art therapy has deep roots in the field of psychology, including treating neuroses and promoting self-actualization, as well as researching and classifying human behavior. Therefore, the field of psychology heavily influences the research and practices of art therapists. This chapter will explore these three philosophical foundations of art therapy as a way to deepen our connection to the collective cultural experience of being an art therapist.

4  *Amy Backos*

*Healer*

As art therapists, we embody the role of healer. Healers play important roles in all religions and cultures—priest, shaman, doctor, chief, witch, elder, and psychotherapist (Jung, 1964; McNiff, 1979). They serve others through helping to reduce sickness, increase health, expel demons, and perhaps most importantly, to heal broken spirits. This is a sacred role that spans history, and art therapy is part of this long tradition of the honored healing arts; these include the laying on of hands, administering herbal or chemical medicines, talking, chanting, dancing, vision-questing, smudging, sweating, fasting, praying, making art and talismans, and pilgrimaging to sacred places. These healing arts rest on the optimistic belief that a person can be soothed, healed, emboldened, or even cured with the help of a guide, intention, treatment, and ritual. For those who have ailments, the *I Ching* teaches, "It furthers one to appoint helpers" (Kopp, 1972, p. 7), and indeed, the role of healer is critical for furthering individuals and communities. Three types of healers will be explored here: shaman, pilgrim, and activist.

What brings each of us to the profession of healer varies, but we can draw on this collective, archetypical identity as healer to lend inspiration, purpose, and personal satisfaction to our work. McNiff (1979) called attention to one aspect of this role of the art therapist: a shaman. Regardless of one's religion, culture, or personal beliefs, this is an early archetypical foundation on which much past and current work rests. The identity of art therapist is more than a healer who administers a single treatment—like a shaman, art therapists also participate in the process and serve as a guide. Unlike cult leaders and gurus who may seek to cultivate dependence from those with whom they work, the psychotherapist, shaman, and art therapist pursue treatment so refined and curative that they ideally, and eventually, render themselves obsolete and unnecessary in the lives of their clients (Kopp, 1972).

Healers accompany others on their own journey towards self-actualization and wellness to help them foster rewarding relationships and meaningful work through art making. Therefore, a second metaphor for our work as healer is that of the co-pilgrim. Ultimately, as art therapists, we are captains of our own voyages, and our meaningful relationships with clients become a vital part of our travels. This allegory of pilgrim and guide captures the stance I take in providing art therapy; I too am on a journey; thus, making art is necessary for me in tending to the aching souls of others; it is necessary for revitalizing myself when the work of therapy becomes painful. Clients seek relief from whatever ails them, and under the guidance of an art therapist they also become the proverbial pilgrim. As Kopp noted, "The contemporary pilgrim wants to be a disciple of the psychotherapist" (Kopp, 1972, p. 7). Using the metaphor of psychotherapy as a journey, modern healers empower clients

*Philosophical Foundations of Art Therapy* 5

with agency as they embody the role of teacher, mentor, therapist, or guide. Conversely, a guru teaches others using stories and metaphors, but the therapy client as pilgrim learns only by telling her or his own story (Kopp, 1972). In this way, art and art therapy help clients to tell their stories by creating coherent trauma narratives (Gantt & Tinnin, 2009) and re-authoring problem-saturated stories (Corey, 2013).

Witnessing the art process and final product can foster a healing and growth-promoting climate. In reflecting on her three-dimensional art, Erin Partridge, Ph.D., ATR-BC, considers the role an art therapist plays as a healer (Plate 1):

> The quick movements and fragile nature of finches obscure their potent symbolism. One thread at a time, a finch weaves and creates a sense of place, a sense of home and a sense of purpose. Finches are collaborative problem-solvers without attachment to a final product; they will continue to do and undo in search of comfort and security. The healer does not provide a premade nest and does not fill in or bandage holes. The healer joins in the weaving, simply holding the end of the thread as the draft is untangled.
>
> (E. Partridge, personal communication,
> April 2, 2017)

Art therapists are not only concerned with helping disenfranchised individuals, but we also engage in actions to impart long-lasting change on the social structures that support and maintain disenfranchisement. Therefore, artists, as community healers and activists, participate in social justice movements and work to help empower and heal disenfranchised communities. Artists have historically played a critical role in calling attention to injustices and oppression, and they assume the role of activist when they engage in social action art therapy (Kaplan, 2007, 2016). Art therapy researchers engaged in social justice include the marginalized and oppressed groups as co-researchers; thus, the voices of their co-researchers are central to the development of the research questions (Partridge, 2016; Potash & Kalmanowitz, 2016). Art therapists around the globe provide communities with opportunities to engage in collective art making for the purposes of fostering social engagement and action (Kaplan, 2007; 2016), crisis management (Anderson, 1995; Gantt & Tinnin, 2009; Howie, 2016), as well as growth and healing (Isis, 2016).

Long a part of the profession of art therapy, social action (Moon, 2016) in art therapy takes on renewed purpose as the world faces pressing attacks against social justice and freedom. Due to the rise of social media, the unparalleled access to information and people (Belkofer & McNutt, 2011), and the evolution in digital art (Orr, 2016), we now have unprecedented opportunities to collaborate with other artists, educators, and art therapists to effect attitude changes in our own communities and throughout the world. We can now easily touch the lives of our friends,

## 6  Amy Backos

families, and online acquaintances with our art and our vision for a better world. We need only look to Lynn Kapitan (2007, 2016), Don Jones, Robert Ault, Catherine and Bruce Moon (2016), and many others for inspiration about activism in art therapy (Potash & Kalmanowitz, 2016). A new generation of young, globally conscious art therapists picks up this call for social action through response art, community engagement, collaboration, and dialogue about the significance and necessity of art's contribution to social discourse.

### Artist

The second foundational pillar in art therapy is occupied by the art therapist's role as an artist. Formal training and apprenticed positions in art provide art therapists with the pragmatic tools of our profession. Our individual creative forces are honed with education in the fine arts and application of the tools to our own artistic ends. We foster our artistic selves for professional development and self-awareness, as well as to remain vitally integrated in the therapeutic process on a shared artistic journey with our clients.

Art has served a critical role throughout humankind, and aesthetics plays a crucial part in the development of civilization (Dissanayake, 1992). With the role that the arts play in discourse, advancement in cultural norms, beliefs, and relationships are possible. Dissanayake (1992) asserted that the role of art is biological and the use of art has evolutionary advantages for individuals and communities. Extrapolating from Diassanayke, understanding art and aesthetics, as well as making, exhibiting, and teaching art, are critical functions to the evolutionary survival of the art therapy profession. Without practicing the language of art, art therapists lose the ability to understand and communicate with others. Art making remains critical to the evolution of individual and collective art therapy work. Specifically, the open studio approach identifies clients as artists and promotes intrapsychic experiences combined with interpersonal interactions and community experiences (Moon, 2002; 2016). Art making allows discovery of personal myth to promote discovery of spiritual creation (Allen, 1995).

To understand the historical role of art and the artist, as well as art's influence on culture and thinking, one must consider the role art making plays in communicating one's inner experience and in reflecting the outer world. For example, art communicates political history through political-action art, the role of religion and spiritual attunement in religious art, and the branding of a company or an idea through media and corporate art. Aesthetics, with its origin in the Greek word, *aisthanomai*, refers to *perceptions of the senses* (Budd, n.d.). Aesthetics can be described in two ways: the philosophy of art and the philosophy of the aesthetic experience in response to nature.

## Philosophical Foundations of Art Therapy 7

Art stems from spirit, and the content of art is spiritual (James, 2008). From this standpoint, artistic beauty surpasses even natural beauty. The idea of art springing from the spirit derives from 18th century philosopher Georg Hegel (David, 2009). His observations are contextualized in terms of art's relationship to religion and spiritual tenets. Cultural and universal symbols are necessary to both communicate and understand the spirit in art. Art therapists utilize these symbols as we create art with our clients; through doing so, we simultaneously value the dignity and sacredness of each of our clients, while also relying on the accepted best practices of our profession. However, Hegel postulated that art must also be conceptualized according to historical and cultural circumstances—an idea that fits well within our postmodern belief system. We attend to and celebrate diversity in culture as well as conceptualize culture within the global profession of art therapy.

We can further understand our modern ideas about aesthetics by reflecting on the judgment of beauty. Kant, a contemporary of Hegel, noted that the experience of beauty is based on three types of aesthetic judgments (Burnham, n.d.). First, disinterested judgment is necessary, whereby something is found to be pleasurable because it is beautiful (not the other way around). We enjoy and find pleasure in what is beautiful. Next, universal judgment must be made; others will come to the same conclusions and agree with the application of the term beautiful, but again, an object does not possess beauty in and of itself. Here, beauty in art can be generally, but not universally, agreed on by others. Finally, art is purposive in its creation, but it does not need to have a particular purpose. In other words, this final judgment implies that art exists for art's sake—we perceive art as if it had a purpose, but no other purpose is necessary, according to Kant, except for the perception of beauty.

In an attempt to capture the definition of art, we must explore the intention of the maker and consider the procedural and functional definitions of art (Davies, 2011). We might procedurally call an object *art* if it has been created properly or vetted by the institutions of art. We can functionally call something art when it provides an aesthetic experience. The former definition suggests art is reserved for museums and trained artists. Using the procedural definition, Art (with a capital A) can be a source of inspiration for art therapy, but it might also leave clients and therapists believing that their art (with a lowercase a) is lacking, insufficient, primitive, or generally not good enough. Conversely, using the functional definition of art suggests that what our clients create is indeed art and should be called such. Functional art can be made by anyone, including children, adults, elders, clients, the differently abled, the disenfranchised communities, and self-taught outsider artists. *Art brut* (raw art) or outsider art, is a term that refers to the work of artists who create independently of the high art market or cultural art scene, as well as those who lack formal training ("What is Outsider Art?" 2017). *Art brut*, a term coined in the 1940s and

8  *Amy Backos*

later expanded on in the 1970s, describes the art of those who display raw creativity, typically practice in isolation, lack outside influence in their art, and may or may not have a mental illness.

Art therapy bridges procedural, high Art (with a capital A) and functional, common art (with a lowercase a), which brings a formal quality to the teaching of art to our clients, while advocating that anyone can create art. However, Budd (n. d.) reminds us that not all creations are necessarily art. Examples of functional art include process-oriented art therapy interventions, or a craft, with craft often being seen as less complex, sophisticated, or meaningful as art. Craft is skill-based and often relies on learning a technique and recreating an object from a template or pattern. It may be seen as subsidiary to art because it may lack spontaneous creative expression. Moreover, it typically serves a functional purpose in addition to aesthetics and is often associated with women's work. However, craft is used in art therapy, and at times, no doubt inspires what Kant calls the experience of beauty based on aesthetic judgments. Three examples of women's textile work illustrate this point: the work of the quilters of Gee's Bend, Alabama; the crochet work of Toshiko Horiuchi MacAdam; and the textile work of textile artist Mandy Greer.

Textile crafts in art therapy have been documented as a means to reduce unwanted symptoms and promote positive mood states (Collier, 2011), as well as a way to call up tactile experiences related to childhood attachment (Findlay, Latham & Hass-Cohen, 2008). Textile and fiber materials in art therapy has focused on women's preference for textiles as intrinsic to the use of the materials (Hinz, 2016). Consider the creative textile work of the quilters of Gee's Bend, Alabama. The quilts were made by generations of African American women who are descendants of Africans enslaved by a cotton farmer. The most prized quilts by these outsider artists, originally crafted out of pragmatic necessity for keeping their families warm, utilize a vibrant, improvised style called "my way," which uses unexpected patterns that are unique to that individual woman's vision for the quilt (Gee's Bend Quiltmakers, n.d.). Quilts from three, and sometimes four, generations of women in Gee's Bend embody art as a way of knowing one's self, others, and one's community (Allen, 1995).

Toshiko Horiuchi MacAdam, who creates child-friendly, interactive, sculptural structures, transforms conventional crochet (Public Art for Kids, n. d.). Her art work embodies architectural sensibility with the goal of engaging children in highly physical sensory play (Meet the Artist, 2012). Textile artist Mandy Greer creates elaborate, ethereal costumes and installations using traditional crochet and other fiber techniques that are combined to create archetypical narratives (About Mandy Greer, n.d.). The craftwork of these quilters and textile artists arguably embodies and inspires the experience of beauty in the viewer.

The evolution and survival of art therapy depends on the continual cross pollination of ideas in our transdisciplinary profession (Talwar, 2016) and by exploring how artists and scientists have interacted in the past to inspire

*Philosophical Foundations of Art Therapy* 9

our future growth. At the time when Freud and Jung were developing their theories, artists and scientists were meeting in salons in Vienna to share ideas about the mind, perception, and the unconscious. The salons were filled with doctors from the Vienna School of Medicine, as well as artists from the Vienna School of Art History, and discussions about evolution and the biological sciences influenced both scientists and artists. Nobel Prize–winning neuropsychiatrist Eric Kandel (2012) identified three artists who were influenced by the exchange of ideas in the Vienna salons: Gustav Klimt, Egon Schiele, and Oskar Kokoscha. Kandel postulated that these artists have much to teach us about the human condition, and furthermore, their art captured elements that are neurologically satisfying to view. He proposed that their art was infused with the knowledge gleaned from their participation in the salons. The constant flow of new information from science and art therapy research has helped to usher in a new age where the "new science of mind has begun to engage with art" (Kandel, 2012, p. 3). Art therapists at Notre Dame de Namur University have adopted the model of the salon, inviting experts in art therapy and in other disciplines (e.g., math, art history, technology, medicine) to engage in dialogue to promote the cross-disciplinary inspiration that Talwar (2016) noted is necessary to the continued growth of the art therapy profession.

Reflecting on the foundational pillar of the artist in our professional identity helps shed light on the relevance of having an art therapist present in a therapeutic art making session. The purpose of having an art therapist present is highlighted when we ask ourselves, "When is artwork finished?" Art historian Alois Riegl suggested an answer: Art is incomplete without the contributions of the viewer's experience and emotional reaction to the artwork (Kandel, 2012; Tallis, 2012). Tallis (2012) remarked that universal standards of beauty do not exist; there is only a subjective experience of beauty and aesthetics. Riegl would also suggest that the art therapist's biological perceptions, cultural beliefs, biases, and emotional responses to client art completes the process of art making (Tallis, 2012). This highlights the critical moment of exchange when an art therapist views art with a client—the therapist not only finds the client's verbal expression about their art relevant, but also the perception and reaction of the art therapist. Not unlike Kant's previously mentioned ideas of aesthetic judgment (Burnham, n. d.), art therapists support the functional qualities of clients' art by witnessing the process and art product, and thus, playing a role in the completion of the art. Through our training as artists and culturally attuned therapists, we further embody Hegel's ideas that art must be conceptualized according to historical and cultural circumstances (James, 2009). Through the lens of cultural awareness and working from a stance of cultural humility (Tervalon & Murray-Garcia, 1998), art therapists provide the finishing touches to the artistic process by viewing and discussing their client's art with them. Thus, by witnessing the emerging art process and final art product, the artist as psychotherapist provides the completion of the art making.

10  *Amy Backos*

Art therapy Master's student, Joelle Fregeau, thoughtfully described how art making is part of her own healing journey and a critical part of her education and transformation to become an art therapist (see Plate 2):

> I am in the process of forming my identity as both an art therapist and psychotherapist. In doing so I have needed to participate in my healing, largely through art and poetry tied to cultural healing. This process, of healing, is in my opinion, crucial to forming a secure and stable identity as an art therapist and psychotherapist and is crucial to providing a safe holding space for clients. In my process of healing through art, I can hold art and aesthetics to further inform how I view the work of clients and then use this knowledge to help guide clients healing. I believe this is paramount and what sets us apart from psychotherapists as art therapists.
>
> (Personal communication, J. Fregeau,
> March 17, 2017)

### Psychotherapist

This third foundational pillar in the discipline of art therapy is that of psychotherapy. The profession of art therapy emerged at a time when psychoanalysis dominated the field of psychology (Rubin, 2016), and Freud's (1913) theories were considered standard in mental health treatment. Our identity as psychotherapists, forged by traditional analytic thought, evolved with the integration of new methodologies and research and was contextualized in our global communities.

Western Freudian thinking postulates that ailments of the mind are treated through therapy, specifically by revealing the unconscious. Although revealing unknown truths about oneself via one's unconscious can be healing and is still relevant to art therapy, other modalities are utilized as well. Social constructs must also be considered, as well as cognitive schemas, or ways of viewing the world that are shaped by one's environment. Therefore, as psychotherapists, art therapists use cognitive behavioral analysis and scientifically supported healing art modalities, including movement, music, drama, and art.

The paradigm of psychotherapy, which stems from the medical model, includes talking with a doctor, taking medication, or talking with a group of other people who have the same disorder. However, both traditional healing, described as the first foundational pillar of art therapy, as well as our postmodern conceptualizations of psychotherapy, highlight similar healing paths. They diverge somewhat from classic analytic psychotherapy in that the beliefs of the person suffering and those of their family influence, and often dictate, the treatments pursued. An ailment leads clients and their families to select a healing method based on their cultural expectations, resources, and previous experiences. Their choice may

## Philosophical Foundations of Art Therapy    11

include spiritual healing, such as consulting with a priest, prayer, as well as engaging in energy work, meditation, chanting, fasting, communing with nature, exorcism, and/or art, medicine, and indeed psychotherapy.

On a recent trip to Central America to provide art therapy, my colleague, Dr. Gwen Sanders, and I worked with a group of our students in a community-centered Catholic church. The open-air church included a community room, an inner garden, and an outdoor area for lunch where children could play. Services were vast: lunch was provided for children and mothers throughout the week, Mass was given every day, and exorcisms were offered on Wednesdays and Fridays. The methods of helping in one snapshot moment included the following: Mass in the church, feeding children, exorcism in the community room, children and adults doing art therapy on the porch, teaching and learning by professors and students, and yoga class in the yard. I became struck with the awareness of the universal human urge to alleviate the suffering of others and to elevate them. No matter where we travel or what we research, we can clearly ascertain the ways in which we humans are instinctually impelled, or called, to collaborate and to help ease the distress, grief, or hunger of others. This impulse exists in tandem with destructive urges in all of us. So it appears in my work, and research supports the notion that there is not just one "culturally appropriate" way to treat a person or to engage them with art materials (Bordonaro, 2016); rather, as psychotherapists, we appreciate the need to contextualize the person, the problem, and the social environment. As art psychotherapists in touch with our role as healers and cultivating an ongoing stance of cultural humility (Tervalon & Murray-Garcia, 1998), we must offer not only what science proposes will heal, but also some of what the client believes will work.

Prior to psychoanalysis, families and religious leaders maintained the role of supporting families and individuals affected by mental illness, grief, or abuse. These practices are still highly relevant today. The idea that Freud's "talking cure" will somehow reveal a solution to what ails is loaded with assumptions that do not account for the need of many individuals to find truths about themselves by means other than through verbal language alone. It also does not account for the stigma and fear of disloyalty to family with which some cultures may view psychotherapy. Talking with a person outside the family or religion remains a challenge for many people across cultures. Stigma about psychotherapy permeates both individualistic and collective cultures on both an individual and community level (Batthje & Pryor, 2011), and providers are not immune to these beliefs (Hansson, 2011). Sharing secrets of the family remains taboo from a collectivist standpoint, while from an individualistic perspective mental illness is perceived as a personal weakness and a stigma. Self-expression through art, however, can bypass the talking and can be referred to as attending "art classes" or visiting the "art lady," as some of the veterans with whom I worked called our sessions; these sessions

12  *Amy Backos*

are free from the self and public shame that often accompanies the idea of going to therapy.

Patti Smith, musician, writer, and artist, described growth and the struggle of thinking as follows: "Eventually we work it out. We recognize in ourselves, our mother's hand, our father's limb. But the mind, that is something else again. Of this we can never be sure" (Smith, 1992, p. 15). This universal experience of uncertainty of thought is counterbalanced with the possibility of knowing through the creation of art. Instead of trying to know ourselves only with further thinking and supplementary words, we can explore our unconscious and tell our stories through images. While Freud influenced the way art therapists think of psychotherapy, Jung (1964) played a critical role for art therapists in the history of psychotherapy, by both using art to understand himself and encouraging his patients to make art. If a client cannot describe a memory or an inner experience, perhaps he or she can draw it (Gantt, 2009). Art, more so than talking, communicates the nonlinear, obtuse, dream, and fantasy imagery that remains critical in revealing the unconscious.

The role of the psychotherapist demands ways of knowing that are numerous and complex. Art therapy student, Ashley Leonard, depicts in her response art (see Figure 1.1) the intricacies and often convoluted ways of perceiving and comprehending her clients at the Veterans' Affairs Medical Center.

*Figure 1.1* The role of the psychotherapist: Ashley Leonard.

## Philosophical Foundations of Art Therapy

Utilizing countertransference to understand our clients is valued in analytic psychology, and response art by art therapists is regarded as useful or even necessary to understanding our clients (Fish, 2012; Sanders, 2016). Thus, the contributions of the art therapist to the art making process of a client is in the viewing of the art and using our trained psychological, emotional, and artistic responses to understand our clients and to communicate with them. These responses have now been revealed through the scientific evidence of neuroscience to be healing. Therapists now know the empathic and emotional responses necessary for psychological understanding and healing (Hass-Cohen & Carr, 2008; King, 2016; Lusebrink, 2010). This evidence can be utilized to build an art therapist's repertoire of evidence-based practices and promote interdisciplinary collaborative research. Finally, integrating the science of mind and art (Kandel, 2012) maintains our relevancy as providers of mental health and confirms the necessity of our identity as artists, and not only clinicians.

## Art Therapy

The intersection of our identities as healer, artist, and psychotherapist is integrated into a profession that is far bigger than the sum of its parts. Bucciarelli (2016) challenged art therapists to become bigger than the roles an art therapist encompasses; this requires each of us to engage in careful consideration of the multifaceted roles we play in the context of the art therapy setting, in the history of humanity, and in contemporary society. Embodying the archetypical role of healers, art therapists must reflect on our sociocultural role as healers in order to provide culturally relevant and appropriate art therapy interventions for our clients from around the world. As artists, we must continually examine the function and role of aesthetics and art in our work as art therapists. As psychotherapists, we are called to science and reliance on best practices for treating mental health. Each of these domains forges us into the discipline of art therapy, where we are obligated to understand the philosophical truths from the past as a way to clear new paths in our profession.

## References

About Mandy Greer. (n. d.). Retrieved from https://mandygreer.wordpress.com/about/

Allen, P. (1995). *Art as a way of knowing*. Boston, MA: Shambhala.

Anderson, F. (1995). Catharsis and empowerment through group clay work with incest survivors. *The Arts in Psychotherapy*, 22(5), 413–427.

Batthje, G. J., & Pryor, J. B. (2011). The relationships of public and self-stigma to seeking mental health services. *Journal of Mental Health Counseling*, 33(2), 161–177.

## 14   *Amy Backos*

Belkofer, C. M., & McNutt, J. V. (2011). Understanding social media culture and its ethical concerns for art therapists. *Art Therapy: Journal of the American Art Therapy Association, 28*(4), 159–164.

Bordonaro, G. P. W. (2016). International art therapy. In D. E. Gussak & M. L. Rosal (Eds.), *The Wiley handbook of art therapy* (pp. 675–682). West Sussex, UK: Wiley.

Bucciarelli, A. (2016). Art therapy: A transdisciplinary approach. *Art Therapy: Journal of the American Art Therapy Association, 33*(3), 151–155.

Budd, M. (n.d). *Aesthetics*. Retrieved from www.rep.routledge.com/articles/overview/aesthetics/v-1 doi: 10.4324/9780415249126-M046-1

Burnham, D. (n.d.). *Immanuel Kant: Aesthetics*. Retrieved from the Internet Encyclopedia of Philosophy website: www.iep.utm.edu/kantaest/#SH2a

Collier, A. F. (2011). The well-being of women who create with textiles: Implications for art therapy. *Art Therapy: Journal of the American Art Therapy Association, 28*(3), 104–112.

Corey, G. (2013). *Theory and practice of counseling and psychotherapy*. Belmont, CA: Brooks/Cole.

Dissanayake, E. (1992). *Homo Aestheticus: Where art comes from and why.* New York: Free Press.

Davies, S. (2011). Art, definition of. Routledge Encyclopedia of Philosophy, Taylor and Francis. Doi: 10.4324/9780415249126-M006-2.

Findlay, J. C., Latham, M. E., & Hass-Cohen, N. (2008). Circles of attachment: Art therapy albums. In N. Hass-Cohen & R. Carr (Eds.), *Art therapy and clinical neuroscience* (pp. 191–206). London, UK: Jessica Kingsley.

Fish, B. J. (2012). Response art: The art of the art therapist. *Art Therapy: Journal of the American Art Therapy Association, 29*(3), 138–143.

Freud, S. (1913). *On the interpretation of dreams*. New York, NY: Palgrave Macmillan.

Gantt, L., & Tinnin, L. (2009). Support for a neurological view of trauma with implications for art therapy. *The Arts in Psychotherapy, 36*(3), 148–153.

Gee's Bend Quiltmakers. (n.d.). Retrieved from www.soulsgrowndeep.org/gees-bend-quiltmakers

Hansson, L. (2011). The interface between people with a mental illness and mental health services: Focusing the role of public stigma and self-stigma in staff-patient relationships. *Psychiatrische Praxis 38*(K09). doi: 10.1055/s-0031-1277736

Hass-Cohen, N., & Carr, R. (2008). *Art therapy and clinical neuroscience*. London, UK: Jessica Kingsley.

Hinz, L. D. (2016). Media considerations in art therapy: Directions for future research. In D. E. Gussak & M. L. Rosal (Eds.), *The Wiley handbook of art therapy* (pp. 135–145). West Sussex, UK: Wiley.

Howie, P. (2016). Art therapy with trauma In D. E. Gussak & M. L. Rosal (Eds.), *The Wiley handbook of art therapy* (pp. 375–386). West Sussex, UK: Wiley.

Isis, P. D. (2016). Positive art therapy. In D. E. Gussak & M. L. Rosal (Eds.), *The Wiley handbook of art therapy* (pp. 90–98). West Sussex, UK: Wiley.

James, D. (2009). *Continuum studies in philosophy: Art, myth and society in Hegel's aesthetics*. London, UK: Continuum. Retrieved from www.ebrary.com

Jung, C. G. (1964). *Man and his symbols*. New York, NY: Doubleday.

### Philosophical Foundations of Art Therapy 15

Kandel, E. R. (2012). *The age of insight: The quest to understand the unconscious in art, mind, and brain, from Vienna 1900 to the present.* New York, NY: Random House.

Kaplan, F. F. (2007). *Art therapy and social action.* London, UK: Jessica Kingsley.

Kaplan, F. F. (2016). Social action art therapy. In D. E. Gussak & M. L. Rosal (Eds.), *The Wiley handbook of art therapy* (pp. 787–793). West Sussex, UK: Wiley.

King, J. (2016). Art therapy: A brain based profession. In D. E. Gussak & M. L. Rosal (Eds.), *The Wiley handbook of art therapy* (pp. 77–89). West Sussex, UK: Wiley.

Kopp, S. B. (1972). *If you meet the Buddha on the road, kill him.* Palo Alto, CA: Science and Behavior Books.

Lusbrink, V. B. (2010). Assessment and therapeutic application of the expressive therapies continuum: Implications for brain structures and functions. *Art Therapy: Journal of the American Art Therapy Association, 27*(4), 168–177.

McNiff, S. (1979). From shamanism to art therapy. *Art Psychotherapy, 6*(3), 155–161.

Moon, B. L. (2016). The sirens of definition: Responding to the call. *Art Therapy: Journal of the American Art Therapy Association, 33*(3), 156–159.

Moon, C. H. (2002). *Studio art therapy: Cultivating the artistic identity of the art therapist.* London, UK: Jessica Kingsley.

Moon, C. H. (2016). Open studio approach to art therapy. In D. E. Gussak & M. L. Rosal (Eds.), *The Wiley handbook of art therapy* (pp. 112–121). West Sussex, UK: Wiley.

Orr, P. (2016). Art therapy and digital media. In D. E. Gussak & M. L. Rosal (Eds.), *The Wiley handbook of art therapy* (pp. 188–197). West Sussex, UK: Wiley.

Partridge, E. (2016). *Amplified voices: Art based inquiry into elder communication.* Available from ProQuest Dissertations and Theses database. (UMI No. 10190347)

Potash, J. S., & Kalmanowitz, D. (2016). Social action research methods and art therapy. In D. E. Gussak & M. L. Rosal (Eds.), *The Wiley handbook of art therapy* (pp. 626–635). West Sussex, UK: Wiley.

Prall, D. (1935). Review: Art as experience by John Dewey. *The Philosophical Review, 44*(4), 388–390. Retrieved from www.jstor.org/stable/2179993

Public Art for Kids. (n.d.). Retrieved from http://netplayworks.com/NetPlayWorks/Home.html

Quirk, V. (2012). *Meet the artist behind those amazing, hand-knitted playgrounds.* Retrieved from ArchDaily website: www.archdaily.com/297941/meet-the-artist-behind-those-amazing-hand-knitted-playgrounds

Rubin, J. (2016). Psychoanalytic art therapy. In D. E. Gussak & M. L. Rosal (Eds.), *The Wiley handbook of art therapy* (pp. 26–36). West Sussex, UK: Wiley.

Sanders, G. J. (2016). *Art response to confusion, uncertainty, and curiosity during group art therapy supervision.* Available from ProQuest Dissertations and Theses database. (UMI No. 10246527)

Smith, P. (1992). *Woolgathering.* New York: New Directions Books.

## 16  *Amy Backos*

Talwar, S. (2016). Is there a need to redefine art therapy? *Art Therapy: Journal of the American Art Therapy Association, 33*(3), 116–118.

Tallis, R. (2012). From neurosis to neurons. *Wall Street Journal.* Retrieved from www.wsj.com/articles/SB10001424052702304023504577319903439493784

Tervalon, M., & Murray-Garcia, J. (1998). Cultural humility versus cultural competence: A critical distinction in defining physician training outcomes in multicultural education. *Journal of Health Care for the Poor and Underserved, 9*(2), 117–125.

What is outsider art? (2017). Retrieved from www.outsiderartfair.com/outsider_art

# 2 Theory and Art Therapy

*Richard Carolan and Karrie Stafford*

## Introduction

Much of what has been written on theory in art therapy has been in relation to a range of theories of psychotherapy. This has led to many of today's art therapists holding egalitarian perspectives and basing their views of art therapy theory and practice on a diverse theoretical backdrop, which ranges from psychoanalytic to postmodern. There is a need for more development of the theory of art therapy that is primarily based on the mechanisms of change that are inherent in, and intrinsic to, the use of art as therapy. Development of theory requires exploring historical foundations, defining the basis of researching and knowing, and establishing principles that serve as the core of the theory.

This chapter proposes principles that can contribute to art therapy theory to develop a more comprehensive understanding of how art may facilitate psychological wellness and change. The principles are based on an exploration of the inherent capacities of art to change and/or improve human life. This exploration will build on core existing theories from art therapy, psychology, philosophy, and anthropology. As the theoretical landscape of art therapy continues to evolve, this chapter aims to help define and highlight the importance of the mechanisms of change inherent in art processes and their role in psychotherapy. A brief discussion of knowing through reductionism, emergentism, and holism will set the framework from which this understanding of art as therapy is based. The following sections will present a brief review of art as an imperative component in the study of the mind. This will lead to the exploration of the role art plays in facilitating change and wellness in psychotherapeutic contexts. The intent is to encourage future development, as well as critique, of art therapy theory and practice that stems from art based on a central, unifying theme, rather than one based on fragmented concepts from psychology which are then applied to art.

## Historical Perspective

It has been historically difficult to measure and to produce evidence of the mechanisms of change in the process of psychotherapy. There is a broad range and a lack of specificity in theories that define the development of individual personality and an overarching focus on pathology rather than on requirements for wellness, growth, and change. Research in the field of anthropology informs us of the human experience and the evolution of a myriad of methods aimed to alter and improve that experience. Modernity required that a science be developed to heal the suffering of the soul. Psychology was to become that science. From psychology emerged psychotherapy.

From the developing field of psychotherapy, the paradigm from which an understanding of psychopathology and healing evolved was grounded on the premise of a "talking cure" (Breuer & Freud, 1893/1956). This paradigmatic structure also became a barrier. The new understanding facilitated exploration and dialogue in the development of the science of psychotherapy, but the barrier to the "talking cure" was the risk that our understanding of the human experience would be limited to only that which we could explain in words. Initial strategies in the "talking cure" involved using words as a means of expanding the possibility of understanding ourselves through "free association." Though dreams and images were part of those associations, in the end, they were articulated and understood through the use of words. Words were not initially used as a means of reducing our experience, but rather as a means of broadening towards other ways of knowing. Talking facilitated access to subconscious and unconscious material, through which insight related to maladies could be developed and pathology mitigated. Accessing content below the conscious layer with discourse would become a fundamental basis of psychotherapeutic practices and would inspire pioneers of art therapy to broaden the avenues to the unconscious to include creative visual expressions in addition to verbal ones.

Publications by Naumburg (1950, 1953, 1987), Kramer (1993), Rubin (2001, 2011), Wadeson (1980), and Arrington (2001), among others, have contributed to our understanding of the range of approaches to art therapy. This work informs our understanding of how art therapy fits into theories and methodologies that are linked to traditional forms of psychologically based psychotherapy, such as psychodynamic therapy or gestalt therapy. Uncovering unconscious material through art has been substantiated through these past decades of art therapy theoretical development, but a much more complex and dynamic understanding of how art may facilitate psychological wellness and change is needed. Exploring the mechanisms of change inherent in the use of art in therapy requires clarity concerning the paradigm that serves as our basis for understanding. We need a language that is not borrowed from other sciences but one that is native to the process that we are attempting to define.

Reductionism, as a means of identifying core elements that are the cause of, or hold the essence of the whole, is a cornerstone of the scientific method. Undeniably, it is the Western world's standard method for identifying truths. Attempting to reduce and "control" how and what we are observing has become synonymous with best practices in research.

Theory and Art Therapy    19

The scientific process, which is based on discovering empirical evidence, is an extraordinary way of knowing; it is considered the best practice for most research protocols. However, applying empirical processes alone to understand the human experience is inadequate. In the early 20th century, Edmund Husserl pointed out the importance of studying consciousness and the inability of Cartesian methods of analysis to adequately understand the human mind. Studying subjectivity through objective means was no longer considered to be the only method of finding truth, and systematic approaches for understanding conscious experiences were then developed.

Art therapy theory recognizes reductionism as fundamental to knowing. It also recognizes holism and emergentism, which emphasize the complexity of psychological phenomena as fundamental to knowing. Susan Langer (1942) noted in *Philosophy in a New Key* that she respected and believed in all that science offered; however, she added that she was not willing to stop there in the pursuit of knowledge. Art in therapy engages a way of knowing that goes beyond the talking cure, where a sense of holism can be achieved and a forum for emergence is preserved.

We have been seduced by the tremendous influence of the scientific process as a way of knowing. This seduction has led us to believe that if we cannot explain something, if we cannot reduce it to its core elements, or predict the interaction of these elements, then we cannot assert that it is true. History has many examples of science being certain of a truth only to realize, as we developed our capacity and our tools for gathering information and integrating information, that those scientific facts were not truth or reality at all.

Matters that infuse human life, such as uncertainty, fluctuation, interpretation, ineffability, and intuition, cannot be ignored in the study of the mind. If we wish to arrive at any holistic sense of the human mind and experience within a relatable and recognizable theory, these matters need to somehow be brought into consideration. Art affords different ways of knowing in areas that include the therapist knowing the client, the client knowing oneself, and knowing the human mind and experience. Limiting our scope of understanding and communicating the therapeutic potentials of art to knowing through reason, while simultaneously ignoring areas such as intuition and imagination, would be an incomplete, and thus a dysfunctional, paradigm. Art offers a means of understanding and communicating human experience that is not confined to linear conceptualizations and that can reflect more accurately the depth of human experience than reductionist means or verbal language alone could do. Kandel (2012), a Nobel Prize–winning neuroscientist, described art as a "distillation of pure experience" (p. 501), which renders it a "desirable complement to, and enrichment of the science of mind" (p. 501). According to Kandel, without creative artistic methods contributing to the science of the mind, conceptions of the mind would be significantly lacking.

20   *Richard Carolan and Karrie Stafford*

Integrating the visual arts into psychotherapy can dilate the limits of purely rational conceptions of the human experience. As the integration unfolds, clarifying mechanisms of change will promote the confluence of art and science and serve to broaden our understanding of best practices within art therapy contexts.

## Theoretical Foundations

The following section reviews and connects key existing theories related to art and mechanisms of change. These theories, though originating from different disciplines, overlap with and reinforce each other, and they offer a clear basis for art therapy theory and practice. The relationship between art and the human mind existed far before theorists began trying to understand it. Exploring art and culture anthropologically, Dissanayake (1995) explained that the behavior of creating art is an inherited tendency, a deeply intrinsic and imperative component of the human experience. The oldest and longest human-known tradition of the hand axe shows the human capacity to externalize thought through careful manipulation of objects in the physical world (Cook, 2013; Dutton, 2009). Selection of materials and the precision executed in the making of these tools indicate that they served, in part, the purpose of showcasing their makers' access to resources, dexterity, and intelligence through the ability to consciously and cleverly craft; these tools carried messages from, between, and about their makers (Dutton, 2009). Dutton proposed that these externalizations of consciousness served as signals of fitness in Darwinian (1859) terms of sexual selection. As art can be defined as any object that an artist intends for aesthetic evaluation (Shimamura & Palmer, 2012), these hand axes are arguably mankind's earliest art.

Fellmann and Walsh (2013) noted that the human mind spontaneously transcends its genetic constitution in the making of meanings from, and representations of, the current concrete situation (p. 65). They described this abstraction process as innate and asserted that in encountering art we witness this transcendence in form. We see a historical relationship between human conscious reality and art, as well as the human proclivity to transcend what is given (see Plate 3). Humans are innately moved to externalize what is internal, to express, move, and relate to others. Art has been a language with profound significance since the earliest times. By looking at the artifacts of our ancestors and at today's artistic expressions, we can see in concrete form the imprint of human consciousness and thus "the evolution of our minds" (Cook, 2013, p. 18).

### Dewey

Dewey (1934), philosopher, psychologist, and educational reformer, urged theorists to avoid isolating art from human experiences. Dewey emphasized that the "actual work of art is what the product does with and in experience" (p. 1). He located knowledge in the experience of making or witnessing art objects. In orienting attention to the experience of art, Dewey relegated the physicality of art to a potential distraction from the "human conditions under which it was brought into being and from the human consequences it engenders in actual life-experience" (p. 1).

Focusing on the lived sensations of the experience of art, Dewey (1934) purported that these sensations are not mere elements of knowledge, as psychologists and philosophers conceptualized them to be. Dewey emphasized a certain kind of knowledge that is sense-based and in an alliance with "emotion, impulse and appetition" (p. 22), and he believed that art facilitated this type of knowing. Dewey's philosophy of truth is based in experience and "accept[ing] life and experience in all its uncertainty, mystery, doubt, and half-knowledge" (p. 35). This philosophy involves movement, spontaneity, and instinct and can become sensuous and rhythmic. Dewey warned against over conceptualizing within philosophical and psychological knowing. He stipulated that objectifying and studying only causal relationships with a lack of focus on elements, such as imagination and felt senses, would result in something so abstract and removed from actual human experience that it could no longer be considered truth.

### Arnheim

Perceptual psychologist Arnheim (1986) described art to be a source for emergent and multilayered meaning, which can prompt and hold multiple meanings at once. Arnheim considered ambiguity in art an asset, as the gaps in understanding are intuitively filled. Intuitive knowing can be characterized as conceptualizing a whole and striving toward a state of equilibrium. He contended that intuition and intellect are two indispensable branches of cognition that are interdependent; they exist on a continuum from direct perception to purely theoretical conceptualization. Arnheim (1986) thought that ignoring intuitive knowing would be "psychologically incorrect and educationally harmful" (p. 13) and suggested that the arts "offer an experience of watching intuition at work" (p. 19). He argued that overreliance on intellectualized knowing results in one-sidedness, and, much like Kandel (2012), he promoted the integration of art into psychology.

### Langer

Philosopher Langer (1942), like Arnheim (1986), emphasized that we find significance in sense-based data and experience before we know rationally and intellectually what we are sensing. In her view, nondiscursive forms are charged with logical possibilities of meaning. She believed that something meaningful or significant is conveyed through art beyond

## 22 Richard Carolan and Karrie Stafford

what can be intellectually grasped; symbolism facilitates expression of that which lies beyond the grasp of words, constituting a language of emotion and intuitive knowing. In this respect, art offers alternative modes of expression to intellectualizing and verbalizing. Like both Dewey (1934) and Arnheim (1986), Langer proposed that art provides an experience of discovery with which one might exercise connection to intuitions and an intentional merger of the mind and the body.

The aesthetic experience involves a form of knowing that is nonrational and irreducible (Hagman, 2005, p. 17). Despite the ubiquity of the aesthetic experience, which Hagman defined as "an emergent phenomenon that arises in the transitional psychological zone in which our creative engagement with the world is lived" (p. 1), this phenomenon largely plays out without intentional, purposeful engagement. Driven by an innate human instinct to "give form and value to the experiences of self-in-relation" (p. 1), each part of human experience involves an aesthetic dimension. This aesthetic dimension is refined and elaborated upon throughout life. Hagman (2005) pointed out that through art the aesthetic experience is most refined. Art therapy offers the opportunity for clients to understand and apply their unique aesthetic, and the refinement of it can be supported for psychological benefit.

As previously discussed, art is an intrinsic component of the human experience which allows consciousness to be externalized and then ineffably conveyed. Art allows for knowing through experience and prompts intuitive and imaginative knowing. Building from, and further discussing, the fundamental principles proposed by Dewey, Arnheim, and Langer, the current authors propose holism, emergence, activation, connection, and reflection as core inherent mechanisms of change in art therapy that may benefit psychotherapeutic practices.

## Art Facilitates Holism in Knowing

Art engages a range of ways of knowing, including knowing through experience, the felt senses, intuition, emotion, and imagination. The variety of ways of knowing involved in artistic encounters can activate the mind-body and help to integrate the whole person in the process of discovery. This quality of holism offers a means of understanding that is multilayered and textured, and within the art therapy context, it can promote not only understanding and communication of psychological material but also its integration. Art, as part of its holistic function, contributes to the achievement and maintenance of homeostasis in the balance of human experience.

It has been argued that there are multiple intelligences (Gardner, 1993) and multiple ways of knowing. Sense perception, intuition, memory, faith, imagination, language, emotion, and reason are included in the task of acquiring knowledge ("Ways of Knowing," 2014). Rationality is clearly

*Theory and Art Therapy*   23

not the only avenue through which one can come to understand. Diverse avenues of understanding are inherent in art therapy contexts, and these avenues of knowing can be engaged for psychotherapeutic benefit.

Art has the capacity to facilitate a multiplicity of experiences of knowing in ways that cognitive linear processes do not. There is a need to balance cognitive linear processes with other ways of knowing that are inherent in human experience (McGilchrist, 2010). Knowing can manifest as attachment to a perspective that we become conditioned to repeat. This repetition may cause limits to the breadth of our understanding, if not the breadth of our experience and even our ability to change. What is required to break this limiting pattern is novel experience and subsequent new pathways of understanding. With its emphasis on broadening access to multiple ways of knowing, art facilitates novel experience as a means of accessing understanding. Encountering art can stir us from a myopia that familiarity induces, letting us peer behind what Langer (1942) referred to as the "curtain of the material world" to a "higher, purer, more satisfying Truth" (p. 265). Art facilitates the leap from the known to the imagined, as it loosens us from the grip of what is expected or anticipated. The art therapy process engages participants in the possibilities on the canvas of cloth as well as the canvas of their lives.

Langer (1942) discussed metaphorically using imagery and art "to exploit their possible significance for the conception of remote or intangible ideas" (p. 266). Like Langer, Hillman (Hillman & Moore, 2013) noted that through art we can depart from binary forms of thinking; art encourages multiplicity in thinking and prompts the use of metaphor. Jung (1961) contended that the use of metaphor is a creative process that can provide access to unconscious material. According to McGilchrist (2010), "Metaphoric thinking is fundamental to our understanding of the world, because it is the only way in which understanding can reach outside the system of signs to life itself. It is what links language to life" (p. 115).

The discoveries of neurobiological variables in relation to art therapy over the last several decades provide testament to the benefits of this multiplicity in knowing. Significant contributions continue to be made by art therapists and other researchers (Chapman, 2014; Gantt & Tinnin, 2009; Hass-Cohen, 2008; Hass-Cohen, Findlay, Carr, & Vanderlan, 2014; King, 2016). While there have been great advances in the field, this work is still in the very early stages of understanding both neurological processes and how these processes correlate with art-based practices. Art facilitates brain functioning as a process of integration (Chapman, 2014) as well as a means of activating brain functions in organizing and communicating experience (Lusebrink, 1990, 2004; Hintz, 2008).

Engaging and integrating multiple aspects of human conscious experience relates to the concept and the experience of *flow* (Csikszentmihalyi, 1997). Csikszentmihalyi described flow as immersion in the creative act.

## 24 *Richard Carolan and Karrie Stafford*

With the right balance of skill and challenge, engaging in art processes can prompt immersive experiences in which the artist's entire conscious experience is saturated with the task of creation. This state allocates attention or psychic energy in a manner that is conducive to high states of wellbeing (Csikszentmihalyi, 1975, 1988, 2014).

Holism allows for a roundedness of knowing in therapeutic contexts, engaging clients and clinicians in experiences beyond conceptualizations through verbal description. This roundedness is a mechanism of change and also provides a context for the following mechanisms: experience and balance.

## Art as an Active, Creative Means of Balance and Experience

Another key element of art is its capacity to facilitate homeostasis. Dissanayake (1995) stated that art has historically aided humans by fostering the integration of experiences and transitions, such as illness and death. Through periods of growth, as well as periods of suffering, the human system is always attempting to maintain or return to homeostasis. This process may involve *holding* and integrating experiences and practices. Because art engages multiple ways of knowing, it can serve as a means of integrating the spiritual, the emotional, and the cognitive. Viewing images and creating images can serve as a means of balancing the system and the human experience, even at times when we cannot understand or explain the interrelatedness of our experiences. While the experience of developing homeostasis might not be achievable nor explainable with the use of words alone, it might be facilitated, captured, and felt in the art process and image.

Art serves a critical therapeutic process by developing alternative pathways of engagement with experience. Suffering often involves the repetition of dysfunctional patterns of thinking, feeling, and behaving. These patterns can become more and more entrenched and subsequently become understood as our "reality"; sometimes the entrenched quality of these patterns can result in feelings of hopelessness and despair. As mentioned previously, art activates the imagination, invites the artist into the unknown, and prompts novel experience. These qualities of art facilitate an escape from the maze of linear patterns of thinking and subsequent feelings that may be incapacitating.

Kramer (1993) believed art could be a transforming life force that allows humans to channel their suffering into creativity. This process shifts the participant from an inactive, absorbing entity, to an active, creating entity. Art can facilitate the development of avenues for channeling the overwhelming or oppressive forces in our lives into active, functioning experiences.

Art therapy contributes to a paradigm shift in the therapeutic process. This shift facilitates the engagement of the artist in the experience of his or her life. It is a means of inviting and supporting the artist in the individual to become active and intentional in the creation of art, and thus it may promote the same empowering stance in life. This emphasis on active engagement is a hallmark of art therapy theoretical concepts. Art therapy allows participants to externalize their internal thoughts and feelings, which provides them with opportunities for expressing, understanding, and communicating these fundamental human functions. This facilitates a kind of empowerment. Through active, engaged experience with psychological material, balance, integration, and thus transformation may be achieved.

## Art as a Form for Holding and Emergence

A fundamental aspect of art is its ability to hold the therapeutic process, to serve as a container that allows internal experience to have external form, which can be viewed, interacted with, and which can continue to be engaged with over time. The image can hold a multiplicity of experiences, feelings, and concepts. It can simultaneously hold what we know and what we do not know. Interpreting the image by translating it into a verbal understanding can close the process, reducing it to limited knowledge. The uninterrupted image, however, maintains possibilities. The engagement with the image held on the canvas allows for a multiplicity of ways of knowing. Holding the image allows intuitive knowing, emotional knowing, imaginative knowing, as well as cognitive knowing. The held image, though stable in form, allows a fluidity of interpretation as an interactive process of these multiple ways of knowing. The art facilitates an open, ongoing process of knowing, rather than reducing it to a more stagnant, interpretive cognitive knowing that fixes it as a fact. Art promotes exploration and learning as well as flexibility in thinking.

As art facilitates an embracing of the unknown, the ambiguous, and the uncertain, it promotes one's ability to imagine one's possibilities. Art as a mechanism of change can hold the ambiguity, and allow the ambiguities and the possibilities of the human experience to be held simultaneously in a nonlinear fashion (see Plate 4).

The holding power of art is a unique and significant part of the art therapy process. It is a mechanism of change that greatly enhances continuity, as well as emergence. The work that is done in creating the image and in relating to the image continues to serve a therapeutic function whenever the person views the image or recalls of the image. Additionally, a continual interactive impact between the artist and the image can occur, which may bring with it new inspiration, imagination, as well as feelings and thoughts related to the artwork. Art therapy facilitates

## 26   Richard Carolan and Karrie Stafford

an active and ongoing process of change in the life of the participant. This mechanism of change can be active while the artist is creating and interacting therapeutically with the image, as well as years later. Stafford (2016) described the ongoing nature of the relationship between an artist and their creations as follows:

> Through making and witnessing art, the artist and audience step across a threshold to a place where *what is* leads to consideration of *what can be*. As artists encounter a work, they find more than a screen to project onto and more than a mirror that holds a reflection; they find an entry to a discovery process.
>
> (p. 9)

In this discovery process, "reality is reinterpreted and reconfigured" (Paul, Graffam, & Fowler, 2005, pp. 46–47). In this art-based ontology, the uncertainty inherent in the art encounter facilitates understanding of self and transformation of subjective reality. Stafford's (2016) research found an important asset of the art encounter is the ability to explore and stay in the unknown. Doing so lends itself to meaning-making and results in movement and flexibility in terms of gleaning self-reflective material. In Stafford's study, insight developed and shifts frequently took place incidentally, without expectation or a set intention to do so. In addition to the unknown being an asset of the art encounter, so too were the elements of chance and potential.

Art gives form to that which exists in human consciousness but that cannot be held by verbal language; thus, it serves as a way of expressing the inner experience of an individual in ways that words cannot. The concept of the unconscious has been a foundation of psychological understanding. The theory of the unconscious postulates that individuals are affected by all of the experiences of their lives whether or not they are conscious of how they are affected. Consciousness involves a more limited segment of the human experience. One is, for the most part, no longer conscious of most of what one thought and felt as a child, yet those experiences still affect one's behavior and experience today; these experiences, though influential, are not conscious. In addition, individuals can be affected by experiences that they have had in their life, which they never experienced consciously. Art serves as a means of holding, integrating, expressing, understanding, and communicating these unconscious experiences. Art therapy serves as a significant bridge between the unconscious and the conscious. What may not be consciously understood may be conveyed through art, which broadens contact with subconscious and unconscious material.

Naumburg (1966), one of the founding pioneers in art therapy, developed the works of the pioneers in psychology, particularly Jung; he saw art as a means of capturing, communicating, and understanding the internal feelings and experiences of the individual that had not, or might never, come into a conscious verbal way of knowing. Jung (1961) wrote about the practice of *active imagination* as critical to the therapeutic process because it facilitates the simultaneous engagement of both the unconscious and the conscious mind in the process of discovery. He viewed painting and sculpture as crucial tools in the process of active imagination. Jung considered that "The patient can make himself creatively independent through this method. . . . By painting himself he gives shape to himself" (Stevens, 1994, p. 109). Jung viewed imagination as the bases of understanding, so through activating it through art, the artist could gain self-awareness.

## Art Invites the Artist

The capacity of art to invite a sense of knowing that is not subject to our current capacity for cognitive understanding allows us to sit in a cave and have a sense of the experience of the cave dwellers who sat there thousands of years before. It is this transcendent aspect of art that allows knowing and engagement with the collective unconscious and its archetypal effect on our current experience (Jung, 1950). Jung's idea of the collective unconscious was that all of human experience is coded in the unconscious of each individual. Invoking the artist within is part of a very long history of engaging with spiritual processes and the numinous. It allows us access to mystery, to thousands of years of religious teaching related to faith, and the wisdom that one needs to see to believe.

The transcendent quality of the art encounter might connect the artist, not only to what is mysterious, but also to the components of the therapeutic relationship between artists—both the client artist and the art therapist as artist. In a way that words typically do not, art engages the felt senses of the perceiver who has an experience of the artist and of themselves in relation to the artwork and or the art process. In the art therapy context, art is used to communicate psychological material (Dalley, 2008); thus it adds dimension to the encounter between client and therapist (Robbins, 2001, p. 58). Knowing through art is evocative of "archaic, preverbal experience of self-in-relation" (Hagman, 2005, p. 26); thus, the art encounter in art therapy is rich with opportunities for therapeutic contact and alignment.

Components of therapeutic practice that hinge on the nature of the therapeutic relationship, such as transference, countertransference, empathy, congruence, unconditional positive regard, and the potential influence of the mirror neuron effect, are heightened, and have an additional level of complexity, in art therapy. The art therapist holds not only the participant, but also the creation of the participant, and the birthing of external reflections of the participant's internal experience. The art therapist witnesses the birth of these external forms of the clients' internal experiences as well

28  *Richard Carolan and Karrie Stafford*

as facilitates their attachment to these birthed images. In effect, the art therapist seeks to provide a safe space in which clients can develop a relationship to the external representations of their internal experience.

However, beyond its facility to represent internal experience, art as a therapeutic tool can transform one's experience through expression, and it can "import" the experience in relation to others (Langer, 1942). Objects of art are viewed as a type of visual language that can transgress social codes of meaning, yet still be meaningful. The artistic import is what an artist *expresses* by means of the depiction of objects or events; it is the visual equivalency of semantics (Langer, 1942).

Hagman (2005) purported that the human aesthetic experience constitutes our formal relationship with the world, and it is the basis of how we organize and experience the world. He proposed that this has its roots in early infantile experiences. Thus, the arts and all other aesthetic experiences are elaborated by multiple levels of subjectivity, including "metasubjective (social), the intersubjective (relational), and the personal (subjective)" (p. 10). Moreover, the "interrelationship between these levels that composes the complexity and profound depth of human aesthetic life" (p. 10). Our relationship with the aesthetic environment, in this view, is how we understand the world. Invoking the artist solicits attention to what is seen, allowing a full, embodied sense of our surroundings. Awakening the witness from passively absorbing what is perceived, the artist actively notices the impact of the visual world, and in turn, has an impact on what is seen.

## Art Facilitates Self-Reflection

As artists are affected by and affect their visual world, they engage in a subjective struggle with their psychological material (Sagan, 2015). This process allows for the intricacies of the human experience to be brought into form. As psychological material is externalized, insight related to this material can be developed; through the struggle itself, self-awareness can be practiced.

Psychotherapy aims to augment an individual's awareness of the self as an arena of conflict and locus of agency (Kirmayer, 2007). The psychotherapist helps broaden and deepen clients' self-awareness by facilitating dialogues about how their thoughts and feelings relate to their personal histories and present lives (Kirmayer, 2007). When art is used as the means to explore and communicate inner material, this dialogue about one's self can be enriched and expanded upon. The concept of the self is generally seen as fluid and subject to constant interpretation, and its location is more a process of choice rather than discovery (Anscombe, 1989; Kirmayer, 2007). Art mirrors the sense of fluidity and subjectivity that exists in conceptualizations of self; therefore, it lends itself to the exploration, understanding, communication, and transformation of the self.

In a recent study (Stafford, 2016), the experience of artist participants confirmed this theory related to the relationship between artist and their art, including that art encounters can make self-concepts more vivid, increase one's sense of self-cohesion, provide personal insight, and increase self-knowledge. Art was also found to expand direct conscious experience and facilitate awareness of felt senses, thus reinforcing the connection between artists and their senses. The findings also showed that the experience of engaging in art for self-reflection is highly idiosyncratic and seems to occur naturally and oftentimes spontaneously (Stafford, 2016). Relationships artists have with their art processes and products are self-perpetuating and intimate. Artists benefit from the veil of interpretation, as this keeps their minds open to what their art might mean or suggest about themselves, and they may also hide from audience members what feels too personal to explicitly share with others (Stafford, 2016). Reshaping the concrete world in an attempt to match one's conscious material helps to embellish the lexicon of the psyche, thus enhancing self-knowledge, which is a cornerstone of the psychotherapeutic process.

## Conclusion

This chapter explored the inherent capacities of art to promote change and wellness and proposed concepts fundamental to art therapy theory by exploring mechanisms of change involved in art processes. Mechanisms of change inherent in the art encounter included holism and emergence, which are conceptualized as not only ways of knowing but which also facilitate growth and wellness within art therapy practices. Another central mechanism discussed in this chapter was the invitation of the artist to take an active role in crafting the experience of making art. The art therapy process activates multiple ways of knowing as a means of empowering awareness and choice. The activation of homeostasis, externalization of psychological material, and enhanced opportunities for intrapersonal and interpersonal connectedness are also fundamental mechanisms of change inherent in the art encounter.

A powerful component of the art therapy process is creating a form that holds the internal experience and offers more than verbal ways of knowing. The created image allows the unknown and the known to be held simultaneously, to continue to evolve, and to be returned to and recalled. It is important that we continue to develop an understanding of theory in art therapy that is built on the mechanisms of change that are inherent in the art therapy process. Central to this development should be a dialectical view, in which both reductionism and holism can be respected. Though they may appear antithetical, both ways of knowing may contribute to the further understanding of art and its role in influencing the human mind and behavior.

## References

Anscombe, R. (1989). The myth of the self. *Psychiatry*, 52, 209–217.

Arnheim, R. (1986). *New essays on the psychology of art*. Berkeley, CA: Regents of the University of California.

Arrington, D. B. (2001). *Home is where the art is: An art therapy approach to family therapy*. Springfield, IL: Charles C. Thomas.

Breuer, J., & Freud, S. (1956). On the psychical mechanism of hysterical phenomena. *The International Journal of Psycho-Analysis*, 37, 8. (Original work published in 1893).

Chapman, L. (2014). *Neurobiologically informed trauma therapy with children and adolescents: understanding mechanisms of change* (Norton Series on Interpersonal Neurobiology). New York, NY: Norton.

Cook, J. (2013). *Ice age art: Arrival of the modern mind*. London, UK: British Museum Press.

Csikszentmihalyi, M. (1975). Play and intrinsic rewards. *Journal of Humanistic Psychology*, 15(3), 41–63.

Csikszentmihalyi, M. (1997). *Finding flow: The psychology of engagement with everyday life*. New York, New York: Basic Books.

Csikszentmihalyi, M. (1988). The flow experience and its significance for human psychology. In M. Csikszentmihalyi & I. S. Csikszentmihalyi (Eds.), *Optimal experience: Psychological studies of flow in consciousness* (pp. 15–35). New York: Cambridge University Press.

Csikszentmihalyi, M. (2014). *Flow and the foundations of positive psychology: The collected works of Mihaly Csikszentmihalyi*. Netherlands: Springer.

Dalley, T. (Ed.). (2008). *Art as therapy: An introduction to the use of art as a therapeutic technique*. New York, New York: Routledge.

Darwin, C. (1859). *On the origin of the species by means of natural selection*. New York, NY: Appleion-Century-Crofts.

Dewey, J. (1934). *Art as experience*. London, UK: Penguin.

Dissanayake, E. (1995). *Homo aestheticus: Where art comes from and why*. Seattle, WA: University of Washington Press.

Dutton, D. (2009). *The art instinct: Beauty, pleasure, and human evolution*. New York, NY: Bloomsbury Press.

Fellmann, F., & Walsh, R. (2013). Emotional selection and human personality. *Biological Theory*, 8(1), 64–73. doi: 10.1007/s13752-013-0093-3

Gantt, L., & Tinnin, L. W. (2009). Support for a neurobiological view of trauma with implications for art therapy. *The Arts in Psychotherapy*, 36(3), 148–153.

Gardner, H. (1993). *Multiple intelligences: The theory in practice*. New York, NY: Basic Books.

Hagman, G. (2005). *Aesthetic experience: Beauty, creativity, and the search for the ideal*. New York, NY: Rodopi.

Hass-Cohen, N. (2008). CREATE: Art therapy relational neuroscience principles (ATR-N). In N. Hass-Cohen & R. Carr (Eds.), *Art therapy and clinical neuroscience* (pp. 283–309). London, UK: Jessica Kingsley.

Hass-Cohen, N., Clyde Findlay, J., Carr, R., & Vanderlan, J. (2014). Check, change what you need to change and/or keep what you want: An art therapy neurobiological-based trauma protocol. *Art Therapy*, 31(2), 69–78.

Hillman, J., & Moore, T. (2013). *The essential James Hillman: A blue fire*. New York, NY: Routledge.

Hintz, L. D. (2008). Walking the line between passion and caution in art therapy: Using the expressive therapies continuum to avoid therapist errors. *Art Therapy, 25*(1), 38–40.

Jung, C. G. (1950). *Modern man in search of a soul* (W. S. Dell & C. F. Baynes, Trans.). New York, NY: Harcourt Brace Jovanovich. (Original work published 1933).

Jung, C. G. (1961). *Memories, dreams, reflections*. New York, NY: Random House.

Kandel, E. (2012). *The age of insight: The quest to understand the unconscious in art, mind, and brain, from Vienna 1900 to the present*. New York, NY: Random House.

King, J. L. (Ed.). (2016). *Art therapy, trauma, and neuroscience: Theoretical and practical perspectives*. New York, NY: Routledge.

Kirmayer, L. J. (2007). Psychotherapy and the cultural concept of the person. *Transcultural Psychiatry, 44*(2), 232–57. doi:10.1177/1363461506070794

Kramer, E. (1993). *Art as therapy with children*. Chicago, IL: Magnolia Street.

Langer, K. S. (1942). *Philosophy in a new key: A study in the symbolism of reason, rite, and art*. Cambridge, MA: Harvard University Press.

Lusebrink, V. B. (1990). *Imagery and visual expression in therapy*. New York, NY: Plenum Press.

Lusebrink, V. B. (2004). Art therapy and the brain: An attempt to understand the underlying processes of art expression in therapy. *Art Therapy: Journal of the American Art Therapy Association, 21*(3), 125–135.

McGilchrist, I. (2010). *The master and his emissary: The divided brain and the making of the western world*. New Haven, CT: Yale University Press.

Naumburg, M. (1950). *Schizophrenic art: Its meaning in psychotherapy*. New York, NY: Grune & Stratton.

Naumburg, M. (1953). *Psychoneurotic art: Its function in psychotherapy*. New York, NY: Grune & Stratton.

Naumburg, M. (1966). *Dynamically oriented art therapy: Its principles and practice*. New York, NY: Grune & Stratton.

Naumburg, M. (1987). *Dynamically oriented art therapy: Its principles and practice*. Chicago, IL: Magnolia Street.

Paul, J. L., Graffam, B., & Fowler, K. (2005). Perspectivism and critique of research: An overview. In J. L. Paul (Ed.), *Introduction to the philosophies of research and criticism in education and the social sciences* (pp. 43–65). Upper Saddle River, NJ: Pearson Prentice Hall.

Robbins, A. (2001). Object relations and art therapy. In J. A. Rubin (Ed.), *Approaches to art therapy: Theory and technique* (2nd ed., pp. 54–65). Philadelphia, PA: Brunner-Routledge.

Rubin, J. A. (2001). *Approaches to art therapy: Theory & technique*. Philadelphia, PA: Brunner-Routledge.

Rubin, J. A. (2011). *The art of art therapy: What every art therapist needs to know*. New York, NY: Routledge.

Sagan, O. (2015). *Narratives of art practice and mental wellbeing: Reparation and connection*. New York, NY: Routledge.

## 32   *Richard Carolan and Karrie Stafford*

Shimamura, A. P., & Palmer, S. E. (2012). *Aesthetic science: Connecting minds, brains, and experience.* New York, NY: Oxford University Press.

Stafford, K. (2016). *The art encounter for self-reflection: An art based phenomenological inquiry* (Unpublished doctoral dissertation). Notre Dame de Namur University, Belmont, CA.

Stevens, A. (1994). *Jung.* New York, NY: Oxford Press.

Wadeson, H. (1980). *Art psychotherapy.* New York, NY: Wiley.

Ways of knowing. (2014). Retrieved from www.theoryofknowledge.net/ways-of-knowing

# 3 Art Therapy and Neuropsychology

*Richard Carolan and Amy Hill*

## Introduction

The last decade has seen important advances in the field of art therapy in terms of developing theory and research on the relationship between neuroscience and art. Multiple books have been published on related topics (Hass-Cohen, 2016; King, 2016), and the *Art Therapy Journal* dedicated an edition to exploring this subject (Kapitan, 2014). This area is a significant emerging trend in discovery for art therapy. This chapter will present some of the advances in what we know and offer perspectives on how to move forward. The intent is to provide a brief overview of the contributions some of the current leaders have made in the field of art therapy and neuroscience.

### Models Informed by Art and Neuroscience

The expressive therapies continuum (ETC; Kagin & Lusebrink, 1978; Lusebrink, 1990, 2004, 2010) is a theoretical model and schematic framework informed by psychological theory and developed by pioneers in the study of human development and cognitive growth (Bruner, 1964; Lowenfeld & Brittain, 1970; Piaget & Inhelder, 1971). As a conceptual model, the ETC was designed for the various fields of art and expressive psychotherapies (Kagin & Lusebrink, 1978). ETC can be used to describe and assess a client's level of creative functioning and to assist art therapists in selecting media and interventions to utilize in sessions. Recent studies in neuroscience and maturational brain functioning have contributed additional evidence to the original model of the ETC. Lusebrink (2004, 2010) later incorporated these findings into the original ETC model by exploring the brain structure and processing systems involved in an individual's movement between levels of creative functioning, as well as the parts of the brain that become activated during a typical art therapy session.

The first three levels of the ETC include the kinesthetic/sensory (K/S level), the perceptual/affective (P/A level), and the cognitive/symbolic (C/S level); these levels reflect the three established systems of human information processing (Kagin & Lusebrink, 1978). The fourth level of the ETC, the creative level (CR), is a synthesis of the first three levels of the continuum. Individuals move throughout the continuum from lower level information processing to more complex cognitive processes and interactions. Kagin and Lusebrink (1978) proposed the ETC as a metatheory; they aligned these aspects of creativity with the five different forms of creativity proposed by Taylor (Taylor & Getzels, 1975).

A variety of theoretical approaches to art therapy can be viewed from the perspective of the ETC. An art therapist can determine how a client processes information through assessment of the formal elements in a work of art, and a treatment plan can identify stepwise transitions and horizontal transformations between each level (Lusebrink, 2010). Art therapists in training can also use the model when selecting art materials to use therapeutically and safely within a session with an individual client, group, or family.

Lusebrink (1990, 2004, 2010) and Hinz (2009) further developed the model by exploring how art making requires activity in different neurological regions of the brain; they observed how various regions are activated depending on the art process and materials used. Lusebrink and Hinz (2016) suggested that the integration between the functions of the left and right hemispheres results in the experience of *wellbeing* or a state of *flow* (Csikszentmihalyi, 2008). Flow can be associated with the integration of emotional and cognitive functions, such that both areas contribute positively to focused attention (Lusebrink & Hinz, 2016).

For almost a decade, Hass-Cohen (2008a) has drawn from clinical neuroscience research to "describe and enhance the therapeutic advantages of arts in action and further illuminate the unique contributions of art therapy to well-being and health" (p. 21). Hass-Cohen views the artwork created in art therapy as a concrete representation of mind-body connectivity, and when created in the presence of an art therapist, the artwork can be an expression of how the self is organized internally and in relationship with others. A state of mind-body connectivity begins in the organization of the nervous system, but art therapists also encourage self-expression and a sense of intra/interpersonal connectivity through art therapy approaches. The *art therapy relational neuroscience* (ATR-N) theoretical and clinical approach (Hass-Cohen, 2016; Hass-Cohen & Clyde Findlay, 2015; Hass-Cohen, Clyde Findlay, Carr, & Vanderlan, 2014; King-West & Hass-Cohen, 2008a) was developed to link developments in clinical neuroscience with art therapy treatment. This framework draws on the affective-sensory experience of art making, which keeps clients grounded in their surroundings and provides relief through the expression of emotions and kinesthetic actions of art making (Hass-Cohen, 2008a). The ATR-N approach includes six theoretical principles informed by the neuroscience of relationships: creative embodiment, relational resonating, expressive communicating, adaptive responding, empathizing, and compassion (CREATE).

## Models for Healing Trauma

Hass-Cohen (2008a) has explored the impact of early attachment on brain development and maturation, the brain's ability to strengthen, renew, and rewire throughout the lifespan, and the importance of regulating and integrating affect through relationships with others. The ATR-N brief assessment protocol was developed to explore the interaction of neurological, emotional, cognitive, social, and cultural factors when assessing for the multiple psychosocial dimensions of chronic pain (Hass-Cohen & Clyde Findlay, 2009). The Check ("Check, Change What You Need to Change and/or Keep What You Want") art therapy protocol was designed to treat trauma through a sequence of directives that provide contextualized exposure to trauma memories in order to support "narrative processing, effective therapeutic engagement, and balancing of stress responses needed to regain autobiographical coherency and resilience" (Hass-Cohen, Clyde Findlay, Carr, & Vanderlan, 2014, p. 76).

The concept of resiliency is used to describe individuals who are able to balance and control their behavioral and neurobiological responses to psychosocial stressors and triggers (Hass-Cohen et al., 2014) and to recover from traumatizing memories and master complex trauma symptoms (Hass-Cohen, 2016). Hass-Cohen (2016) has developed a number of ATR-N principles and traumatology informed arts-based interventions (Hass-Cohen, 2016; Hass-Cohen & Clyde Findlay, 2015; Hass-Cohen et al., 2014; King-West & Hass-Cohen, 2008) that allow clients to achieve and maintain actual and perceived safety during contextualized traumatic memory processing. These interventions also help clients increase social connections, decrease the risk of relapse, and creatively consolidate and change autobiographical memories. While much of her work focuses on the treatment of trauma, the ATR-N CREATE guidelines and protocols are characterized by the following principals that can contribute to positive outcomes: (a) safety, comfort, and pleasure; (b) positive emotions and cognitions; (c) repetitive opportunities for mastering control and protection; (d) relational security and social communication; (e) self-acceptance and compassion; (f) memory reconsolidation; and (g) mind-body transformative integration (Hass-Cohen, 2016).

With increased understanding in neurodevelopment, attachment, and the treatment of trauma, art therapists have begun to develop new methods and multidisciplinary models of treatment. Based on findings that the brain first encodes information in the right hemisphere visually (Ogden & Minton, 2000) and that the most common recall of traumatic material is in visual form (Cohn, 1993), Chapman (2014) developed a neurodevelopmental model of art therapy (NDAT) treatment for toddlers, children, and adolescents who have experienced acute and chronic relational trauma. Drawing on recent understandings in neurobiology, brain development, and traumatic memory recall, as well as how the right hemisphere of the brain develops and its role in nonverbal symbolic

## 36  *Richard Carolan and Amy Hill*

and unconscious affective processes, Chapman's approach to treatment is grounded in an understanding of the physical, psychological, and cognitive reactions to trauma.

In 1988, prior to the development of the NDAT, Chapman developed the Chapman art therapy treatment intervention (CAATI) in response to a need for a brief method to reduce PTSD symptoms in children and adolescents who were hospitalized following urban community violence (Chapman, 2014). The intervention was designed to help children who were experiencing the neurochemical dysregulation of a stress response; they were assisted in remembering, expressing, and integrating acute traumatic episodes by illustrating their experiences and developing a coherent narrative with each drawing. The CAATI includes four components; a kinesthetic scribble, a sequential drawing depicting the traumatic event, a discussion of each drawing extending to adjustment after the hospitalization, and a retelling of the story using the images.

Chapman incorporated Lusebrink's ETC model to direct youth from the lower level kinesthetic activity of drawing to the affect/perceptual level, in which accompanying affect is organized and normalized. The next level of information processing, cognitive/symbolic, becomes activated through the use of language, analytical thought, and problem solving, as the youth attempt to formulate a coherent narrative. The creative level, which is a synthesis of the previous three levels, can be reached when the information related to the traumatic event is activated in conjunction with early brain development, which can lead to a reduction of PTSD symptoms (Chapman, 2014).

Chapman developed the NDAT for use with children who require long-term treatment due to multiple traumatic exposures, losses, and disrupted or dysfunctional living situations, but the model was shaped by the theoretical constructs that first comprised the CAATI model. In the NDAT, treatment remains focused on the activation of sensory nonverbal neural pathways in the right hemisphere of the brain, along with the verbal neural pathways in the left hemisphere, to utilize the integrative capacity of the brain in healing (Chapman, 2014). NDAT is a long-term treatment, and once safety and trust are established, it consists of four stages. Unlike short-term treatment models, the NDAT first activates the lower structures of the brain in order to address early trauma and disrupted attachment before integrating interventions that develop the parts of the brain responsible for affect and cognition.

Each stage of the NDAT can be viewed as a continuum (Chapman, 2014). The *self-phase* is the starting point of therapy and includes assessment, attention to safety, and highly structured interventions that provide ego containment, avoid regressive experiences, and strengthen the physical body and the sensory and motor systems. In the *problem phase*, the focus shifts to emotions, and therapeutic emotional homeostasis becomes the main goal as the child begins to develop a safe and secure relationship with the therapist in order to explore art as a symbolic and metaphorical expression (Chapman, 2014). In the *transformation phase*, the focus moves to cognitive homeostasis; as affect and behaviors are stabilized, a cognitive understanding of the past is developed, and higher-level contemplation of affect-laden content can help to redefine beliefs about the self and integrate fragmented memories. Finally, the *integration phase* is structured around the termination of treatment after coping skills have been developed, a support system has been identified, and a continued refinement of self-regulation and emotional processing have led to symptom reduction.

Linda Gantt has incorporated trauma treatment with art therapy for decades (Gantt & Tinnin, 2007). She focuses her trauma treatment theory on the structure of the human brain, as well as on animal survival mechanisms (Gantt & Tripp, 2016). Gantt has incorporated recent neurobiology research into her art therapy approach to working with early developmental trauma (Gantt & Tripp, 2016). Gantt asserted that foundation traumas (i.e., those traumas occurring before three years of age) must be processed before other traumatic events can become the focus of treatment.

Gantt and Tinnin developed *intensive trauma therapy* (ITT) in their outpatient clinic in West Virginia; ITT is based on their *instinctual trauma response* theory (Gantt & Tripp, 2016) and is grounded in the understanding that traumatic memory is encoded through visual imagery and bodily sensation, which can compromise cognitive functioning when unresolved (Gantt & Tripp, 2016; van der Kolk, 2006a, 2014). In contrast to earlier assumptions that trauma occurring in infancy or in young children could not be experienced or remembered, Tinnin and Gantt (2014) have called attention to the enduring capacity of early trauma based on the structure of the developing human brain, especially before the age of three, when the corpus callosum has acquired its myelin sheath, which allows the left and right hemispheres to communicate. Their work draws from contemporary theories developed by child psychiatrist Daniel Siegel (1995, 1996, 1999, 2001) and neuro-psychoanalyst Allan Schore (1994, 1997, 2001a, 2002, 2003, 2009).

The ITT clinic was designed to offer intensive treatment for clients; a treatment team works with each client for seven hours per day for five to 10 days, with art therapy being the primary mode of treatment (Gantt & Tripp, 2016). This treatment allows traumatized individuals to create coherent autobiographical stories with a beginning, middle, and end based on fragmented trauma memories. The basic tenets for working with preverbal trauma (Gantt & Tripp, 2016) are as follows: (a) preverbal traumatic memories are stored in the nonverbal mind, (b) preverbal memories are blocked from awareness by verbal cerebral dominance and are inaccessible to verbal probes, and (c) in the nonverbal mind, imprints of trauma memory lack narrative structure and therefore lack narrative closure.

## 38    Richard Carolan and Amy Hill

A universal response to overwhelming, life-threatening events is referred to as the *instinctual trauma response* (ITR; Tinnin, Bills, & Gantt, 2002; Tinnin & Gantt, 2014). The ITR model of treatment uses three components to process each trauma in the same order chronologically (Gantt & Tripp, 2016). The graphic narrative (GN) is a structured series of drawings that represent each component of the ITR, as well as the body sensations; these drawings include at minimum before and after scenes, and preferably a drawing for the startle, the thwarted intention to fight or flee, the altered state of consciousness, the automatic obedience, and the attempts at self-repair (Gantt & Tripp, 2016). This initial component is used to process a trauma story and bring the trauma to a close. During the next component, the re-presentation of the GN, the art therapist displays the temporal sequence of drawings on the wall and repeats the story to the client, being careful not to provide interpretation or commentary. In the final step, an externalized dialogue (ED) takes place between internal parts of the client (Gantt & Tripp, 2016). Variations can include video dialogue, puppets, drawn portraits, sculpture, or writing using different colors of ink and the dominant and nondominant hands. The authors asserted that art therapy can provide a holding place to safely contain difficult feelings associated with trauma work, including a fear of dysregulation due to the intense range of feelings that could be unearthed as well as patterns of distrust in intimate relationships (Gantt & Tripp, 2016). This approach provides a structured template for art therapists and for individuals to use outside of sessions.

When psychological trauma disrupts bodily systems, the long-term impact on the mind and the body can extend well into adulthood (Anda et al., 2006). Belkofer and Nolan (2016) combined neuroscience research with their experience utilizing art therapy with children who have experienced severe trauma to demonstrate that "the contemporary frameworks for understanding the brain return mental health clinicians to considerations of the body" (p. 158). They identified how process-oriented approaches to art therapy treatment can target the underlying components of trauma, which allow clients to increase awareness of their own bodies in order to regulate difficult emotions.

Difficulties with self-regulation are a key feature of severe trauma and cause children to struggle within their own bodies (van der Kolk, 2006b). Belkofer and Nolan examined how levels of hyper- and hypo-arousal and dysregulated systems of the brain (Glaser, 2000; Klorer, 2005; Perry, 2009) are associated with variations in neurophysiology (Siegel, 1999). They also examined how clinical neuroscience and interpersonal neurobiology have contributed to attachment theory (Schore, 2001b) to allow clinicians to better understand how relationships shape the brain (Siegel, 1999). Through this exploration, Belkofer and Nolan (2016) encouraged art therapists to address mental health as "an interpersonally influenced mind/body holistic experience" (pp. 159–160) and to incorporate and emphasize bodily elements of the arts in treatment to reach the state of interpersonal connection—"therapeutic attunement" (Kossak, 2009, p. 14)—with clients.

Tripp (2007) developed a short-term art therapy approach for the treatment of trauma-related disorders using a modified eye movement desensitization and reprocessing (EMDR) protocol with alternating tactile and auditory bilateral stimulation; their treatment was informed by research in neurobiology, attachment theory, sensorimotor therapy, and EMDR. Tripp's therapeutic approach integrates dual attention focusing, heightened somatic awareness, art making, and narrative. The client is asked to select a disturbing memory, and affective material is brought to conscious awareness through ongoing bilateral tactile and auditory stimulation (Tripp, 2007). The client then engages in art making while focusing on an image, a negative self-referencing belief, and the emotions and sensations that accompany the memory. According to Tripp, the creation of a series of consecutive drawings or paintings allows the individual to track new cognitions, which paves the way for new avenues of awareness (p. 178). Tripp (2016) further developed a somatically-informed bilateral art therapy protocol for trauma treatment, combining elements of art therapy, sensorimotor psychotherapy, EMDR, and interpersonal neuroscience; this protocol focuses on the body in order to assess and facilitate the resolution of traumatic memories.

### Measuring the Brain

Researchers have made significant advances in the last several decades in developing accurate measurements of the brain. The measurements are focused on measuring electrical activity or fluid activity (water, blood). These instruments allow researchers to compare brain composition and activity to brains of individuals with similar age and gender, as well as to compare a specific brain to itself under different conditions. These systems of measurement often require extensive skill in "reading" the results. The meaning of the results is also complicated because different diagnostic categories may have vastly different neurological results. The most common means of neurobiology includes the following.

#### Electroencephalogram (EEG)

When using electroencephalogram (EEG), electrodes are placed on the scalp to identify neural firings between regions, which measure frequency of firings and variation in function and connectivity. Synchronized activity reflects functional connectivity. Nonsynchronized activity may suggest areas that need attention.

#### Computed Tomography (CT)

Computed tomography (CT) is an x-ray technique which uses brain images that are enhanced by mathematical computer programs.

40　*Richard Carolan and Amy Hill*

A drawback of this approach is that it produces poor images, and there is a radiation impact.

### Magnetic Resonance Imaging (MRI)

The magnetic resonance imaging (MRI) procedure is able to show anatomical brain changes. It measures soft tissue and the movement of water in the brain in response to magnetic activity. This approach eliminates exposure to radiation. The brain normally contains consistent structural integrity and volume relative to age and gender. Structural differences may be representative of issues that lead to cognitive and/or emotional difficulty. The MRI measures the relationship between blood flow and neural activity using magnetic resonance to find changes in blood oxygenation. It is an indirect measure of brain activity because the rate of change in neural activity compared to change in blood flow is vastly different. This procedure allows for a comparison of the brain's resting state with specific activation states (visualization/facial expression).

### MRI-Spectroscopy (MRS)

The MRI-spectroscopy (MRS) uses magnetic fields to identify unique characteristics of specific molecules, which results in the identification of the biochemical make-up of a region; it is able to evaluate its strength and can track its neuroplasticity. The MRS can track specific biochemical changes that occur before and after a particular intervention.

### Diffusion Tensor Imaging (DTI)

Diffusion tensor imaging (DTI) is a magnetic resonance technique that identifies the integrity of primary myelinated axonal brain pathways that connect brain regions. This procedure evaluates the water molecules within axons.

### Single Photon Computed Tomography (SPECT) and Positron Emission Tomography (PET)

Both the single photon computed tomography (SPECT) and positron emission tomography (PET) use gamma cameras to view radioactive tracer molecules called ligands in the brain.

### Understanding the Landscape of Neurobiology and Art

The significant progress that has been made regarding the means of measuring brain activity anchors our understanding of the complexity of neuroscience and the potential for the interaction between the science and the art of art therapy. We need to understand this process in the macro as

*Art Therapy and Neuropsychology* 41

well as the micro view. The brain is an extraordinary organ that cannot accurately be reduced to predictable patterns of electrical and chemical interactions. As the brain grows and develops neural pathways, there is ongoing interaction with external and internal environmental factors. The attraction and repulsion in relation to environmental variables may well be synchronistic with the attraction and repulsion in the chemical and electrical activity in the brain. The brain adapts to its environment, even to the point of restructuring its anatomy and function (Lukasz, 2016). While we each have the same brain anatomy, each brain is unique.

Lusebrink (2016) noted that the brain developed two different types of neural systems—one for emotionally based responses and the other for objective perceptual evaluation. She discussed the separate (but related) processing of information from these systems (i.e., emotional, objective) in different parts of the brain and their subsequent reintegration into a different brain area (i.e., dorsolateral prefrontal cortex). The relationship between the different sections of the brain, from both evolutionary and developmental perspectives, can provide an important source of information that can lead to a more macro view of neuroscience.

The focus on trauma has helped us understand the still active survival functions of the primitive brain. We place less emphasis on understanding the communication functions of the preverbal brain in both primitive species of humans as well as in the brains of infants. The extraordinary neural functioning in preverbal language communication is an area that seems to be considered less significant, yet it is a critical component of neural functioning related to art. When discussing the left brain—right-brain relationship, Gantt and Tripp (2016) suggested that the left-brain verbal mind assumes dominance. The left-brain dismisses all of the critical right brain functioning as "it," while claiming ownership of "I" (Gantt & Tripp, 2016). Gantt further stated, "As Shore explains (2009) before the left hemisphere dominates, the right hemisphere preforms the crucial role of developing the emotional self and forming a secure attachment" (Gantt & Tripp, 2016). However, there may be inherent losses in this process. McGilchrist (2009) noted how the left brain creates a version of the world that is separate from experience:

> Language enables the left hemisphere to represent the world "off-line," a conceptual version, distinct from the world of experience. . . . Isolating things artificially from their context brings the advantage of enabling us to focus intently on a specific aspect of reality and how it can be modelled, so that it can be grasped and controlled. But its losses are in the picture as a whole. Whatever lies in the realm of the implicit, or depends on flexibility. Whatever can't be brought into focus and fixed, ceases to exist as far as the speaking hemisphere is concerned.
>
> (p. 124)

## 42 *Richard Carolan and Amy Hill*

Returning to the studies on neuroscience and trauma, we know that in crisis, or in life-threatening situations, the right hemisphere responds to stimuli more quickly than the left. Belkofer and Nolan (2016) added that "one could argue that an overemphasis on the mind (thinking and explaining) as opposed to the body (feeling and experiencing) has thrown mental health out of balance."

### *Artist—Scientist Researcher*

One of the areas that may be valuable in current neuroscience inquiry by art therapists is the integration of the artist/scientist as researcher. The reductionism of science can be balanced by the emergent discovery process intrinsic in the arts. An example of a nonreductionist approach would be an increased focus on a systems perspective as a way of understanding the human experience. As we continue to learn about the brain as a functioning system, we may find this information is applicable to understanding all human systems (and perhaps systems in nature other than human systems). The concept that a person can have an active influence on changing the structure of their own brain on the one hand seems extraordinary, yet on the other hand we have known that art and the therapeutic process can have a powerful influence on the person's experience of life; would that not presuppose changes in the brain?

The field of neuroscience continues to make important advances in developing hypotheses about what we know more clearly than what we do not know. Neurobiology, as in all science, is a reflection of the instruments that generate data. It is postulated that it is a scientific fact that a neuron is either on or off, "is or isn't" (King, 2016). Is that a fact or is it an understanding based on our means of measuring? There has always been a human drive to know, to "break the code" of understanding the complexity of human experience. The extraordinary Human Connectome Project hopes to map the typical human brain and its 100 billion neurons, each with about 10,000 connections. It is as if the river of life were still, as if it were finite, yes or no, on or off, and once we decipher the code we will have the answer—as if to scoop a cup of water from the river and analyze it in detail in the laboratory is to know the river.

The concept of "action potentials" that are critical to brain communication is a complex process. 10,000 to 100,000 inputs are activated, leading to the communication process, which involves the action potential moving down the axon and thus causing the release of neurotransmitters. This is the "on or off" neuron activity; the action potential moves down the axon or it does not. However, implicit in this simple "yes or no" is the action of the 10,000 to 100,000 input stimuli. This is an interesting phenomenon when we look at it in terms of the desire for predictability in human behavior. We want to know that this stimulus will cause that action. The function of the brain itself seems to indicate that the impact of a given input can depend on 10,000 to 100,000 other variables.

Art therapy should have a basis anchored in neuroscience, and there should be a collaborative function between the two fields where each enhances the understanding of the other. We must embrace advances and the hunger for knowledge and evidence from a broad perspective. It is important to remember that one of the most significant advances in neurology in the last century, for which Portuguese neurologist Egas Moniz was awarded the Nobel Prize in 1949, was the development of "evidence-based" procedures for lobotomies. It is extraordinary to consider that lobotomies for mental illness were considered best practices until the 1960s. Another practice that is currently still in use in the United States and throughout the world is electroconvulsive therapy. This procedure creates seizure activity in the brain, and there is evidence that it can be helpful for depression that is considered treatment-resistant. Yet we are still uncertain as to how or why it is helpful.

We have certainly made important progress in attempts to measure brain activity. There are regions of the brain that are more active in relation to different activities. We know which regions of the brain have more dominant activity in relation to the senses and also in relation to different functions. We are able to measure both location and degree of activity. We have an understanding of how the brain takes sensory input and transforms it into electrical signals that impact sensory pathways forming neuronal signals, and how different brain areas integrate the sensory input and send it to another area of the brain that manages behavioral response. Examining components of the creative art process, such as cognitive processes, memory, awareness of space, and kinesthetic activity, and furthering our knowledge of where these processes are located in the brain, allows us to have a fuller understanding of neurological activity involved in the art process.

However, there is also research supporting the understanding that artistic production is not localized to certain neurological regions; art involves activation throughout the brain (Belkofer, 2012). We know that the art process is kinesthetic, tactile, and sensory, and as such, it activates and facilitates the integration of multiple brain areas and functions. King (2016) identified the following primary tenets of art therapy related to neurobiology:

1. The bilateral and multidirectional process of creativity is healing and life enhancing;
2. The materials and the methods utilized affect self-expression, assist in self-regulation, and are applied in specialized ways;
3. The art making process and the artwork itself are integral components of treatment that help to understand and elicit verbal and non-verbal communication within the attuned therapeutic relationship.

One area of future development in research and art is in neuroesthetics and how the brain functions during activity that is not goal-oriented.

## 44   *Richard Carolan and Amy Hill*

Recent research in the function of the default mode network and the viewing of art is promising for the field of art therapy (Hutton, 2014). Future research will certainly develop clarity on the relationship between neurological activity and therapeutic work, with different art materials as well as different art processes. This information can then be correlated with measurements of neurological activity and mood states, which will contribute to future directions in designing art-based neurological interventions for mood disorders. This same type of research can also be refined for work with cognitive disorders. The organic evolution of the human brain in response to environmental stressors provides us with a good deal if we keep in mind the ineffectiveness of reducing this knowledge to formulas and remember that measuring brain activity is not the royal road to the end of human suffering; however, it is very promising in terms of providing us with important information and guidance in understanding the human systems and its levels of integration. Neurological studies also offer hope in terms of understanding the brain activity involved in different ways of knowing. Examining the neurological relationship between cognitive knowing, emotional knowing, intuitive knowing, and imaginative knowing offers exciting trends in which art can play a contributing role.

## References

Anda, R. F., Felitti, V. J., Bremner, J. D., Walker, J. D., Whitfield, C., Perry, B. D., Dube, S. R., & Giles, W. H. (2006). The enduring effects of abuse and related adverse experiences in childhood: A convergence of evidence from neurobiology and epidemiology. *European Archives of Psychiatry and Clinical Neuroscience, 256*(3), 174–186.

Belkofer, C. M. (2012). *The impact of visual art making on the brain* (Unpublished doctoral dissertation). Cambridge, MA: Lesley University.

Belkofer, C. M., & Nolan, E. (2016). Practical applications of neuroscience in art therapy: A holistic approach to treating trauma in children. In J. King (Ed.), *Art therapy, trauma, and neuroscience* (pp. 157–172). New York, NY: Routledge.

Bruner, J. S. (1964). The course of cognitive growth. *American Psychologist, 19*, 1–15.

Carlson, N. R. (2001). *Physiology of behavior* (7th ed.). Boston, MA: Allyn & Bacon.

Chapman, L. (2014). *Neurobiologically informed trauma therapy with children and adolescents: Understanding mechanisms of change.* New York, NY: Norton.

Christian, D. (2008). The cortex: Regulation of sensory and emotional experience. In N. Hass-Cohen & R. Carr (eds.), *Art therapy and clinical neuroscience* (pp. 62–75). Philadelphia, PA: Jessica Kingsley.

Cohn, L. (1993). Art psychotherapy and eye movement desensitization reprocessing (EMDR) technique: An integrated approach. In E. Virshup (Ed.), *California art therapy trends*. Chicago, IL: Magnolia Street Publishers.

Csikszentmihalyi, M. (2008). Flow: The psychology of optimal experience. New York: Harper.

Fuster, J. M. (2003). *Cortex and mind: Unifying cognition*. New York, NY: Oxford University Press.

Gantt, L., & Tinnin, L. (2007). Intensive trauma therapy of PTSD and dissociation: An outcome study. *The Arts in Psychotherapy, 34*(1), 69–80.

Gantt, L., & Tripp, T. (2016). The image comes first: Treating preverbal trauma with art therapy. In J. King (Ed.), *Art therapy, trauma, and neuroscience* (pp. 157–172). New York, NY: Routledge.

Gazzaniga, M. S., Ivry, R. B., & Mangun, G. R. (2002). *Cognitive neuroscience: The biology of the mind* (2nd ed.). New York: W. W. Norton & Co.

Glaser, D. (2000). Child abuse and neglect and the brain—A review. *Journal of Child Psychology and Psychiatry, 41*(1), 99–116.

Hass-Cohen, N. (2008a). Partnering of art therapy and clinical Neuroscience. In N. Hass-Cohen & R. Carr (Eds.), *Art therapy and clinical Neuroscience* (pp. 21–42). Philadelphia, PA: Jessica Kingsley.

Hass-Cohen, N. (2008b). CREATE: Art Therapy Relational Neuroscience principles (ATR-N). In N. Hass-Cohen & R. Carr (Eds.), *Art therapy and clinical neuroscience* (pp. 283–309). Philadelphia, PA: Jessica Kingsley.

Hass-Cohen, N., & Loya, N. (2008). Visual system in action. In N. Hass-Cohen & R. Carr (Eds.). *Art therapy and clinical neurosciences* (pp. 92–110). Philadelphia, PA: Jessica Kingsley.

Hass-Cohen, N., & Findlay, J. C. (2009). Pain, attachment, and meaning making: Report on an art therapy relational neuroscience protocol. *The Arts in Psychotherapy, 36*(4), 175–184.

Hass-Cohen, N. (2016). Secure resiliency: Art Therapy Relational Neuroscience trauma treatment principles and guidelines. In J. King (Ed.), *Art therapy, trauma, and neuroscience* (pp. 100–138). New York, NY: Routledge.

Hass-Cohen, N., & Findlay, J. C. (2015). *Art therapy & the neuroscience of relationships, creativity, and resiliency*. The Interpersonal Neurobiology Series. New York: Norton

Hass-Cohen, N., Findlay, J. C., Carr, R., & Vanderlan, J. (2014). Check, change what you need to change and/or keep what you want: An art therapy neurobiological-based trauma protocol. *Art Therapy: Journal of the American Art Therapy Association, 31*(2), 69–78.

Hinz, L. D. (2009). *Expressive therapies continuum: A framework for using art in therapy*. New York: Routledge.

Hughdahl, K., & Davidson, R. J. (Eds.). (2003). *The asymmetrical brain*. Cambridge, MA: MIT Press.

Hutton, N. (2014). *Art and the default mode network*. Retrieved from http://thebeautifulbrain.com/2014/02/art-and-the-default-mode-network/

Kagin, S. L., & Lusebrink, V. B. (1978). The expressive therapies continuum. *Art Psychotherapy, 5*, 171–180.

Kapitan, L. (2014). Introduction to the neurobiology of art therapy: Evidence-based, complex, and influential. *Art Therapy: Journal of the American Art Therapy Association, 31*(2), 50–51.

King-West, E., & Hass-Cohen, N. (2008). Art therapy, neuroscience, and complex PTSD. In N. Hass-Cohen & R. Carr (Eds.), *Art therapy and clinical neuroscience* (pp. 223–253). Philadelphia, PA: Jessica Kingsley.

King, J. L. (Ed.). (2016). *Art Therapy, trauma, and neuroscience: theoretical and practical perspectives*. New York, NY: Routledge.

## 46 Richard Carolan and Amy Hill

Klorer, G. P. (2005). Expressive therapy with severely maltreated children: Neuroscience contributions. *Art Therapy: Journal of the American Art Therapy Association, 22*(4), 213–219.

Kossak, M. (2009). Therapeutic attunement: A transpersonal view of expressive arts therapy. *The Arts in Psychotherapy, 36*(1), 13–18.

Lowenfeld, V., & Brittain, W. L. (1970). *Creative and mental growth* (5th ed.). New York, NY: Macmillan.

Lukasz, K. M. (2016). Neuroscience concepts in clinical practice. In J. King (Ed.), *Art therapy, trauma, and neuroscience* (pp. 157–172). New York, NY: Routledge.

Lusebrink, V. B. (1990). *Imagery and visual expression in therapy.* New York, NY: Plenum Press.

Lusebrink, V. B. (2004). Art therapy and the brain: An attempt to understand the underlying processes of art expression in therapy. *Art Therapy: Journal of the American Art Therapy Association, 21*(3), 125–135.

Lusebrink, V. B. (2010). Assessment and therapeutic application of the expressive therapies continuum: Implications for brain structures and functions. *Art Therapy: Journal of the American Art Therapy Association, 27*(4), 168–177.

Lusebrink, V. B., & Hinz, L. D. (2016). The expressive therapies continuum as a framework in the treatment of trauma. In J. King (Ed.), *Art therapy, trauma, and neuroscience* (pp. 42–66). New York, NY: Routledge.

McGilchrist, I. (2009). *The master and his emissary.* New Haven, CT: Yale University Press.

Ogden, P., & Minton, K. (2000). Sensorimotor psychotherapy: One method for processing traumatic memory. *Traumatology, 6*(3), 149–173.

Piaget, J., & Inhelder, B. (1971). *Mental imagery in the child.* New York, NY: Basic Books.

Schore, A. (1994). *Affect regulation and the origin of the self: The neurobiology of emotional development.* Mahwah, NJ: Erlbaum.

Schore, A. (1997). Early organization of the nonlinear right brain and development of a predisposition to psychiatric disorders. *Development and Psychopathology, 9*(4), 595–631.

Schore, A. (2001a). The effects of early relational trauma on right brain development, affect regulation, and infant mental health. *Infant Mental Health Journal, 22*(1–2), 201–269.

Schore, A. (2001b). Effects of secure attachment relationships on right brain development, affect regulation, and infant mental health. *Infant Mental Health Journal, 22*(1–2), 7–66.

Schore, A. (2002). Dysregulation of the right brain: A fundamental mechanism of traumatic attachment and the psychopathogenesis of post-traumatic stress disorder. *Australian & New Zealand Journal of Psychiatry, 36*(1), 9–30.

Schore, A. (2003). *Affect dysregulation and disorders of the self.* New York: W.W. Norton.

Schore, A. (2009). Attachment trauma and the developing right brain: Origins of pathological dissociation. In P. Dell & J. O'Neil (Eds.), *Dissociation and the dissociative disorders: DSM-V and beyond* (pp. 107–141). New York: Routledge.

Siegel, D. (1995). Memory, trauma, and psychotherapy: A cognitive science view. *Journal of Psychotherapy Practice and Research, 4*(2), 93–122.

Siegel, D. (1996). Dissociation, psychotherapy and the cognitive sciences. In J. Spira, (Ed.). *The treatment of dissociative identity disorder* (pp. 39–80). San Francisco, CA: Jossey-Bass.

Siegel, D. (1999). *The developing mind: How relationships and the brain interact to shape who we are.* New York: Guilford.

Siegel, D. (2001). Toward an interpersonal neurobiology of the developing mind: Attachment relationships, "mindsight," and neural integration. *Infant Mental Health Journal*, 22(1–2), 67–94.

Taylor, I. A., & Getzels, J. W. (1975). *Perspectives in creativity.* Oxford, England: Aldine

Tinnin, L., Bills, L., & Gantt, L. (2002). Short-term treatment of simple and complex PTSD. In M. B. Williams & J. G. Sommer (Eds.), *Simple and complex post-traumatic stress disorder: Strategies for comprehensive treatment in clinical practice* (pp. 99–118). Binghamton, NY: Haworth Press.

Tinnin, L., & Gantt, L. (2014). *The instinctual trauma response and dual brain dynamics: A guide for trauma therapy.* Morgantown, WV: Gargoyle Press.

Tripp, T. (2007). A short term therapy approach to processing trauma: Art therapy and bilateral stimulation. *Art Therapy: Journal of the American Art Therapy Association*, 24(4), 176–183.

Tripp, T. (2016). A body-based bilateral art protocol for reprocessing trauma. In J. King (Ed.), *Art therapy, trauma, and neuroscience* (pp. 173–194). New York: Routledge.

van der Kolk, B. A. (2006a). Post-traumatic stress disorder and the nature of trauma. In M. Solomon and D. Siegel (Eds.), *Healing trauma: Attachment, mind, body and brain* (pp. 168–195). New York: W. W. Norton.

van der Kolk, B. A. (2006b). Clinical implications of neuroscience research in PTSD. *Annals of the New York Academy of Sciences*, 1071(1), 277–293.

van der Kolk, B. A. (2014). *The body keeps the score: Brain, mind, and body in the healing of trauma.* New York: Viking.

# 4 Art Therapy Pedagogy

*Amy Backos and Richard Carolan*

## Introduction

A consideration of the emerging trends in art therapy education requires reflecting on a broad landscape that includes the role of both teachers and students, the latter of whom are graduate students and professional lifelong learners. We must define art therapy education, the role of teaching, learning, and apprenticeship, as well as understand who we are educating. In essence, we must carefully define and consider *the how* and *the what* of education in art therapy. This chapter builds on theories and philosophies previously explored in earlier chapters of this book. Concepts explored in more detail include theories of education that influence our work, the multiple roles and responsibilities of the educator, the role of the art therapy student in learning, and the role of art therapy professionals as lifelong learners. Finally, we will suggest future directions in learning and pedagogy that highlight emerging trends in art therapy standards and practices.

## Education in Art Therapy

Hilgenheger (1993) distinguished between education and teaching as follows: He defined education as a holistic enterprise that encompasses both development of the character and the process of the learner, while he defined teaching more narrowly in terms of communicating new knowledge and developing current understandings and skills. The practice of art therapy requires that the therapist focus on the character and process of the learner; it follows that emerging trends in art therapy education need to take responsibility for the more holistic definition and not the narrower focus of teaching.

Education in art therapy addresses a far broader audience then the art therapy student. We must include art therapy professionals who stay abreast of current trends and best practices through continuing education classes, reading art therapy journals, attending conferences, and engaging with professional organizations. Additionally, we must educate members of allied professions about the uses and benefits of art

*Art Therapy Pedagogy* 49

therapy—gatekeepers of fiscal support—as well as the general public, if they are to be well-informed consumers. It appears that educators should be experienced—those who are most qualified to address the broad responsibilities of art therapy education.

We must carefully attend to whom we are educating in order to address the understanding the learner requires. Art therapy educators must encourage students to embody many roles: the artist, the clinician, the educator, the scientist, the researcher, and the interdisciplinary. It is the role of the educator to invite, engage, and facilitate the process of each of these aspects for the student, as the student learns to embrace and honor each of these aspects and to collaborate with others. The content of the academic inquiry becomes the ground of the educational process, and it is the role of the educator to engage and stimulate the different ways of knowing that are native to the different components of the learner. The art therapy educator, then, must be fluent in the language of art, clinical practice, science, research, social justice, and of related disciplines.

Gerber (2016) recommended a dialectic paradigm: a conversation between pragmatism and constructivism. The former is more scientifically based, while the latter has a more philosophical influence. This parallels Langer's (1942) view of the importance of accepting science, but not being willing to stop where the edge of science dictates one must stop. Perhaps art therapy education requires broader conversations than what we know through scientific accruement and what we can construct through experience. Art therapy education in graduate school should also address what can be imagined and what can be created, and this imagination must be cultivated throughout our careers. We should perhaps develop a different perspective on the charge towards truth—recognizing that what we call "truth" is a postmodern construct and a holding ground for currently accepted standards, which are based on limited measurement tools.

Pedagogy addresses the science and art of education: the theory and the practice. Our understanding of pedagogy is influenced by theories of human development. Piaget's theory of cognitive development (1970), Bruner's (1996) theory of culture, and Vygotsky's (1978) theory of learning through social interaction are significant contributions to current theories of pedagogy. In speaking about the strategic component of instructional design, Gagne (2015) postulated there are different learners, and naturally, different learning strategies. While he defined different categories of learning, he also identified "instructional events," each with related cognitive processes. He proposed nine events with associated cognitive process that support students in learning new material by linking it to previously learned information or to previous experiences. These include engaging the student, having expectations or goals and conveying those to the students, helping students to retrieve previous learning, presenting the lesson, helping to guide the learner through the experience, and "eliciting performance" (para. 3). The final steps are giving feedback, assessing, and then helping the student generalize the experience.

"Five Standards of Effective Pedagogy" (2017) include the following:

1. Emphasis on joint productive activity on the part of both teachers and students
2. Competency in a common language of literacy across the curriculum
3. Contextualizing teaching to skills and lived experience
4. Developing complexity in cognitive processes
5. Use of dialogue and teaching through conversation

We can identify the increasing depth and mastery that graduate learning entails by reviewing "Bloom's Taxonomy of Learning" (2015). The levels of knowledge begin with a recall of previously learned information, then moving through understanding, and applying, analyzing, evaluating, and creating. Creating is the process of building on diversity and implementing new integrated models. We propose that these two factors—building on diversity and implementing new models—are at the core of art therapy education, and in doctoral education in particular. This education goes far beyond mastery of material, and these two ways of thinking define the creative origins of the profession and are at the heart of the emerging trends in the field.

To visually conceptualize the stages of integrating knowledge, we look to a painting by Doris Arrington, art therapist, HLM, psychologist, and artist. In her painting, *Eight Steps of Women* (see Plate 5), she depicts the stages of development using size and shoes that are typically worn according to one's age. The bottom steps are filled with baby shoes, pink boots, and saddle shoes. These might best reflect the early stages of students as they learn philosophical foundations and theory. Foundational areas are meant to be learned for developing a shared understanding of language and mastery of content that is conceptualized by experts in the field. The middle stages hold running shoes and high heels. This is representative of the action stages, whereby we integrate our lived experience with the theory. This middle section of the steps represents increasing complexity—its challenging to run hard or even walk in heels. The final, top step, holds Birkenstocks; these are shoes that symbolize thoughtful comfort and a sense of knowing oneself as an unselfconscious embodiment of wisdom. These later stages are reflective of complexity in cognitive processes as well as dialogue and teaching through conversation.

Pedagogy for art therapy educators, both professors of art therapy at a university and trainers at conferences, requires that we engage the diversity of learners. We capitalize on the strengths inherent in diversity to fully value and develop all the components of the effective art therapist. Art therapy benefits from diversity. When the voices of all in the profession are heard and valued, not only the voices of the dominant group,

*Art Therapy Pedagogy*   51

new ideas emerge and push the field forward. Furthermore, we benefit when we engage in diverse ways of knowing; related to the learner, the educational process must call upon the complexity within the scientist while collaborating with the artist.

### Art Therapy Educator

Having had the opportunity to work with and train art therapy students over the course of many years, we have learned that one of the most important conversations involves supporting the student in reflecting on not only what they know, but what they do not know they know. Students are often led by an internal wisdom, which comes to the foreground in active engagement and is effectively implemented. At times, it is only in reflection that the theory and concepts related to their interventions becomes integrated. The early stages of Bloom's taxonomy are processed, then let go of, as the student moves to a later stage and a developmentally more complete understanding ("Bloom's Taxonomy," 2016). The multiple stages are then integrated at different times. I (Richard) trained many years ago at the Gestalt Institute. In the first semester of training we learned Gestalt theory and technique. In the second semester, we were trained to let go of the theory and the technique. The lesson was that if the theory and technique were in the forefront of one's awareness, it would hinder the ability to be attentive and aware in the moment. The theory and technique needed to be in your "bones" not in your head. B. F. Skinner, the preeminent expert on learning, defines it as such: "Education is what survives when what has been learned has been forgotten" (Nelson, 2007).

Gerber (2016) addressed how integrating ways of knowing occurs by discussing extrinsic and intrinsic knowledge in the context of the dialectic between pragmatic and constructivist perspectives. One of the more difficult challenges as educators is communicating with students in a way that facilitates meeting them where they are on this intrinsic-extrinsic continuum, not where we might think they should be. The levels of education might create some recommendations for this balance; it is likely that more emphasis needs to be put on extrinsic knowledge in the earlier levels of the educational process, with more emphasis on intrinsic on the later levels. Referring again to the Gestalt training, we were first taught the theories and definitions; then, when they were integrated, we shifted focus from them to allow focus on intrinsic knowing. While we emphasize to students the importance of attending to and honoring intuitive knowing as artists and therapists, we also emphasize that everything we feel in our gut is not necessarily based on intuitive knowledge; some of it is based on stomach acid! Our intuition is composed of, among other things, ancestral knowledge and family folklore. These beliefs must be examined and compared to scientific practice, and our cultural beliefs must be explored and well.

## 52 Amy Backos and Richard Carolan

Emerging trends in art therapy education require that educators show up as artists, as scientists, and as researchers with interdisciplinary awareness, and engage students in conversations in each of these areas. Through pedagogy, art therapy educators stimulate dialogue and engagement, such that each learner is required to have dialogue with, and integrate, these different bases of knowledge within the self. Learning how to learn involves facilitating conversations between these stakeholders within the individual's knowledge base and helping that individual contextualize this knowledge within his or her lived experience.

Reflexive of Paulo Freire's seminal work, *Pedagogy of the Oppressed* (1970), modern art therapy education provides opportunities for generating knowledge in concert with others. Freire considered learners as co-creators of knowledge, not merely as empty containers that are waiting for knowledge to be deposited into them like a bank. This concept is particularly relevant when we consider the valuable knowledge of individuals and the shared wisdom of underrepresented and minority communities, including people of color, students, women, LGBTQ, poor people, and other oppressed groups. Through a careful analysis of the relationship between the colonizer (oppressor) and the colonized (oppressed), Freire concluded that depositing knowledge without creating shared knowledge strips the humanity from both the educator and the learner. He advocated for cultural synthesis, a term he used to describe working together to solve societal problems and liberating the oppressed. Indeed, this shared creation of knowledge in art therapy and the valuing of community wisdom allows the profession to grow and strengthen its knowledge base.

Educators must consider their role and their issues related to power. Is the role of the educator to be leading, to be directing, or to be accompanying the student on the journey? One must also consider how this role differs according to the population of students. The role of the teacher will differ significantly when teaching undergraduate students compared to graduate and doctoral level students. The issue of culture must also be integrated into our understanding of our role as educators. The concept of *teacher* is regarded differently by various cultures, as is the process of learning. The educator cannot assume that what he or she says in the classroom is heard as intended without engaging with the students. Similarly, the educator should elicit and respect the intrinsic knowledge that emanates from those that have significantly different life experiences. It is critical that diverse cultural and intrinsic wisdom becomes part of the learning dialogue. One might be able to teach different cultures a similar extrinsic perspective, but to truly educate, the teacher must be intentional in integrating awareness of the cultural variables of the learner into the teaching.

Teaching, according to Zen teacher Suzuki Roshi (1970), requires lecture, practice, and silence. While we are responsible for preparing teaching material in the classroom, we also provide opportunities for practicing art and psychotherapy in practicums and internships. Then how do we incorporate fertile and fruitful, reflective silence into our teachings where students are able to contemplate and integrate their work?

Within the creative dialectical space, students are encouraged "to deconstruct, reconstruct, and synthesize multiple forms of knowledge, be open and receptive to emergent knowledge and the anxiety of not knowing, cultivate curiosity and imagination" (Gerber, 2016, p. 798). Yet perhaps it is incumbent on the educator to do more than encourage the learner in these areas of discovery. The responsibility of orchestrating the environment and designing a strategy for educational engagement with a cohort of learners is also an exciting privilege. While working as therapists, we are not likely to demand that the patient understand the language and the strategy of therapy. We do not demand that they come to us in terms of *the how* and *the what* in communication; we go to them. It seems that this should also be the stance of the educator in working with students.

Content in art therapy education must address the continuum between the restrictive oppression of a pedagogy of compliance and the requirement of rigorous standards that facilitate interdisciplinary collaboration. The pedagogy of compliance is pervasive in our educational system, and art therapy risks limiting discovery because of our angst concerning a narrow understanding of *evidence-based* standards combined with our drive towards growth. The funding-based "teaching to the test" pedagogy does not necessarily correlate with excellence in practice. The inspirational educator, Maria Montessori (2013), spoke to this as follows:

> If an educational act is to be efficacious, it will be only that one which tends to help toward the complete unfolding of life. To be thus helpful it is necessary rigorously to avoid the arrest of spontaneous movements and the imposition of arbitrary tasks.
>
> (para. 7)

The role of educators in the development of the field of art therapy requires broad-based reflection. The profession of art therapy has the responsibility of defining the parameters of the field, of considering the relationship between art therapy and other professions, and of addressing marketability. Membership organizations, such as the American Art Therapy Association, have taken on the responsibility of defining educational standards that they promote in order for schools to be "approved" by them. The Art Therapy Credentials Board establishes the educational requirements to become "registered" as an art therapist. Does it follow then that educators should follow a pedagogy of compliance in designing their educational process and curriculum according to the membership organizations guidelines, or for that matter, the credentialing boards requirements?

## 54  Amy Backos and Richard Carolan

The current trend among the gatekeepers with respect to educating art therapists is to establish educational standards based on perceived marketability of graduates. The membership organization supports art therapists becoming licensed practitioners. Licensure will increase marketability, which is desirable by art therapists, and it also allows access to art therapy by a portion of the population who may not be able to access art therapy services through private pay. While these seem important priorities for a membership organization, it is less clear if this should be the primary area of emphasis for educators, who must teach not only the areas of competency, but also the nuances of being a therapist and an artist. Developing educational standards for any profession serving the public requires balance between two areas. The first is external standards established by individuals in power whose responsibility it is to protect the public and who may not be familiar with the intricacies of the profession. The second standard comes from experts in the field. The gatekeepers who guard and protect the public and the profession require competency in designated areas of the known. Educators in art therapy are committed to inquiry into the unknown, of the possibilities and the imagined. Educators need to also adhere to the university standards and practices in designing and implementing the educational experience. Educators must also comply with the regional educational standards under which the university or college is accredited. The task for educators is to identify how to serve two different masters: the creative artist with intuitive knowledge and the regional and national standards. We are reminded of Plato following his students; how do we follow the elder chief, a circle of wise women, and also "teach to the test?"

The educator's role is to hold knowledge of the most current theory and practice in the field, to be well versed in the external guidelines established by gatekeepers of the educational process, and to create a learning environment that holds all of this, while simultaneously engaging each student there to stimulate imagination, creativity, and a dialogue. "We especially need imagination in science. It is not all mathematics, nor all logic, but it is somewhat beauty and poetry" (Montessori, 2013, para. 21).

Educating the art therapist necessitates a pedagogy that engages the artist. We are only teachers, not educators, when we only require them to memorize facts to be regurgitated for an exam. This focus will result in well-trained test takers, not therapists. There is no evidence that therapy is efficacious through the regurgitation of facts to the client whose soul is suffering.

### Art Therapy Students

Students who take an active role in their education and who do not confuse being taught with learning can integrate material and apply the

Art Therapy Pedagogy 55

concepts in the therapy office. Bloom identifies levels of learning in the *cognitive, affective*, and *psychomotor* domains ("Bloom's Taxonomy," 2016). This shift in cognitive learning from recalling and understanding to synthesizing and evaluating happens through the course of a graduate art therapy program and internship. Similarly, student's affective experiences develop from receiving and responding to emotional material, along with organizing and internalizing a personal value system. This develops throughout formal education and throughout our lifetimes as students of art therapy. Bloom further described the acquisition of psychomotor skills, which applies to art making. New students of art begin by learning through imitation and learning to manipulate material via instruction, and then they develop skills of articulation and naturalization, whereby they become experts in the media while art making becomes automatic to their experiences in the world ("Bloom's Taxonomy," 2016).

Through the apprenticeship training of practicums and internships, we teach art therapy students to become client advocates, helping others navigate complicated mental health, legal, educational, and other systems. We also coach students on educating other professionals and the public on art therapy and the strategies of using art to promote health, reduce mental health symptoms, and increase wellness. Finally, learning to advocate for others takes on a more sophisticated and nuanced role when art therapists are able to work towards social justice and related causes using their skills and knowledge as art therapists.

### Professionals as Lifelong Learners

Mandated continuing education requirements by the Art Therapy Credentials Board (2013) and other respective licensing bodies ensures that we are continuing our role as students, but we are ultimately responsible for our own continued cognitive, affective, and artistic learning. We as art therapy practitioners are responsible for the following: synthesis and integration of art therapy and psychotherapy material; maintaining the ongoing process of internalizing and refining our personal, professional, and emotional values; and creating original artistic outcomes. We are responsible for developing our own wisdom and perspectives. Furthermore, identifying psychological theory remains critical for therapeutic success, and maintaining ongoing alignment with one's chosen psychological theory and art therapy approach prevents drift into diluted or ineffective uses of scientifically derived approaches and helps us remain engaged in the creative and therapeutic processes of art therapy.

As professionals, we support clients in reaching a position of self-actualization by adopting a Rogerian stance of genuineness, accurate empathetic understanding, and unconditional positive regard. Another way to conceptualize this position, which is designed to value the uniqueness and sacredness of each individual, is through the Buddhist stance of

## 56   Amy Backos and Richard Carolan

*shoshin* or *beginner's mind*. Through this lens, we approach opportunities for learning with nondefensive openness and without preconceived notions. "In the beginner's mind there are many possibilities, but in the expert's there are few" (Suzuki, 1970). As professionals, we can avoid complacency, apathy, and possibly burnout, by reminding ourselves of the richness of our original mind and attitude towards art therapy. A beginner's mind maintains an active and lifelong interest in art making, engaging with clients, and in developing personally and professionally. Finally, studying and fostering a beginner's mind helps us avoid the trappings of intellectualism which may promote—in negative terms—the clinification of art therapy, whereby we become enamored with the psychotherapeutic aspects of our work to the point where we neglect the creative and artistic components that initially drew us to the work. The beginner's mind (Suzuki, 1970) supports the interest in novelty and flow (Csikszentmihalyi, 2014), which art making can satisfy.

## Future Directions in Art Therapy Education

The future of art therapy education has shifted radically in the last decade with the wide availability of art and psychological information on the internet, increased global connections between art therapists, and the advent of doctoral level education in art therapy. We can now rely on the free and open access to material, and our job has shifted to teaching others to develop information literacy, whereby clinicians and researchers learn to sift through vast amounts of literature to hone in on what is relevant, accurate, and engaging. Our global society also allows for a critical analysis of how art therapy education is positioned within the dominant culture. Additionally, with a postmodern perspective, we have new opportunities to explore what defines knowledge and how it is reciprocally created between teacher and learner.

## References

Art Therapy Credentials Board. ATR-BC. (2013). *Recertification standards*. Retrieved from www.atcb.org/resource/pdf/Recert%20Standards%201-1-2013.pdf

Blooms Taxonomy. (2016). Retrieved from www.maxvibrant.com/bloom-s-taxonomy/bloom-s-taxonomy

Bloom's Taxonomy of Learning. (2015). Retrieved from www.nwlink.com/~donclark/hrd/bloom.html

Bruner, J. S. (1996). *The culture of education*. Cambridge, MA: Harvard University Press.

Csikszentmihalyi, M. (2014). *Flow and the foundations of positive psychology: The collected works of Mihaly Csikszentmihalyi*. New York: Springer.

Five Standards of Effective Pedagogy. (2017). Retrieved from www.tolerance.org/supplement/five-standards-effective-pedagogy

## Art Therapy Pedagogy   57

Freire, P. (1970) *Pedagogy of the Oppressed.* New York: Bloomsbury.

Gagne (2015). *Conditions of learning.* Retrieved from www.instructionaldesign. org/theories/conditions-learning.html

Gerber, N. (2016). Art therapy education: A creative dialectic intersubjective approach. In D. E. Gussak & M. L. Rosal (Eds.), *The Wiley handbook of art therapy* (pp. 794–801). West Sussex, UK: Wiley.

Hilgenheger, N. (1993). Johann Friedrich Herbart. *Prospects: The Quarterly Review of Comparative Education, 23*(3/4), 649–664. Retrieved from www. ibe.unesco.org/fileadmin/user_upload/archive/publications/ThinkersPdf/ herbarte.pdf

Langer, K. S. (1942). *Philosophy in a new key: A study in the symbolism of reason, rite, and art.* Cambridge, MA: Harvard University Press.

Lusebrink, V. B. (2004). Art therapy and the brain: An attempt to understand the underlying processes of art expression in therapy. *Art Therapy: Journal of the American Art Therapy Association, 21*(3), 125–135.

Maria Montessori. (2013). Retrieved from www.great-quotes.com/quotes/ author/Maria/Montessori

Nelson, P. (2007). *A salute to teachers!* Retrieved from *Monitor on Psychology* website: Retrieved www.apa.org/monitor/jan07/soe.aspx

Piaget, J. (1970). *Science of Education and the Psychology of the Child.* New York, NY: Orion Press.

Suzuki, S. (1970). *Zen mind, beginner's mind.* Tokyo: Weatherhill.

Vygotsky, L. S. (1978). *Mind in society: The development of higher psychological processes* (M. Cole, V. John-Steiner, S. Scribner, & E. Souberman, Eds., A. R. Luria, M. Lopez-Morillas & M. Cole with J. V. Wertsch, Trans.). Cambridge, MA: Harvard University Press. (Original manuscript published 1930–1934)

# 5 The Road Ahead

## Preparing for the Future of Art Therapy Research

*Girija Kaimal*

## Introduction

This chapter is intended to provide an overview of current and future directions for research in art therapy to help prepare art therapy researchers and to deepen the impact of research both within and outside of the art therapy field. Art therapists will increasingly find themselves in fields other than direct mental healthcare, including wellness services, burnout prevention, human resource services, entrepreneurship, telehealth, indigenous art, minority populations, international settings, community studios, museums, and integrative models of care. In this climate of economic considerations in healthcare, art therapists will also need to conduct cost-benefit analyses, as well as epidemiological and health outcomes studies. Art therapists will also find that they serve as a nonpharmacological option to manage health, especially in integrative models of care. Future research in art therapy will need to integrate and innovate from methods in the medical sciences, social sciences, and humanities in a creative way that captures the uniqueness of our field. They will need to be able to develop research tools to analyze artistic expression, digital media creations, and virtual reality data, along with traditional qualitative and quantitative measures of human health, behavior, and change. In sum, art therapists must be prepared to conduct systematic inquiry using a range of mixed methods approaches. The next section discusses current trends.

## Art Therapy Research Today

### Influences of Other Disciplines

Art therapy research has been influenced by a range of disciplines, including the fine arts, social sciences, humanities, education, and the medical sciences (Junge, 2010; Ulman, 1975). These influences are embedded in philosophical perspectives that can, at times, be in conflict or limited in alignment and purpose. For example, research in the humanities often focuses on representing the human condition and capturing the

The Future of Art Therapy Research 59

human experience, while social and medical sciences might focus more on scientific methods that place a premium on randomized controlled designs. These differences in perspectives and values affects research that are generated. In one case, the focus might be on individual case examples and artistic representations, while in the other, the individual human experience might be subsumed in order to identify overall generalizable patterns across large groups. In an effort to address these challenges, there have been calls for identifying research methods that capture the unique attributes of art therapy rather than adopt existing methodologies from other disciplines (Junge & Linesch, 1993; Kaiser, 2015). Although ideal, this approach risks reinvention of the wheel and delays the opportunity to approach art therapy research through diverse and mixed methodologies.

### Approaches to Research in Art Therapy

The arts therapies have more structures in place to guide clinical work, licensure, and credentialing for professional practice (American Art Therapy Association [AATA], 2017a) than for research, particularly funded research. The Master's degree has been the terminal degree for art therapy clinical practice, and preparation programs have varied in their levels of emphasis on research and support of active research agendas for educators and clinical practitioners. Art therapy research has traditionally been rooted in the clinical practice paradigm of case reports, theoretical perspectives, and descriptive and observational studies (Robb, 2015). In particular, traditional research mainly included descriptive case studies, which was inspired by the earlier psychoanalytic origins of the field (Junge & Linesch, 1993; Kaiser, 2015; Talwar, 2016). There are also recognized challenges with the perceived ability of arts therapists to conduct research (Linesch, 1995), including limited educational support and opportunities for research (Kaiser, St. John, & Ball, 2006), relatively lower levels of interest in research compared with clinical practice (Robb, 2015), apprehensions about lack of time, statistical skills, funding, and training in conducting research (Betts & Laloge, 2000), and unacknowledged fears, anxieties, and a culture of resistance to conducting research (Huet, Springham, & Evans, 2014).

### Supporting Research as a Priority for the Field

Art therapy research is increasingly gaining attention within and outside the field. This is evidenced by the emergence of new journals in the field and the AATA's acknowledgment through standards, awards for research, and through elevating the research committee into one of the seven main committees of the association in its recent strategic plan. Clinicians are increasingly leaning to research evidence to advocate for their practice in the workplace, recognizing that research is the only way we

60   *Girija Kaimal*

can seek compensation and ensure reimbursement for our work. In a recent example, the state of Wisconsin declined the use of art therapy services for children with autism, citing the lack of adequate evidence-based research (AATA research committee, personal communication, July 7, 2015). Such examples highlight the urgent need to develop a stronger research base in our field.

Over the past 10 years, the trend in research has been shifting toward aligning with research traditions in the social and behavioral sciences; evidence of such trends include the hosting of peer-reviewed conference presentations of research, the increasing emergence of funded experimental studies, and an emerging commitment to diverse research paradigms, perspectives, and populations. More recently, experimental studies have been emerging in art therapy literature, but the continual challenges of integrating research paradigms of art making, research, and clinical practice tend to put philosophical values underlying the methods in conflict (Puetz, Morley, & Herring, 2013; Slayton, D'Archer, & Kaplan, 2010).

At present, most art therapy research conducted as part of Master's thesis requirements tend to remain on library shelves or online abstracting sites. Many researchers publish their work in related disciplines, such as education, social work, disability studies, and trauma studies. Kaiser (2016) encouraged art therapists to write and publish in peer-reviewed journals in addition to the ongoing trend of writing books and book chapters, which might not be as rigorously peer-reviewed beyond the initial book proposal stage. Although books have limited digital access, comprehensive handbooks can be valuable resources that provide an overview of the state of field, as well as provide opportunities for independent scholarship and inquiry. Journal articles are more apt for research and often have more visibility and access because of global indexing and keyword searches available through the publishers.

### Current Dissemination Options

Several art therapy journals presently allow for peer-reviewed research and dissemination. Some journals offer free open access, including *Journal of Clinical Art Therapy*, *International Journal of Education and the Arts*, and *Art/Research International: A Transdisciplinary Journal*. Others require subscription, such as *Art Therapy*, *Arts in Psychotherapy*, *International Journal of Art Therapy*, *Arts and Health*, *Journal of Allied Arts and Health*, and *the Canadian Journal of Art Therapy*. The journals offer articles as open access if the authors are willing to pay. Costs of open access range from $1800 to $3000. Open access enables readers from around the world to access research without having to pay for subscriptions or individual articles. The majority of journals that publish art therapy research tend to have a minor impact, as measured by traditional measures like *impact factors*. Impact factors refer to the ratio of the number of papers cited versus papers published. Thus, high impact factors imply that the journal articles were cited many more times than the total number of articles published. At present, only two journals have an *impact factor* (i.e., a measure of how frequently research from the journal is cited); they are the *Arts in Psychotherapy* and *Arts and Health*. Dissemination is also increasingly evident in social media, such as blogs, Facebook, online news forums, blogs, and Twitter. Because of the options of online sharing and social media, in addition to impact factors, journals now also have an *altmetric score*, which is a measure of its impact in the popular media.

Art therapy journals are increasingly offering multi-media options in online versions of the journal. Many researchers and clinicians also use personal websites and blogs to reach broader audiences and minimize the criticisms of denseness and jargon in academic work. Intuitive Creativity (n. d.) hosts a list of top fifty art therapy blogs written by art therapists (Art Therapy Alliance, 2017), and the Art Therapy Alliance (2017) is another platform.

### Emergent Within-Field Researcher Capacity

In the past decade, a handful of educational institutions have recognized the need for advanced research in art therapy (Gerber, 2006). Systematic and sophisticated research in any field requires doctoral level education. Doctoral preparation can help art therapy researchers develop skills, as well as experience, in developing a research agenda for the needs of the field. It does, however, need to be distinguished from Master's level research endeavors. Research in art therapy has traditionally been focused on preparing Master's level clinicians who complete required basic coursework in research methods. The goals for Master's level education is for students to become informed consumers of research. At the doctoral level, however, the goals are to develop a cadre of future researcher-clinician leaders who can serve the needs of the field. The five doctoral programs in the United States in art therapy at present (i.e., Florida State University, Lesley University, Drexel University, Notre Dame de Namur University, and Marymount University), as well as those in other countries, help support and develop researchers who understand the need for research in art therapy. Having doctoral programs in art therapy helps to retain scholars in the field because if they receive their doctorates in other disciplines, they tend to leave the profession (N. Gerber, personal communication, November 8, 2014). Potential researchers have been lost from art therapy when they have continued their research work through doctoral education in other fields, such as psychology, social work, and education.

## 62   Girija Kaimal

## Emergent Funding Opportunities for Art Therapy

Despite efforts to lobby for funding and set a research agenda (Kaiser & Deaver, 2013), there are few federal agencies or private foundations that explicitly support research in art therapy, and the formal calls for proposals are few and far between. Although funding support for art therapy is still limited compared to other health-related fields, there have been a few requests for proposals (RFPs) announced in the last six years. The Department of Defense's Defense Advanced Research Projects Agency (DARPA) had a call in 2011. Moreover, a larger scale funding opportunity, the first of its kind, was posted by the National Institutes of Health (2015), seeking proposals for the study of arts-based approaches to palliative care. A recent funding opportunity for an arts and health research lab was offered by the National Endowment for the Arts (2016). These cross-sector efforts are helping to build a foundation of evidence for arts and health. Funding for pilot studies continues to be an unmet need for the field, and many art therapy researchers fund their scholarship efforts through pro bono commitments of time and study expenses.

## The Road Ahead: Preparing for the Future of Art Therapy Research

The scope of art therapy practice is increasingly moving beyond mental health settings into broader artistic ways of knowing in the context of the therapeutic relationship (Moon, 2016; Talwar, 2016), as well as in terms of art's impact on society, the mind, health, and behavior (Spooner, 2016). These broader practices of art therapy, which include the study of arts and health across disciplines, will affect the scope of art therapy research. In light of the changing scope of practice, new tools for research, dissemination, and advanced preparation of scholars will be needed. Future directions and related needs are summarized in Figure 5.1.

### New Areas of Clinical Practice and Research

### Expanded Scope of Clinical Practice

Art therapy is inherently interdisciplinary; it brings together the traditionally unrelated disciplines of art and psychotherapy. In addition, contemporary approaches in art therapy practice have extended to diverse contexts in community, educational, and international settings (Howie, Prasad, & Kristel, 2013; Talwar, 2016); social justice (Kapitan, 2015; Talwar, 2010), workplace, and organizational settings; and telehealth (Collie & Cubranic, 2011). Talwar (2016) emphasized that it is no longer adequate to refer to *art psychotherapy* and *art as therapy* as the main components of art therapy. In particular, she referred to the need to be open to new paradigms of care, including considering art as not only self-expression, but also a representation of social, cultural, and political

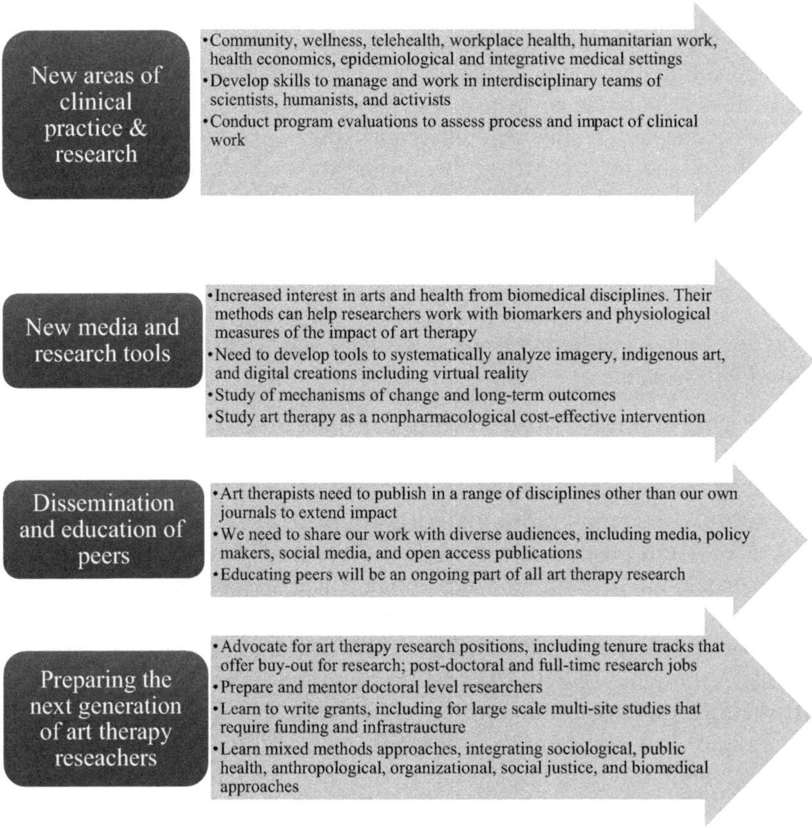

# The Future of Art Therapy Research    63

**New areas of clinical practice & research**
- Community, wellness, telehealth, workplace health, humanitarian work, health economics, epidemiological and integrative medical settings
- Develop skills to manage and work in interdisciplinary teams of scientists, humanists, and activists
- Conduct program evaluations to assess process and impact of clinical work

**New media and research tools**
- Increased interest in arts and health from biomedical disciplines. Their methods can help researchers work with biomarkers and physiological measures of the impact of art therapy
- Need to develop tools to systematically analyze imagery, indigenous art, and digital creations including virtual reality
- Study of mechanisms of change and long-term outcomes
- Study art therapy as a nonpharmacological cost-effective intervention

**Dissemination and education of peers**
- Art therapists need to publish in a range of disciplines other than our own journals to extend impact
- We need to share our work with diverse audiences, including media, policy makers, social media, and open access publications
- Educating peers will be an ongoing part of all art therapy research

**Preparing the next generation of art therapy reseachers**
- Advocate for art therapy research positions, including tenure tracks that offer buy-out for research; post-doctoral and full-time research jobs
- Prepare and mentor doctoral level researchers
- Learn to write grants, including for large scale multi-site studies that require funding and infrastraucture
- Learn mixed methods approaches, integrating sociological, public health, anthropological, organizational, social justice, and biomedical approaches

*Figure 5.1* Future clinical trends and related opportunities for researchers.

realities. These multiple modes of practice necessitate a more integrative model for art therapy research in the future. As art therapy programs are beginning to offer courses as part of counseling degrees, as well as hybrid programs that include online and face-to-face coursework, art therapy practice will move even farther beyond traditional mental health fields to more community, organizational, and international settings. Researchers will therefore need to be able to work in a range of approaches, including participatory and indigenous methodologies.

Art therapists will increasingly find themselves in fields other than direct mental health settings, including health and wellness services, burnout, human resource services, and integrative models of care. Art therapists will also find that they serve as a nonpharmacological option to manage health, especially in integrative models of care. Future research in art therapy will need to integrate methods from medical sciences, social sciences, and the humanities in creative ways that capture the uniqueness of our field. Mixed methods studies

64  *Girija Kaimal*

that integrate artwork with qualitative and quantitative data offer an opportunity for art therapy researchers to serve as leaders. As a result, research in interdisciplinary contexts, including organizational, international, humanitarian, and community settings, could become particularly relevant. Art therapy researchers will need to navigate methodological, cultural, and contextual factors when designing studies that differentiate the role of a trained art therapist from those who use the arts in therapeutic ways. In the increasing climate of healthcare cutbacks, additional areas of study will be cost-benefit analyses of art therapy services and health economic studies measuring the monetary impact of art therapy on patient care and client care.

## Aligning Individual Research Interests with Research Paradigms Outside of the Field

Approaches to research in art therapy are quite diverse. Just as the philosophies of practice differ, the philosophies of research also vary. Reviews of publications in art therapy journals indicate a range of perspectives and approaches, from traditional case studies to arts-based research, critical theory, and post-positivist studies. Case studies were essential early in the profession to communicate among colleagues, but now as a profession with several decades of clinical history, we need more sophisticated research approaches (A. Backos, personal communication, December 7, 2016). Although research is gradually gaining a more prominent role in art therapy, there continue to be tensions between the kinds of research that align with art therapists' interests and the types of studies that receive federal funding. For example, art therapists tend to focus on individuals and small groups; they prefer to examine processes of change at these levels, which are often best analyzed with qualitative or arts-based approaches. Art therapists often conduct these studies on their own time and without funding support. Federal funding, however, is still mainly limited to post-positivist approaches and large-scale randomized control trial designs. Although funders are receptive to qualitative data, most are still inclined to support statistical analyses and traditional research designs. Such fundable studies require art therapists to build capacity and work with researchers from other disciplines who might have more experience with clinical trials. Smaller scale studies might continue to be funded by foundations, donors, and nonprofit organizations. Continued advocacy and outreach is essential to integrate a spectrum of methods, including mixed methods research designs in art therapy research.

## New Media, Artwork, and Research Tools

### Artwork as Data

The artwork in art therapy has for decades been inspired by the fine arts and fine arts tools (Kaimal, Gonzaga & Schwachter, 2016; Moon, 2002), but there are art therapists who are increasingly using new expressive tools, including crafting (Huss & Cwikel, 2005), and digital media (Carlton, 2016; Kaimal, Rattigan, Miller, & Haddy, 2016; Orr, 2016), as well as photographs, videos (Carlton, 2015, 2016), and graphic and comic formats (Carlton, in press). In the future, researchers will potentially use virtual reality immersive contexts of self-expression.

Art therapists need to develop tools that can help us systematically analyze these data. Most software for data analysis are designed to analyze either text or numeric data. We need tools that can help capture and code nuances of digital, virtual reality, as well as images of crafting and other indigenous media. Sandak, Huss, Sarid, and Harel (2015) recently used a mathematical model to capture aspects of the art therapy interaction. The tool was, however, simplistic and could only capture very basic aspects of drawing. Art therapists need to be alert and responsive to new tools that allow for tracking eye gaze, hand movements, and physiological arousal to be attuned to the many ways in which we can analyze artwork and the therapeutic interaction.

### Objective Measures Including Biomarkers

With the advances in neuroscience, art therapists have proposed theoretical frameworks and clinical approaches that integrate existing knowledge about biological and neural systems and structures to art therapy practice (Hass-Cohen & Findlay, 2015; King, 2016; Lusebrink, 2014). The actual empirical studies using biological indicators are, however, rare. Some studies have used biological assessments such as qEEG (Belkofer, VanHecke, & Konopka, 2014; Kruk, Aravich, Deaver, & deBeus, 2014), heart rate variability (Stinley, Norris & Hinds, 2015), or salivary cortisol levels (Kaimal, Ray, & Muniz, 2016). There is increasing interest in using biological indicators. Salivary and blood plasma indicators of health and immune function, heart rate variability, and brain imaging studies offer ways to reduce the perceived biases of self-report data. In addition, using standardized measures could help address some of the perceived biases of nonvalidated author-generated instruments and tools. These studies are also resource intensive and will require external funds for professionals to conduct the studies, which further highlights the need for art therapists to be skilled in grant writing for funded research studies.

### Beyond Outcome Studies

In a systematic review of research in the creative arts therapies (CATs), Puetz, Morley, and Herring (2013) found that the CATs have received less empirical attention compared with other complementary therapies. The few studies to date on cancer patients indicate that CATs help reduce anxiety, pain, and depression, as well as improve quality of life, but there is limited evidence of any sustained change at follow up (Puetz et al.,

66   *Girija Kaimal*

2013). Further research is needed that examines long-term improvements in quality of life and outcomes in the creative arts therapies, as well as a deeper understanding of how these changes arise. Research studies that provide outcomes are valuable; however, examining mechanisms of change is an emerging area to consider. Of note is that several calls for proposals from the NIH have focused not only on outcomes, but they have increasingly emphasized the need to examine mechanisms of change in the CATs. Mechanisms of change are traditionally understood and explained through statistical methods of mediation analyses (Gratz, Bardeen, Levy, Dixon-Gordon, & Tull, 2015; Kazdin, 2007). To study the mechanisms of change, researchers need to consider all the factors that are known to affect outcomes in art therapy. For example, to explicate "how" therapeutic change occurs in art therapy we need to design studies that will lead to a greater understanding of how creative self-expression and the therapeutic relationship interact to change identified symptoms and/or conditions. We will need to go beyond proving the effectiveness of art therapy (outcomes) and be able to explain "how" art therapy helps participants reduce symptomatology, improve health, and sustain wellbeing. In order to do so, we will need to have a range of methods and tools, including arts-based data, as well as biomarker and qualitative indicators.

The AATA (2017b) maintains annual updated bibliography of outcome studies, as well as one on art therapy assessments. These are listings of studies organized by topic area. These are useful resources, but there needs to be development of more systematic review articles that summarize research into concise, critical assessments. Such reviews can be focused on quantitative studies (meta-analyses) or qualitative studies (meta-syntheses). Because many studies in art therapy tend to be qualitative, researchers might also consider guidelines on how to create such review articles (Edwards & Kaimal, 2016). Having distilled review documents can help researchers within and outside the discipline get a snapshot of the current state of research, methodology, and areas for further inquiry.

### Ongoing Dissemination and Education of Peers

Becoming comfortable and proficient in writing, documenting, and ongoing learning is essential for successful research. Instead of waiting for the perfect words to emerge, scholars and researchers might consider developing the habit of writing every day or at least a few days a week. Art therapists could use their artwork as a reflective tool, which could provide motivation to document and process their clinical practice, personal development, and research efforts (Kaimal, 2015). I often have a stash of paper and doodling pens that I use when I take breaks from working or writing to reflect and engage in a personally meaningful exercise. Research thus becomes a way to enhance and deepen our skills rather

The Future of Art Therapy Research   67

than something that appears to contradict the creative work we do. One of the unique contributions of our field could be the inclusion of art into reflective practice and dissemination in traditional journals (including with impact factors) and multi-media dissemination options within and outside of the discipline. Educating peers and advocating for art therapy research could be an ongoing part of our service to the field. For example, a "call for comment" was recently issued by the National Institutes of Mental Health (NIMH, 2016) seeking suggestions for new areas of research. Calls for comments and similar public forums constitute areas in which art therapists can advocate for research funding support. Funding support is essential to conduct larger scale studies, as well as studies with underserved populations in terms of demographics and diagnostic categories.

## Preparing the Next Generation of Art Therapy Researchers

The future of art therapy research lies in the timely preparation of the next generation of researchers. The field needs to be mindful of the depth of training required in doctoral programs to ensure that we are building capacity in the field. Doctoral level researchers need to have skills, sophistication, and the ability to handle complex ideas and approaches beyond the scope of Master's level researchers and clinicians. Specific suggestions are included below.

### Creating Positions That Enable Research

Because the generally accepted terminal degree in art therapy at present is a Master's degree, the education of exemplary clinicians is the priority. Relatedly, AATA is focused on licensure and working towards job protections for clinicians in the field. Although doctoral level education is increasingly the norm for faculty in art therapy programs, there are few pathways to a research career for art therapists interested in research. As a field, art therapy needs to advocate for tenure-track positions with buy-out time for research, as well as post-doctoral positions for aspiring scholars. Advocating for positions focused on research (and not just teaching and mentorship of students), are essential if we are to build a cadre of practicing researchers who can contribute substantially to the field.

### Program Evaluations: A Bridge from Practice to Research

One way to link clinical practice to research is to integrate art therapy clinical practice with program evaluation (Kaimal & Blank, 2015). This can be a simple first step that helps art therapists integrate data collection

68   *Girija Kaimal*

and analysis and then develop an agenda for research. An initial way to develop systems for program evaluation in clinical practices is to identify evaluation questions that art therapists might have about their work and feedback they seek from their clients. Graduate students can be taught program evaluation methods as a stepping-stone to more systematic research studies. Program evaluation is also a way to engage in reflection on clinical practice. It can include and/or combine qualitative, quantitative, or arts-based methods. Program evaluations can also provide pilot data for researchers to explore larger scale studies.

### Diversity and Innovation in Methods

There is an increasing trend of looking to experimental designs and outcome-based studies to produce the kind of evidence that will win awards and funding. That is one dimension of research in art therapy. However, what distinguishes us as a field is the integration of art media, self-expression, and creativity in therapeutic practice. Moreover, including innovative data sources and analytic strategies that incorporate artwork, analysis of visual data, narratives, digital tools, and mathematical models will be integral to differentiating our work in the future. Doctoral level researchers in art therapy will need to be proficient in mixed methods approaches (Kapitan, 2015) that integrate methods from other disciplines, such as sociology, anthropology, and public health, and indigenous approaches (Chilisa, 2012), such as participatory action research, which integrates community voices into research approaches (Kapitan, 2015). These approaches are relevant to contexts of practice that might differ from traditional mental health care settings. Community-based approaches to health and wellbeing are best served when stakeholders are actively involved in collecting and analyzing data relevant to the effectiveness of the interventions. The researcher's tool kit needs to include both traditional methods, as well as new ways to understand the efficacy and impact of art therapy. This is an opportunity for art therapy researchers to develop customized software and analytic tools that help us analyze creative and human behavioral data.

### Learning to Manage and Work in Interdisciplinary Teams

Finding and sustaining partnerships of complementary skill sets is essential to furthering the scope and research of art therapy. Working by ourselves as art therapists limits our access to resources; it limits the impact of our research and the levels of analysis we can implement. Art therapists have expertise in the expressive and therapeutic aspects of art; however, we are not proficient in all aspects of research methodology. It is imperative that we learn to work with colleagues in other fields whose expertise might serve to better define the contributions and outcomes of art therapy. This includes colleagues in related fields of social science,

The Future of Art Therapy Research  69

biostatistics, neuroscience, health economics, human biology, psychology, the fine arts, the humanities, and art education. Working with colleagues in other fields involves challenges and opportunities. When philosophical perspectives are aligned, and the colleagues respect art therapy, the collaborations work out well. However, when these paradigmatic stances, expertise, and capacities are at odds with one another (Kaimal, Barber, Schulman, & Reed, 2012), collaborations can fall apart. For example, if the art therapist, who operates from constructivist perspective, works with colleagues who are purely post-positivist, the collaboration might prove to be challenging. Exploring these subtle differences in perspectives is essential to successful partnerships. Mixed methods approaches, which typically involve multiple paradigms and/or pragmatic approaches to research, are well suited to interdisciplinary collaboration. Working within a research team with other collaborators further ensures that key findings and lessons learned are shared with the community within and outside art therapy. In addition, being an effective researcher requires a leadership stance; it requires an art therapy researcher who is fearless about exploring frontiers, negotiating the mazes of funding sources, reviews, and peer reviews, while also building a reservoir of inner strength, resilience, and resolve for the work.

## Conclusion

Art therapy clinicians and researchers need to work in partnership to develop a credible evidence base for our field. As the expanded scope of art therapy reaches beyond mental health sectors into community, organizational, and international settings, the field will bring new opportunities for innovative mixed methods research practices. The five new doctoral programs available in the US at present and some Master's programs that emphasize systematic research could help develop much needed capacity in our field. In addition, working in interdisciplinary contexts with new media and with colleagues from related social science, humanities, and medical fields can help bolster acceptance and integrate art therapy into health and educational settings. Art therapists must also be willing and constantly prepared to educate non-art therapists about the work we do and how we know what we know about the healing potential of the creative arts. The ability of work to build and sustain research collaborations within and across disciplines in diverse settings and innovative methodologies is the key to the future of art therapy research.

## References

American Art Therapy Association. (2017a). Retrieved from www.arttherapy.org
American Art Therapy Association. (2017b). *American Art Therapy Association research committee and art therapy outcome bibliography*. Retrieved from http://arttherapy.org/upload/outcomebibliographyresearchcmte.pdf

## 70  Girija Kaimal

Art Therapy Alliance. (2017). *Welcome to the Art Therapy Alliance.* Retrieved www.arttherapyalliance.org/

Belkofer, C. M., Van Hecke, A. V., & Konopka, L. M. (2014). Effects of drawing on alpha activity: A quantitative EEG study with implications for art therapy. *Art Therapy: Journal of the American Art Therapy Association, 31*(2), 61–68. doi:10.1080/07421656.2014

Betts, D. J., & Laloge, L. (2000). Art therapists and research: A survey conducted by the Potomac Art Therapy Association. *Art Therapy: Journal of the American Art Therapy Association, 17*(4), 291–295. doi: 10.1080/07421656.2000.10129765

Carlton, N. R. (2015). Expansive palettes. In J. Cohen, L. Johnson, & P. Orr (Eds.), *Video and filmmaking as psychotherapy* (pp. 69–80). New York, NY: Routledge.

Carlton, N. R. (2016). Grid + pattern: Sensory qualities of digital media. In R. Garner (Ed.), *Digital art therapy: Material, methods and applications.* London, UK: Jessica Kingsley.

Carlton, N. R. (in press). Illustrating stories: Using graphic novels in art therapy practice and research. In S. Imholz & J. Sachter (Eds.), *Psychology's New Design Science and the Reflective Practitioner.* New York, NY: Oxford University Press.

Chilisa, B. (2012). *Postcolonial indigenous research paradigm: Indigenous research methodologies.* Thousand Oaks, CA: Sage.

Collie, K., & Cubranic, D. (2011). An art therapy solution to a telehealth problem. *Art Therapy: Journal of the American Art Therapy Association, 16*(4), 186–193. doi: 10.1080/07421656.1999.10129481

Edwards, J., & Kaimal, G. (2016). Using meta-synthesis to support application of qualitative methods findings in practice: A discussion of meta-ethnography, narrative synthesis, and critical interpretive synthesis. *The Arts in Psychotherapy, 51*, 30–35. doi:10.1016/j.aip.2016.07.003

Gerber, N. (2006). The essential components of doctoral level education for art therapists. *The Arts in Psychotherapy, 33*(2), 98–112. doi:10.1016/j. aip.2005.08.002

Gratz, K. L., Bardeen, J. R., Levy, R., Dixon-Gordon, K. L., & Tull, M. T. (2015). Mechanisms of change in an emotion regulation group therapy for deliberate self-harm among women with borderline personality disorder. *Behaviour Research and Therapy, 65*, 29–35. doi:10.1016/j.brat.2014.12.005

Hass-Cohen, N., & Findlay, J. C. (2015). *Art therapy and the neuroscience of relationships, creativity, and resiliency: Skills and practices (Norton Series on Interpersonal Neurobiology).* New York, NY: Norton.

Howie, P., Prasad, S., & Kristel, J. (2013). *Using art therapy with diverse populations.* London, UK: Jessica Kingsley.

Huet, V., Springham, N., & Evans, C. (2014). The art therapy practice network: Hurdles, pitfalls and achievements. *Counseling and Psychotherapy Research: Linking Research with Practice, 14*(3), 174–180. doi: 10.1080/14733145.2014.929416

Huss, E., & Cwikel, J. (2005). Researching creations: Applying arts-based research to Bedouin women's drawings. *International Journal of Qualitative Methods, 4*(4), 1–16.

## The Future of Art Therapy Research 71

Intuitive Creativity. (n.d.). *Expressive art inspirations: Reflections on the creative path*. Retrieved from http://intuitivecreativity.typepad.com/expressiveartinspirations/top-50-art-therapy-blogs.html

Junge, M. (2010). *The modern history of art therapy in the United States*. Springfield, IL: Charles C. Thomas.

Junge, M., & Linesch, D. (1993). Our own voices: New paradigms for art therapy research. *The Arts in Psychotherapy*, 20(1), 61–67. doi:10.1016/0197-4556(93)90032-w

Kaimal, G. (2015). Evolving identities: The person(al), the profession(al) and the artist(ic). *Art Therapy: Journal of the American Art Therapy Association*, 32(3), 136–141. doi:10.1080/07421656.2015.1060840

Kaimal, G., Barber, M., Schulman, M., & Reed, P. (2012). Preparation of urban high school principals in Philadelphia through multi-organizational partnerships. *Journal of School Leadership*, 22(5), 902–921.

Kaimal, G., & Blank, C. L. (2015). Program Evaluation: A doorway to research in the creative arts therapies. *Art Therapy: Journal of the American Art Therapy Association*, 32(2), 89–92. doi: 10.1080/07421656.2015.1028310

Kaimal, G., Gonzaga, A. M. L., & Schwachter, V. (2016). Crafting, health and well-being: National trends and implications for art therapists. *Arts and Health*, 9(1). 81–90. doi: 10.1080/17533015.2016.1185447

Kaimal, G., Rattigan, M., Miller, G., & Haddy, J. (2016). Implications of national trends in digital media use for art therapy practice. *Journal of Clinical Art Therapy*, 3(1), 6. http://digitalcommons.lmu.edu/jcat/vol3/iss1/6

Kaimal, G., Ray, K., & Muniz, J. M. (2016). Reduction of cortisol levels and participants' responses following artmaking. *Art Therapy: Journal of the American Art Therapy Association*, 33(2), 74–80. doi:10.1080/07421656.2016.1166832

Kaiser, D. H. (2015). What should be published in art therapy? What should art therapists write about? *Art Therapy: Journal of the American Art Therapy Association*, 32(4), 156–157. doi:10.1080/07421656.2015.1107376

Kaiser, D. H. (2016). Why art therapists should care about peer review. *Art Therapy: Journal of the American Art Therapy Association*, 33(2), 56–57. doi:10.1080/07421656.2016.1176845

Kaiser, D. H., & Deaver, S. (2013). Establishing a research agenda for art therapy: A Delphi study. *Art Therapy: Journal of the American Art Therapy Association*, 30(3), 114–121. doi:10.1080/07421656.2013.819281

Kaiser, D. H., St. John, P., & Ball, B. (2006). Teaching art therapy research: A brief report. *Art Therapy: Journal of the American Art Therapy Association*, 23(4), 186–190. doi:10.1080/07421656.2006.10129331

Kapitan, L. (2015). Social action in practice: Shifting the ethnocentric lens in cross cultural art therapy encounters. *Art Therapy: Journal of the American Art Therapy Association*, 32(3), 104–111. doi:10.1080/07421656.2015.1060403

Kazdin, A. (2007). Mediators and mechanisms of change in psychotherapy research. *Annual Review of Clinical Psychology*, 3, 1–27. doi:10.1146/annurev.clinpsy.3.022806.091432

King, J. L. (2016). *Art therapy, trauma and neuroscience: Theoretical and practical perspectives*. New York, NY: Routledge.

Kruk, K. A., Aravich, P. F., Deaver, S. P., & deBeus, R. (2014). Comparison of brain activity during drawing and clay sculpting: A preliminary qEEG study.

Art Therapy: Journal of the American Art Therapy Association, 31(2), 52–60. doi:10.1080/07421656.2014.903826

Linesch, D. (1995). Art therapy research: Learning from experience. Art Therapy: Journal of the American Art Therapy Association, 12(4), 261–265. doi:1 0.1080/07421656.1995.10759176

Lusebrink, V. (2014). Art therapy and the neural basis of imagery: Another possible view. Art Therapy: Journal of the American Art Therapy Association 31(2), 87–90. doi:10.1080/07421656.2014.903828

Moon, B. L. (2016). The sirens of definition: Responding to the call. Art Therapy: Journal of the American Art Therapy Association, 33(3), 156–159. doi:1 0.1080/07421656.2016.1199247

Moon, C. (2002). Studio art therapy: Cultivating the artist identity in the art therapist. Philadelphia, PA: Jessica Kingsley.

National Endowment for the Arts. (2016). Program solicitation: National Endowment for the Arts research labs. Retrieved from www.arts.gov/program-solicitation-national-endowment-for-the-arts-research-labs

National Institutes of Health. (2015). Arts-based approaches in palliative care for symptom management (R01). Retrieved from Department of Health and Human Services website http://grants.nih.gov/grants/guide/pa-files/PAR-14-294.html

National Institutes of Mental Health. (2016). Request for information (RFI): NIMH request for brief perspectives on the state of mental health research. Retrieved from https://grants.nih.gov/grants/guide/notice-files/NOT-MH-16-015.html

Orr, P. (2011). Technology training for future art therapists: Is there a need? Art Therapy: Journal of the American Art Therapy Association, 23(4): 191–196. doi:10.1080/07421656.2006.10129329

Puetz, T. W., Morley, C. A., & Herring, M. P. (2013). Effects of creative arts therapies on psychological symptoms and quality of life in patients with cancer. Journal of the American Medical Association (JAMA Internal Medicine), 173(11), 960–969. doi:10.1001/jamainternmed.2013.836.

Robb, M. (2015). An overview of historical and contemporary perspectives in art therapy research in America. In D. E. Gussak & M. L. Rosal (Eds.), The Wiley Blackwell handbook of art therapy (pp. 609–616). Oxford, UK: John Wiley.

Sandak, B., Huss, E., Sarid, O., & Harel, D. (2015). Computational paradigm to elucidate the effects of arts-based approaches and interventions: Individual and collective emerging behaviors in artwork construction. PLoS ONE, 10(6), e0126467. doi:10.1371/journal.pone.0126467

Slayton, S. C., D'Archer, J., & Kaplan, F. (2010). Outcome studies on the efficacy of art therapy: A review of findings. Art Therapy: Journal of the American Art Therapy Association, 27(3), 108–118. doi:10.1080/07421656.2010.10129660

Spooner, H. (2016). Embracing a full spectrum definition of art therapy. Art Therapy: Journal of the American Art Therapy Association, 33(3), 163–166. doi.org/10.1080/07421656.2016.1199249

Stinley, N., Norris, D. O., & Hinds, P. (2015). Creating mandalas for the management of acute pain symptoms in pediatric patients. Art Therapy: Journal of the American Art Therapy Association, 32(2), 46–53. doi:10.1080/07421656.2015.1028871

Talwar, S. (2010). An intersectional framework for race, class, gender, and sexuality in art therapy. *Art Therapy: Journal of the American Art Therapy Association, 27*(1), 11–17. doi:10.1080/07421656.2010.1.129567

Talwar, S. (2016). Is there a need to redefine art therapy? *Art Therapy: Journal of the American Art Therapy Association, 33*(3), 116–118. doi:10.1080/0742 1656.2015.1068632

Ulman, E. (1975). Art therapy: Problems of definition. In E. Ulman & P. Dachinger (Eds.), *Art therapy in theory and practice* (pp. 3–13). New York, NY: Schocken.

# 6 Transcending Media
## Tangible to Digital and Their Mixed Reality

*Natalie Carlton with Teresa Sit and Dustin Ryan Yu*

As digital and new media scholarship grows, art therapists are exploring emerging edges and multiple facets of creative and communicative materials that channel therapy-driven goals (Garner, 2016). Digital media are interrelated computer-mediated devices, software, and tools that support customizable activities that assist with the creation of on- or off-line art forms. This chapter describes the ways in which intermedia applications have inspired art making and practical media expansions for current and future approaches in art therapy. Teresa Sit and Dustin Ryan Yu wrote two segments that are embedded within the center of this essay, and their insights have contributed valuable examples and rich descriptions.

Digital media range from concrete to more abstract tools, processes, locations, platforms, and products. Some of the explicit hardware *tools* of digital media are computers, smartphones, iPads, virtual reality (VR) headgear, creative interface components (e.g., digital keyboards, cameras, and stylus drawing surfaces) and storage hard drives. Some of the implicit *processes* of digital media are found within various drawing, graphic design, and audio/visual editing software, and their simplified iPad app versions, in addition to animation and/or gameplay activities. Social media sites, such as Facebook, Snapchat, LinkedIn, Instagram, and other computer-mediated communication platforms—which are accessible by digital devices—are invisibly embedded locales and pathways of communication where multiple individuals or groups bring information or self-approximates together, to share and interact discriminately or indiscriminately.

Within the structural to expressive properties of computer-mediated technologies, there are imaginative and relational, thus, sensory spatial qualities, which are designed into the media and are resultant from our interactions with them. Many forms of hybrid new media are "filtered through a computer, in parts or in whole" (Ehinger, 2016, p. 115) and specifically encourage interactivity, learning, identity display, character play, and user dialogue and exchange—sometimes via the internet and within site specific digital and interactive platforms (social media) or virtual community sites (Cohen, Johnson, & Orr, 2015; Garner, 2016; Miller, 2017).

Two examples of virtual community sites are Minecraft (2017) and Second Life (2017), while Instagram (2017) and Medium (n. d.) are interactive platforms where image-makers and/or writers deliver and mix content. Creative use and *fan labor* (2016) by early adopters (including art therapists) can evolve a software or digital media tool past its original intended use and into a variety of applied practices (Choe, 2016; Imholz & Sachter, in press). Much like with any other art form, a consistent challenge for art therapists using materials therapeutically is the dedicated time and energy needed to substantiate their own creative explorations and experimentations with that media (Carlton, 2016; Edmunds, 2012). For digital media, Sundararajan (2014) discussed how vital the interplay of the computer's cognitive environment and artistic explorations are for customized and inventive uses. Such experimentation with finding the limitations of, and articulating possible innovations to, the media's design and use can drive powerful dialogues between art therapists, computer engineers, and software designers (Imholz & Sachter, in press). Furthermore, imagining and applying the therapeutic use of any material requires flexible approaches, curiosity into what a media holds for different clients, and some technical execution skills to heighten the art and therapeutic interaction (Edmunds, 2012; Partridge, 2016). Creativity does not live in devices or materials but rather in our protracted interactions of immediacy with them.

While some art therapists find digital media extremely adaptable to context, client, and therapeutic applications, others have characterized digital media as one-dimensional, nonsensory, and flat compared to the "traditional" multisensory activities of drawing with pencil and paper (Klorer, 2009; Orr, 2012; Potash, 2009). There are obvious, insidious, and subtle social transformations occurring within "paper to pixel" shifts, and further research is needed in the areas of digital and tangible intermedia applications, rather than presumed material hierarchies or separations (Carlton, 2016). Digital media present many conundrums due to their omnipresence, commercialization, and advertising that often touts them as intuitive, affordable, and time-saving, whereas they are not automatically understandable, easily malleable, financially feasible, or accessible to all, nor are they more inventive than previous remediated media.

We will describe specific examples of combined media applications by applying the terms *tangible* and *digital media* simultaneously and defining their mixed use as *transcending media*. These are a variety of media that are pushing future possibilities in creative forms—as well as in the production of communication and dissemination exchanges—that hold inherent value for art therapy approaches and material use. However, to authenticate any communication exchange back and forth across the tangible-digital material boundaries, our fingers, hands, and bodies must channel interconnections between the media, the self (actively manipulating or

76   *Natalie Carlton, et al.*

moving within the apparatus), and audience (Q. Rivenburgh, personal communication, October 6, 2016). For example, imagine the fictional, recreational, (and sometimes product-laden or anthropological) ways that computers extend our bodies and minds into avatar embodiments, such as character play in Second Life (2017). The definition of avatar is from the descent of a deity into human form:

> and then to any embodiment (such as that of a concept of philosophy), whether or not in the form of a person. In the age of technology, "avatar" has developed another sense—it can now be used for the image that a person chooses as [their] "embodiment" in an electronic medium.
>
> (Merriam-Webster, 2017, para. 3)

Such embodiments in new media often lead users into a cyberspace matrix of interactive worlds, created by the user individually or within a group and community effort. These embodiments can rematerialize across multiple platforms and formats to destabilize a person's identity, which is formed by typical classifications or "real world" lived realities. Through the acts of crossing back and forth between mixed reality structures, many virtual world participants perceive an interplay between the *outworld* and *inworld* avatar selves adaptive and liberating within changing contextual experiences with other participants (Despres, 2015).

Art therapist Partridge (2016) researched group communication engagement for older adult research participants collaboratively interacting with a digital projector and scanner device called the HP Sprout (Westover, 2014). Partridge noted that one of her primary research intentions was to investigate whether art interaction, via the conduit of technological tools and processes, would assist in understanding older adults' communication strengths and needs (Partridge, 2016, p. 189). She found that the HP Sprout projector and touch pad generated strong interactive group mural making. The process raised critical conversations amongst the group participants about ageism, disability, how caregivers sometimes infantilize them, and desires for greater community and relations. Partridge described the therapeutic art process with the HP Sprout as follows:

> The sensitivity of the touch pad and the immediacy of working with their fingers gave participants an experience similar to the more controlled medium of drawing combined with more expressive finger painting. They were often so immersed in the experience that they forgot it was a digital system. Several participants lifted up their fingers to check for paint after making the first mark. Even staff participants wiped their hands or rubbed their fingers together when they completed their images. However, the sensitivity of the touchpad was

also difficult for those with limited wrist and arm mobility or low muscle-tone; they struggled to make intentional marks because their wrist or arm was resting on the touchpad. The use of a painting bridge assisted with this barrier.

(p. 188)

Digital media qualities are increasingly being described as adaptive to context and having applications in art therapy that are relational, communicative, and that increase self-awareness in clients (Ehinger, 2016; L'Esperance, 2016), and enhanced digital literacy and skill building for the art therapy community is greatly needed (Choe & Carlton, 2017; Choe, 2016; Ehinger, 2016; Partridge, 2016).

Scholarship of technology in the art therapy field, from the historical to the contemporary, is varied and layered. The earliest writings about the use of technology within therapeutic sessions were focused on videotape (McNiff & Cook, 1975; McNiff, 1981), Polaroid to film-based phototherapy applications (Krauss & Fryrear, 1983; Weiser, 1999; Wolf, 1976), and digital collage and computer drawing programs (McLeod, 1999; Weinberg, 1985). In the last decade, digital media reflective practices have further investigated the use of iPad apps, digital drawing, photography, video, and animation (Austin, 2010; Choe, 2014, 2016; Ehinger, 2015, 2016; Partridge, 2016; Thong, 2007; Tilberg, 2014; Wolf, 2007). Some long-standing debates have centered on the devaluation of "virtual artwork" (Carlton, 2015a, p. 23), perceptions of missing and intangible therapeutic qualities (Asawa, 2009; Klorer, 2009; Orr, 2006; Peterson, 2010), challenging confidentiality measures and digital literacy requirements (Alders & Allen, 2010; Belkofer & McNutt, 2011; Choe & Carlton, 2017), low adaptation rates by art therapists (Asawa, 2009; Edmunds, 2012; Peterson, 2010; Orr, 2006, 2012), and general fears regarding the assimilating and automating effects of technology (Austin, 2009; Kapitan, 2009).

For contemporary digital media innovators in art therapy, the question is not *if* but *how better?* Current practices and protocols are being crafted and articulated to better suit our clients, supervision relationships, and reflective practices (Choe & Carlton, 2017; Garner, 2016; Lee, 2015; Miller, 2017; Partridge, 2016). Digital media are flexible and spreading. Some focus has moved from the distinct qualities of specific hardware or software, to questioning and relaying the multi-dimensional interactions possible within virtual reality expansions, media re-mixed hybrids, and social media locales and platforms (Garner, 2016; Miller, 2016, 2017). What multiple relational and creative possibilities intersect in the borderland of material and virtual realities? In considering these possibilities, we should give attention and pause in equal parts to how we show up in these intermediary spaces to learn and build community and interactions with one another.

## 78  *Natalie Carlton, et al.*

### Embracing Zeroes & Ones

by Teresa Sit

Art therapists are dedicated to learning and developing skills and identity within their own artistic practices, which they then model—through methods and use of materials, safety, and innovation—to their clients (Garner, 2016). Keeping up with the most recent updates in technology is not the central drive in my use of digital media, but making innovative use of available and accessible tools is. Using digital media in combination with other traditional materials represents a critical resourcing of what is available and financially practical for the art therapy practice or clinical site.

Most art therapists agree that it can be difficult to get new programming *started*. Scheduling clients, securing space and materials, and obtaining funding are all necessary preparations for providing care, and these are not easy tasks. Moreover, utilizing new media tools, software, and supplies in art therapy settings can represent additional challenges. Well established and supported art therapy settings continue to have limitations with respect to the literacy, capacity, and the budgeting needed for digital media use. A studio budget might purchase a high-end fine art printer, but replacing the ink cartridges can cost hundreds of dollars at a time. Added to the costs of printing papers are the creative editing software packages and updates, the savviness needed to discern and choose firewall protection and password-protected storage options, and the space required for single or multiple computers (if you plan on running group sessions). Art therapists must be thoughtful and resourceful in how they select, access, maintain, and provide digital media, as well as other creative materials.

Creative social media applications can provide both affordability and approachability for clients in the art therapy studio (Choe, 2014, 2016; Miller, 2016). Smartphone users can capture, edit, and distribute their images without ever touching a computer, scanner, or printer. These devices and applications are developed for broad audiences and uses. Clients who are interested in doing photography during art therapy sessions will need guidance in order to protect and intentionally limit the sharing of these final products (Choe & Carlton, 2017). The multi-part process of learning digital literacy also includes how clients develop nuance for how they *read* photographic imagery, as well as generating and manipulating it. Ironically, the abundant presence of photographic content on social media has shortened our attention span for it. I coach clients on taking their time with digital media, and I reinforce this by incorporating breathing techniques, inserting breaks into editing sessions, and frequently asking clients to spend time writing journal entries or captions to their finished works. This encourages a healthy, more positive relationship with technology overall; moreover, it challenges users to be more conscious or mindful of how they interact with technology daily at work, home, or in a therapy milieu.

Resourcing communication exchange through self-produced digital media messages and products into the wider world outside of therapy are being utilized for both clients and therapists (Miller, 2016, 2017). Advocacy, public education, and stigma-breaking narratives of self and community-produced empowerment are growing exponentially on the internet—usually through a combination of images with text, or videos and music ("DJ with Down Syndrome Turns Offensive Quote into Positive Message," 2017). Sharers of work created with apps or for social media platforms typically have options to set parameters around the visibility of artworks, as well as control regarding the audience's ability to comment on, or contribute to, the published work.

For the art therapy setting, the therapist is responsible for keeping their clients aware of the risks and vulnerability that come along with any internet use and creative digital media production (Choe & Carlton, 2017). Art therapist and social media researcher Gretchen Miller (2017) recently concluded, "as social media and the Internet becomes less restricted, increasingly borderless, and more flexible, these grey areas that currently exist will require ongoing guidance more than ever" (p. 190). Miller's vision for the future inclusion of social media use in art therapy practices and graduate education squarely includes enhanced *digital social responsibility* that would take greater advantage of the vast interconnection possibilities that internet platforms offer to individuals and groups. For example, the *blog* provides an instantaneous and potentially cost-free outlet for creating and displaying works of art. The blog's diary format compels immediacy but also reflection on works posted as finished or ongoing content. In this way, blogging encourages sustained interactivity between the artist, artwork, and audience. Art therapists are delineating how to ethically use social media platforms within therapy sessions (Choe, 2016; L'Esperance, 2016), while the larger community of art therapists and clients of art therapy are actively using these internet communications for many purposes, including personal or professional advocacy and creative goals (Miller, 2016, 2017).

When my best friend was relocated cross-country by his wife's advancement at work, we began a photographic back-and-forth response game to keep in touch and create a digital space to foster our relationship. Our *Shutter To Think* exchanges consisted of each of us taking turns posting a blog photograph on a weekly basis. Photos were frequently accompanied by poetry, prose, or a simple written reflection. One photo would inspire the next, like a game of word association. Most of the time, we let the images do the talking (Figure 6.1 and 6.2). In addition to being a creative outlet, this exercise provided a sense of purpose in our own art making as well.

*Figure 6.1* "Untitled."
Photograph by Patrick Mooney, April 13, 2015.

*Figure 6.2* "Confidence."
Photograph by T. Sit, April 21, 2015.

Even more accessible than blogging are photography-driven social media platforms that provide space to create chronological photo archives or imagery-based shorthand communication systems. Users can post single or multiple entries and manipulate photos using built-in editing tools or writing a caption. Instagram, Facebook, Twitter, Tumblr, DeviantArt, Swarm, and Flickr additionally all take advantage of *hashtags*—the # symbol followed by a word or phrase—which, when clicked, show alternate posts sharing the same hashtag. This intentional content sharing can build a community with like-minded social media artists or participants and allow for spontaneity, such as taking, editing, and sharing a photograph while commuting or going about everyday activities. Better yet, taking the time to look for an image each day reminds me to slow down and be mindful and aware of my surroundings and the community I share these moments with. I believe creative social media outlets can be indispensable tools and communication platforms. As the relationship between man and machine builds, art therapists must deeply examine the relationship between communication and art-sharing that may transgress what we have known as possible.

## Video Appropriation

by Dustin Ryan Yu

Video and digital media are increasingly dominating our everyday lives, and using these artistic mediums with clients in our art therapy practice has become an ongoing point of discussion. As human beings, we have a need to relate to others, to ideas and ways of thinking, and to identify the communities in which we exist. Building and resolving one's identity can be difficult, and we may be able to better utilize the fact that we live in a digital era of abundant information.

In 2014, during my first semester in a graduate art therapy program, I developed a video-based intervention that had little to no published research in the field. This came from my own engaged creative process when I made a video collage about my hybrid cultural identities (Figure 6.3) and then ultimately integrated this process into my thesis research. As a Canadian-born Hongkongese student with a confused identity, I wondered about the many individuals in the world who have experienced acculturation, or simply identify with two or more cultures from vastly different aspects. Online-sourced video collage (OSVC) is an art therapy intervention technique that integrates video appropriation and video editing, using videos taken from the internet as art material that allow clients to intentionally manipulate, collage, and recontextualize their own personal narrative (Yu, 2016). In combination with the appropriated video files, video editing software can then be applied to

82  *Natalie Carlton, et al.*

*Figure 6.3* Stills from "Cultura Ego." Video by Dustin Ryan Yu.

support specific and purposeful clip trimming and placement of appropriated videos to portray one's experiences. In combining the approach of narrative therapy (White & Epston, 1990) with core principles of interventions, such as Landgarten's magazine photo collage (1993), this art therapy intervention targets video as a raw material and a means to stimulate our sense of connection with relatable experiences, as well as to potentially result in therapeutic benefits through self-exploration.

With the implementation of this OSVC intervention, a client would initially identify a goal or topic of exploration and proceed to use the internet to access specific information about the topic that would yield new and relatable experiences. Based on the assumption that other internet users are uploading their subjective realities, clients can potentially employ multiple videos as a foundation for their artwork, eventually creating meaningful and expressive artwork that can help them reflect more deeply about their identity. These means of therapy could not only reduce language barriers for therapeutic benefits, but they could also allow various leadership roles to emerge (e.g., editor or director), as well as promote the use of technology to better help us meet clients where they are at.

In this research, the anticipated benefits of this process included not only empowerment through art making for myself as an artist, but they also extended into skill-building and mastery through guided video-making, reflection on one's own sense of identity, and gaining broader understanding of "fit" within our communities. Additionally, when implemented in therapy, the space can help cue forgotten memories safely, provide controlled emotional distancing through video playback and review, and help individuals ultimately re-author their narrative to work towards their clinical treatment goals. There are countless ways of expanding this intervention, including the incorporation of other art mediums or perhaps their use in group formats. As art therapists, we must continue to challenge our material-based competencies and praxis to provide the best services to help clients reach their potential. Doing so can help answer the question art therapists are always asking: How can art therapy be more accessible and match our clients' needs and realities?

## Art Making in Virtual Reality

The phenomena of virtual reality art making and how these new materials integrate into future art therapy approaches will be examined and experimented within the next several years. I was afforded recent sessions using the "Tilt Brush" (2016) virtual painting software with the HTC Vive. Entering the VR world requires donning a headset that covers one's eyes and upper head and holding small controls in both hands (Figure 6.4). The VR participant manipulates and chooses customizable colors, lines, and features from the hand-controlled VR "palette," while drawing and creating in a three-dimensional space that is bordered by a grid (seen through the VR headgear) to define the parameters of the creative space. One immediate observation I had was how this virtual space erased my limbs because only the spatial grid and created forms are visible while in the headgear. There are layering visual and audio effects that are customizable within the hand controls and facilitated by the fine and gross motor physical movements of the participant's hand, arm, and body posture, which all create the "painting" in three-dimensional space. Some choices in the media applications include thinner or thicker paint lines and strokes, added embellishments, such as fire, glitter, or smoke, other variabilities of color, shape, line quality, and pulsing lights that create light play and shadow. The virtual "paint stroke" forms can be overlaid quickly and become three-dimensional working "images" or "shapes" that can be further scaled large or small. The VR participant can move within or around the forms of the image or stand back and apart from the imagery. One can "walk into" the painted elements and have the sensation of the created lines, forms, and colors running through and around one's body in a way that is distinct from non-virtually immersive art making. (Figure 6.4).

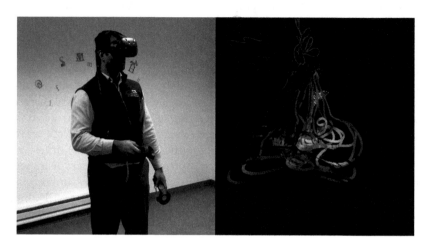

*Figure 6.4* The HTC Vive headset and hand controls (left) and a Tilt Brush drawing in virtual space, as seen on the computer monitor (right).

There are predetermined shapes that can be loaded into the digital workspace, and the participant can explore, interact with, and add or delete elements within these virtual artworks made by others and available through the software. Multiple participants can make virtual artworks together by taking turns with the headgear and hand controls. Multiple participants making artworks simultaneously has not been engineered into the software yet, but this capacity will certainly be developed in the future.

The therapeutic applications of virtual reality art making are at their beginning stages of use (Lohrius, 2017). I believe they include a vital awakening of numerous creative possibilities that engage aspects of imaginal and critical thinking, and relating through the new media. The immersive qualities of VR create a quiet and meditative space around the participant and offer an altered mental state by being "inside" self-generated and manipulated imagery. The light and color play as well as the layering effects of lines, objects, and spatial mergers and separations create playful and free spaces to manipulate, to add or delete and erase elements, and move around within. How the participant is held in the self-created space is distinct and unusual to previous art forms and diversifies how we might discuss and understand projection and the processes of witnessing an artwork unfolding. Virtual reality tools that are literally carried on body parts and made with gestures within the creative space accentuate a vital full body immersion into the imagery. The doorway to the imagination seems a little wider as VR artworks and processes offer distinct and hybrid forms of three-dimensional immersions that further complicate the practices and effects of virtuality (Carlton, 2016).

With the implementation of VR art making and role playing platforms in art therapy, clients could initially explore the tools and capacities of the media and then set goals for exploration. For example, goals for children could be to work through grief, anger, or anxiety by displaying or creating their "superpowers" and other self-projections (Austin, 2010; Carlton, 2015b; Ehinger, 2015). Through completing three-dimensional projections of their body movements, character play and imagination, child clients may create new virtual viewpoints and fantasy metaphors about their lived experiences and relations that could be resourced and literally reviewed and re-manipulated over time and therapeutic process (Carlton, 2015b). Based on the software library of other virtual creators uploading their imagery and subjective worlds to a database, a therapy participant could potentially explore multiple scenes and additional hybrid fantasy worlds as foundations for their own artworks; this would lend ego and form to things that are often difficult for children to draw and give words to. The therapist could also join and witness the child in their created artwork world to increase the shared experience for therapeutic benefits, allow the child to have a leadership role in his or her three-dimensional world, encourage executive decision-making and functioning for the client as editor or director, and promote the use of technology for enhanced digital literacy and creative narrative capacity for therapy participants.

## Integrations

Artistic computer users have demonstrated the ways in which digital media contain both straightforward, tangible structures that can morph into intangible levels of *unfixedness* and unbounded qualities. These ever-changing parameters can mystify attempts to define any physical matter understanding of their multifaceted and pluralistic art forms and thus therapeutic applications. These fluid boundary qualities can be problematic in the use of some digital applications due to concrete privacy requirements that are challenging for both art therapists and clients to outright "control" within prevailing art therapy ethics and aesthetic values (Choe & Carlton, 2017), as well as traditional sensory expectations (Carlton, 2016). These augmentations and complications all contribute to why interested art therapists are building digital media literacy and knowledge through exploratory methods amidst reflective critique.

The new paradigms of thinking, relating, and creating are emerging through the variable applications of digital media that add to vital media choice discussions within art therapy (Carlton, 2014; Choe, 2014; Moon, 2010; Orr, 2010; Partridge, 2016), which are also activating interdisciplinary mixing and scholarship sharing (Carlton, Lee, Yu, & Lanctot, 2016; http://digitalsymposium2016.wixsite.com/home). We are situated in a contemporary gestalt where internet commons and relational qualities are wired into digital media and distinct from previous generations of materiality (Carlton, 2016; Miller, 2017; Orr, 2010). Media scholar

Elo (2012) described how our digitized fingers or touch screen controls have replaced the mechanical switch to further complicate our sense of touch and disembodied "realness" in cyberspaces. Media educator Lòpez (2012) has discussed our collective internet experiences as "illusions of immediacy" (p. 106), in which worldwide events and images are brought to us in vector approximations, or re-represented, filtered, and framed spectacles. There are perceptual grounds of visual and aural representation and connectivity being reinvented by digital media that are supplanting previous forms of exchange and truth. "Traditionally, words have been privileged as the proper mode of explanation, as the tool of thought" (Sousanis, 2015, p. 54), whereas computerized apparatuses are re-ordering our senses, and sense of reality, by multiple forces and contexts (McLuhan as cited in Carlton, 2015a).

We often define the terms of digital media but not their whole possibilities; we readily use and identify computer-mediated materials and outputs but cannot always articulate the way media content and effects shapeshift human communication and consciousness, as much as their products are innovating forms and outputs. As both younger and older generations, we are responding to their ubiquitous effects and developing greater capacity for digital literacy in our computer-mediated work, home, and school environments (Choe, 2016). Digital media are infinite circuit combinations of "off or on," "zeros and ones," respectively. Many media have had long histories of remediating previous forms and "reassembling" our consciousness and worlds as we adapt within them (Carlton, 2015a). The boundaries between any "traditional" media and "new" media have always been permeable, interchangeable, adaptable, and engaging to many creative and communication forms. There are also distinct qualities that hybrid media bring to creativity and communication:

> [Digital media] allow me a lot of control over how my work is ultimately seen. They also allow me to easily fix mistakes, re-size images, and collage images together seamlessly. They give me the additional options of posting online or flexing my sculptor brain to create an object.
>
> (R. Clinton, personal communication, October 8, 2016)

Virtual and material interactivity that create crisscrossed boundaries and margins to mixed worlds can contain valuable enlightenment and perspectives that defy being of any "one world." Such material engagement uses both concrete and malleable objects, such as handheld and keyboard tools and related hardware, as well as the more abstract interior pathways of networks and interactive vector grids, which together project and form the stimuli of computers. Though unseen and considered "unreal" in our largely material world, virtual experiences continue to be felt as real and are becoming more embodied by participants who employ and learn within them. A colleague recently imagined that our behind the screen pathways and materials from the internet are pulses of information being sent along "threads in a cosmic fabric" (D. Dunston, personal communication, October 7, 2016). There are added realities and sets of experiences many of us build daily in the digital cosmos of our and others' making. As a result, there is a consciousness being woven by experimentation and critique within our ever-growing, mixed reality worlds. The future of new media requires a looking through, and not directly at, the possibilities and challenges while asking questions we barely comprehend.

## References

Alders, A., & Allen, P. (2010, November). *Ethics of representation: Ethical movie making in art therapy.* Paper presented at the 41st Annual Conference of the American Art Therapy Association, Sacramento, CA.

Asawa, P. (2009). Art therapists' emotional reactions to the demands of technology. *Art Therapy: Journal of the American Art Therapy Association, 26*(2), 58–65.

Austin, B. (2009). Renewing the debate: Digital technology in art therapy and the creative process. *Art Therapy: Journal of the American Art Therapy Association, 26*(2), 83–85.

Austin, B. (2010). Technology, art therapy, and psychodynamic theory: Computer animation with an adolescent in foster care. In C. H. Moon (Ed.), *Materials & media in art therapy* (pp. 199–213). New York, NY: Routledge.

Belkofer, C. M., & McNutt, J. V. (2011). Understanding social media culture and its ethical challenges for art therapists. *Art Therapy: Journal of the American Art Therapy Association, 28*(4), 159–164.

Carlton, N. (2016). Grid + Pattern: The sensory qualities of digital media. In R. Garner (Ed.) *Digital art therapy: Materials, methods, and applications* (pp. 22–39). Philadelphia, PA: Jessica Kingsley.

Carlton, N., Lee, S. C., Yu, D., & Lanctot, D. (2016, March 12). *Creative digital media in therapeutic processes symposium.* This symposium brought together artists, art therapists, and an empathy game creator to present and evidence how digital animation, video, and photo editing are currently being used for therapeutic processes and healing narratives, School of the Art Institute (SAIC), Chicago, IL. Retrieved from http://digitalsymposium2016.wix.com/home

Carlton, N. R. (2014). Digital culture and art therapy. *The Arts in Psychotherapy, 41*(1), 41–45.

Carlton, N. R. (2015a). *Digital media use in art therapy* (Doctoral dissertation). Available from ProQuest Dissertations and Theses database. (UMI No. 3682148)

Carlton, N. R. (2015b). Expansive palettes. In J. Cohen, L. Johnson, & P. Orr (Eds.), *Video and filmmaking as psychotherapy* (pp. 69–80). New York, NY: Routledge. Retrieved from www.filmandvideobasedtherapy.com

Choe, N. (2014). An exploration of the qualities and features of art apps for art therapy. The *Arts in Psychotherapy, 41*(1), 145–154.

Choe, N. (2016). Utilizing digital tools and apps in art therapy sessions. In R. Garner (Ed.), *Digital art therapy: Material, methods, and applications* (pp. 54–66). New York, NY: Routledge.

## 88   *Natalie Carlton, et al.*

Choe, N., & Carlton, N. R. (2017). Behind the screens: Why informed consent and digital literacy matter. Manuscript in preparation.

Cohen, J., Johnson, L. & Orr, P. (2015). *Video and filmmaking as psychotherapy.* New York & London: Routledge. www.filmandvideobasedtherapy.com

Despres, D. (2015, August 12). *The Drax files: World makers* [Episode 31: Tom Boellstorff; Video file]. Retrieved from www.youtube.com/watch?v=zhrE5MYbeOs

Edmunds, J. D. (2012). *The applications and implications of digital media in art therapy: A survey study* (Unpublished Master's thesis). Philadelphia, PA: Drexel University.

Ehinger, J. (2015). Filming the fantasy: Green screen technology from novelty to psychotherapy. In J. Cohen, L. Johnson, & P. Orr (Eds.), *Video and filmmaking as psychotherapy: Research and practice* (pp. 43–56). New York, NY: Routledge.

Ehinger, J. (2016). Therapeutic technology re-envisioned. In R. Garner (Ed.), *Digital art therapy: Materials, methods, and applications* (pp. 115–123). Philadelphia, PA: Jessica Kingsley.

Elo, M. (2012). Digital finger: Beyond phenomenological figures of touch. *Journal of Aesthetics*, 4. Manuscript in preparation.

Fan Labor. (2016). Retrieved from https://en.wikipedia.org/wiki/Fan_labor

Garner, R. (2016). *Digital art therapy: Materials, methods, and applications.* New York, NY: Routledge.

Imholz, S., & Sachter, J. (in press). *Psychology's new design and the reflective practitioner.* New York, NY: Springer.

Instagram. (2017). Retrieved from www.instagram.com

Kapitan, L. (2009). Introduction to the special issue on art therapy's response to techno-digital culture. *Art Therapy: Journal of the American Art Therapy Association*, 26(2), 50–51.

Klorer, P. (2009). The effects of technological overload on children: An art therapist's perspective. *Art Therapy: Journal of the American Art Therapy Association*, 26(2), 80–82.

Krauss, D. A., & Fryrear, J. L. (1983). Phototherapy introduction and overview. In J. L. Fryrear & D. A. Krauss (Eds.), *Phototherapy in mental health* (pp. 3–23). Springfield, IL: Charles C. Thomas.

Landgarten, H. B. (1993). *Magazine Photo Collage: A multicultural assessment and treatment technique.* New York, NY: Brunner Mazel Publishers.

Lee, S. C. (2015). *The supervisory relationship: Exploring the use of video as an adjunctive tool in art therapy* (Unpublished Master's thesis). The School of the Art Institute of Chicago, Chicago, IL.

L'Esperance, N. (2016). Art therapy and technology: Islands of brilliance. In R. Garner (Ed.), *Digital art therapy: Material, methods and applications* (pp. 82–93) London, UK: Jessica Kingsley.

Lòpez, A. (2012). *The media ecosystem: What ecology can teach us about responsible media practice.* Berkeley, CA: Evolver Editions.

Lohrius, J. (2017). Step into, through and around your art with virtual art making. Workshop presented at the 48th annual conference of the American Art Therapy Association, Albuquerque, New Mexico.

McLeod, C. (1999). Empowering creativity with computer-assisted art therapy: An introduction to available programs and techniques. *Art Therapy: Journal of the American Art Therapy Association*, 16(4), 201–205.

McNiff, S. A. (1981). Video enactment in the expressive therapies. In J. L. Fryrear & B. Fleshman (Eds.), *Videotherapy in mental health* (pp. 79–92). Springfield, IL: Charles C. Thomas.

McNiff, S. A., & Cook, C. (1975). Video art therapy. *The Arts in Psychotherapy*, 2, 55–63.

Merriam-Webster (2017). *Avatar*. Retrieved from www.merriam-webster.com/dictionary/avatarwww.merriam-webster.com/dictionary/avatar

Mighty. (2017). Retrieved from https://themighty.com/2016/10/casey-rochell-dj-with-down-syndrome-turns-offense-to-positive-message/

Miller, G. (2016). Social media and creative motivation. In R. Garner (Ed.), *Digital art therapy: Materials, methods, and applications* (pp. 40–53). Philadelphia, PA: Jessica Kingsley.

Miller, G. (2017). *The art therapist's guide to social media: Connection, community, and creativity*. New York, NY: Routledge.

Minecraft. (2017). Retrieved from https://minecraft.net/en-us/

Moon, C. (2010). Introduction, A history of materials and media in art therapy, and Theorizing materiality in art therapy. In C. H. Moon (Ed.), *Materials & media in art therapy* (pp. xiii–88). New York, NY: Routledge.

Orr, P. P. (2006). Technology training for art therapist: Is there a need? *Art Therapy: Journal of The American Art Therapy Association*, 23(4), 191–196.

Orr, P. P. (2010). Social remixing: Art therapy media in the digital age. In C. H. Moon (Ed.), *Materials & media in art therapy* (pp. 89–100). New York, NY: Routledge.

Orr, P. P. (2012). Technology use in art therapy practice: 2004 and 2011 comparison. *Arts in Psychotherapy*, 39, 234–238. doi: 10.1016/j.aip.2012.03.010

Partridge, E. (2016). *Amplified Voices: Art-based inquiry into elder communication*. Notre Dame de Namur University, Belmont, CA

Peterson, B. (2010). The media adoption stage model of technology for art therapy. *Art Therapy: Journal of the American Art Therapy Association*, 27(1), 26–31.

Potash, J. S. (2009). Fast food art, talk show therapy: The impact of mass media on adolescent art therapy. *Art Therapy: Journal of the American Art therapy Association*, 26(2), 52–57.

Rochell, C. *DJ with down syndrome, turns offensive quote into positive message*. (2017). Retrieved from The Mighty website: https://themighty.com/2016/10/casey-rochell-dj-with-down-syndrome-turns-offense-to-positive-message/

Second Life. (2017). https://go.secondlife.com/

Sousanis, N. (2015). *Unflattening*. Cambridge, MA: Harvard University Press.

Sundararajan, L. (2014). Mind, machine, and creativity: An artist's perspective. *Journal of Creative Behavior*, 48(2), 136–151. doi:10.1002/jocb.44

Thong, S. (2007). Redefining the tools of art therapy. *Art Therapy: Journal of the American Art Therapy Association*, 24(2), 52–58.

Tilberg, A. L. (2014). *Digital art therapy with children in a community mental health agency*. (Unpublished Master's thesis). Ursuline College: Pepper Pike, Ohio.

Tilt Brush: Painting From a New Perspective (2016, May 3). Retrieved from www.youtube.com/watch?v=TckqNdrdbgk

Weinberg, D. (1985). The potential of rehabilitative computer art therapy for the quadriplegic, cerebral vascular accident and brain trauma patient. *Art Therapy: Journal of the American Art Therapy Association*, 2, 66–72.

Weiser, J. (1999). *Phototherapy techniques*. Vancouver, CA: PhotoTherapy Centre.

Westover, B. (2014). *Hands on with the weird but intriguing HP Sprout*. Retrieved from PC Magazine website: www.pcmag.com/article2/0,2817,2471169,00.asp

90  *Natalie Carlton, et al.*

White, M., & Epston, D. (1990). *Narrative means to therapeutic ends.* New York, NY: Norton.

Wolf, R.I. (1976). The Polaroid technique: Spontaneous dialogues from the unconscious. *The Arts in Psychotherapy, 3*(3), 197–201.

Wolf, R. I. (2007). Advances in phototherapy training. *The Arts in Psychotherapy, 34*(2), 124–133. doi: 10.1016/j.aip.2006.11.004

Yu, D. R. (2016). *Online-sourced video collage in therapy with Asian immigrants experiencing acculturation difficulties: A literature review and proposal* (Unpublished Master's thesis). The School of the Art Institute of Chicago, Chicago, IL.

# Part II
# Practice

# 7 Ethics in Art Therapy

*Lisa Manthe and Richard Carolan*

## The General Ground

Understanding and upholding ethics in the field of art therapy requires reflection on the meaning and scope of ethical practice. Ethical standards in the field of art therapy have multiple purposes. They serve as a guideline for practitioners by identifying standards of practice, and they also serve as a means of protecting the public that participates in art therapy practices (Art Therapy Credentials Board [ATCB], 2017). Ethical standards represent the collective wisdom of the profession. This definition differs from law, which represents the collective wisdom of the community the laws serve. Personal values are the third critical variable in the consideration of ethical practices; they represent the wisdom of the individual practitioner.

Art therapists are required to abide by the law, adhere to the wisdom of the profession that they represent, and work in harmony with their personal values. This is easier to accomplish when these three guidelines fall in a synchronistic pattern. It is more difficult when there are grey areas: those "between areas" that do not clearly fit or synchronize. Conflict between core areas of law, ethics, and personal values present other areas of difficulty. It is these gray areas that Moore (1994) referred to when he identified ethics as *care of the soul*. It is the uncertainty between these areas that Moon (2006) wrote about when he discussed deontological legalism, antinomianism, and theological contextualism.

Art therapy moves further into the quagmire of ethics through its responsibility to address practices that involve the emotions and the imaginal capacities. The documents and conversations regarding ethics in art therapy primarily address the confines of art therapy as a science; they do not address art therapy as an art. Pathways in art therapy deal with areas other than those that fit into the paradigm of predictability. The premise that art is a language of the unconscious, and that the practice of art therapy by design addresses novel experience and imaginal possibilities, requires that we reflect on issues of ethics beyond the ethical principles embedded in psychology, while at the same time honoring those principles. Figure 7.1 serves as a representation of the evolving frameworks art

*Figure 7.1* "Inter-intra." Representing the evolving ethical frameworks we are in dialogue with, as we encounter ethical challenges.

therapists must be in dialogue with in order to find resolution to the ethical challenges we encounter. The ethics of place, of media, of technology, of social justice, and of evidence are aspects of the broader spectrum of the ethics of art therapy that are addressed in this chapter.

## Ethics and Culture

Literature addressing issues of culture in therapy often focus on cultural competence, multiculturalism. and cultural humility, which are all needed areas of reflection (Calisch & Hiscox, 1998). However, there is less emphasis on how to define and understand the parameters of cultural context and how culture serves as our way of knowing. That cultural variables are the ground of our sense of reality and truth is an ethical issue. *Culture* refers to the following:

> The cumulative deposit of knowledge, experience, beliefs, values, attitudes, meanings, hierarchies, religion, notions of time, roles, spatial relations, concepts of the universe, and material objects and possessions acquired by a group of people in the course of generations through individual and group striving.
>
> ("Culture," n. d., para.1)

*Ethics in Art Therapy*  95

The work of therapy is a practice that necessarily includes relationship with the cultural variables that serve as the basis of each participant's lived experience and way of knowing. Ethical considerations include the core elements that concern the nature of the relationship, and culture serves as the basis of what we see and how we understand what we hear. Verbal language serves as the flagship of culture. What is said and what is heard is defined by culture. While art is a language that is embedded in culture, it also allows greater possibility of transcending culture. The image can serve as its own entity separate from the artist, and it can be experienced by the viewer as more of an unknown, uncertain communication, which thus allows for possibility and invites the artist and the participant to step into new territories of communication.

Ethics in art therapy includes consideration of the practice of moving into unfamiliar language, beyond the embedded cultural variables of verbal language. Art allows for us to strive to maintain awareness of the cultural pull towards "knowing" based on the language of our culture, while also seeking new possibilities of transcending these limitations in working with the individual toward some other way of knowing and experiencing. Art is a focal area that needs to be further explored in the inquiry of ethical art therapy. Culturally aware art therapy practices must strive towards using art as a means of discovering how our reality as clinicians and participants is a product of the lens of our culture.

## Ethics and Social Responsibility

Cliff Joseph (2006) wrote about the art therapist's and mental health worker's need to have *transcultural insight*, by which he meant a deep understanding of the particular ethnic and social factors that may influence an individual. It is through this insight that art therapists come to understand the influence of the sociopolitical forces on clients' relationships and mental health, which must be attended to with empathic and compassionate understanding and creative problem solving.

Art therapists are in the unique position to offer the clients tools through art to rebuild their lives and rise up against societal oppression and the self-negation that ensues from it. A unique power of art is its ability to uncover the deception of social forces (Joseph, 2006). Knill, Levine, and Levine (2005) spoke of the "aesthetic responsibility" (p. 138) of art therapists to provide interventions that help individuals who have lost their creativity regain what they have lost by helping them transcend their limitations and become aware of their untapped opportunities. Art challenges the hopelessness in individuals by creating windows to different ways of situating their understanding and identity.

The social forces weighing on staff and clients within agencies and practices need also be addressed; this might entail creating dependable opportunities for art making for clients and staff. It is also critical to

# 96    Lisa Manthe and Richard Carolan

help individuals develop and strengthen their voices through the powerful communication of the image within individual and group interventions. Giving individuals the opportunity to address social forces through their art teaches them to externalize and depersonalize the forces. It creates a template for social change, invests, and inducts a trust and belief that they are the artists of their souls. This author (Lisa Manthe), as an art therapist faced with clients from these entrenched social forces, must make sure that I create opportunities for my own creativity as well. Creating my own art allows me to connect to the creative force and address the social forces that weigh so heavily on my clients and myself.

As art therapists, we are faced with a social responsibility to address these social inequities with our unique capabilities. As others are faced with the sociopolitical fallout of decisions that they had no power to influence, what is our obligation to provide creative statements that resituate their power? It is through art and creation that we demand unity and reject reality (Camus, 1956). We need to create interventions that inspire and reflect the hope we hold for our clients. Camus (1956) spoke to how the beauty of the artistic rebellion carries the light of hope and illuminates evolution. Art explores, expresses, and evaluates what is unseen and unrecognized in society. This tacit knowledge offers the hope of creation (Camus, 1956) and untapped possibilities. Art therapy represents a new way of knowing that exposes opportunities to unvoiced solutions. Creating solutions to social issues through interdisciplinary collaboration and new ways of knowing is the creative rebellion we need to take on (Camus, 1956). As art therapists, we are role models for our clients, and the artistic process is a role model for us.

## Ethics of Place

As complex social and political forces change the boundaries of art therapy, an ethical art therapist is forced to consider the implications of space on the provision of service. Historically, art therapists engaged with their practice within the walls of an office, medical facility, or art therapy studio (Vick, 2003; Waller, 2013). However, currently, many art therapists find themselves working on the edges, providing services in refugee camps, community projects, disaster areas, and within homes, prisons, nature, and the internet. Each of these settings demands us to remain in discourse with ourselves and those we serve regarding the implications and special ethical considerations of the setting. Issues of physical safety, confidentiality, contextual meaning, emotional safety, and ownership of image demand careful consideration. The places where we provide art therapy services are the holding environments in which we provide care. The ethical guidelines of AATA, ATCB, BATA, and other international organizations directly address the needs for adequate ventilation, access to water, and proper lighting in the provision of art therapy services, but do they adequately

*Plate 1* The role of the healer by Erin Partridge.

*Plate 2* The role of the artist: Response art by Joelle Fregeau.

Plate 3  *Grace*.

*Plate 4  Woman in water.*

*Plate 5 Eight Steps of Women* (re: Erickson) by Doris Arrington.

*Plate 6 Muñecas quitapenas* (worry dolls).

*Plate 7 Nicaragua.*

*Plate 8 Recycled waste from my life.*

speak to the range of sites we are now practicing within? The places that we choose or that are chosen for us to engage in art therapy carry implicit meaning to those we serve regarding our values and purpose. What are the differences in the areas that we intentionally co-create with those we serve and the areas we are directed to serve with or without our input?

The places in which we serve have profound neurobiological and theoretical implications that need to be considered. Place, when seen in this light, becomes an extension of the materials we provide, a thoughtfully planned-out intervention. Nature-based art therapy draws on the use of place to provide an experience of whole body, mindful contemplation, which engages the artist in a "haptic" state and directly addresses issues of trauma and attachment (Berger & Lahad, 2013). In this intentional breaking of the barriers of the office walls, the nature-based art therapist communicates an engagement with the ever-changing physical world. What does that communicate to those whom we serve, and how do we ethically prepare ourselves and those we serve for those experiences?

A stark contrast to nature-based services are art therapy services provided in a death row prison community, where art therapy groups are conducted in several one-person wire modules. Art materials are very limited and passed through a small opening in each module. The art therapist in this instance has little power over place, despite it having a profound effect on services. The art itself stands in contrast to the setting, as it offers hope and belief in the powers of creativity.

A refugee setting is yet another place over which the art therapist has little power, which again has profound implications for service. Physical and political safety are powerful issues that can affect art therapy services in a refugee camp, both for the art therapist and those he or she may serve. Clear dialogue regarding physical and emotional safety, confidentiality, and the possible social effects of participation is essential to ethical practice.

The effects of the art therapy image in the transformation of place is also a profound ethical consideration. Intentional collaborative art pieces can become instruments of social justice by amplifying and articulating the voices of the marginalized (Partridge, 2016). Art therapy images can alter personal relationships to place through the profound power of illuminating preverbal and unconscious material. The interrelationship between image, place, and artist needs to be thoughtfully considered in practice. As we expand the boundaries of place in the provision of art therapy services, we need to carefully consider and attend to the ethical considerations unique to each place.

## Ethics of Materials

Materials in the ethical practice of art therapy need to be a core consideration as well. Materials are the primary vehicle of communication and engagement in the therapeutic process (Moon, 2011). Different materials evoke different neurobiological engagement, cultural context, developmental and social contexts, and defenses. (Lusebrink, 2010; Moon, 2011; Orr, 2005; Robbins, 2000; Seiden, 2001). Choice with respect to materials and who chooses materials should be thoughtfully and intentionally made by art therapists. Materials that reflect thoughtful engagement with our clients' emotional, physical, and social developmental needs can inspire creativity, deep process, and the experience of mirroring by the therapist (Robbins,2000). Materials can empower clients to redefine themselves through the use of personal metaphor and narrative process.

The plethora of materials in the current art world, as well as the expansion of processes available, reflects the multiple definitions and perspectives that co-exist. When we welcome the expansion of the boundaries of materials in our clinical practices, we welcome the possibility of engaging the authentic self of our client. We need to be fully aware of the range of experiences possible with the materials offered. It is also essential that we have had our own art making experiences with the materials to serve as a guide. Materials should be seen as an intervention, and they need to be thoughtfully considered as they can cause fragmentation (Chapman, 2014; Lusebrink, 2010; Robbins, 2000), personal injury (Springham, 2008), and further marginalization.

Materials communicate our held values, both about our clients and ourselves. A wide range of materials, including fine art materials and repurposed art materials, allow individuals to situate art making outside the confines of socioeconomic privilege and allow potential access and acceptance to all. A wide range of possible materials can communicate our respect for, and our trust in, our clients. It allows all to feel welcome and equally celebrated. Art therapists need to thoughtfully consider how the materials meet the therapeutic needs of the client in every situation. When art making is seen outside of the past Eurocentric boundaries of privilege, it can foster a flattening of the power in the therapeutic relationship. This can lead to our clients feeling comfortable to assert their needs and express themselves with materials that address those needs.

As artists and art therapists, we need to thoughtfully consider our own biases to materials and aesthetics and find ways to sensitively bracket them in our therapeutic relationships. Our potential countertransference to materials, whether positive or negative, can interfere with our client's primary creativity and therapeutic process. Along with this comes an obligation to be aware of, and in dialogue with, our own cultural background and how it may affect our choice of materials and process.

Art therapists are providing services outside the boundaries of what could be conceived of when the field was first developed. Our materials and practices need to reflect the ever-evolving global landscape. Art therapy services are no longer confined to offices or medical facilities. Art therapy services are conducted in refugee shelters and outdoor environments, and each unique place and population will have unique material needs to contemplate. Appropriate materials in one context could present a danger in another. The art materials offered need to be relevant and appropriate to the population, place, and social or cultural context. As materials evolve, art therapists need to incorporate the use of technology and other emerging fields of materials.

Art therapy services are never a static process; they constitute a dynamic relationship between the artist, the art, and art therapist. Keeping in mind the wisdom of the field, a skilled art therapist can offer specific materials to a client, which allows that person to utilize the art process to heal and resolve salient emotional issues. Allowing our clients to utilize us as creative resources in engagement with materials can offer them the experience of truly being seen.

## Ethics and Technology

Technology is another area that requires profound ethical considerations with respect to its clinical uses. It is developing at such a rapid pace that its implications must be continually chased down. The ethical mandates of art therapy developed by our organizations will, by nature, always be afterthoughts. The swiftness in which the technological field is developing forces the practitioner to be continually focused on, and in dialogue about, the ethical implications of using technology within every clinical situation. It is essential that art therapists engage in ethical conversations regarding the parameters of confidentiality, emotional and physical safety, permanence, culture, the potential absence of physical presence, informed consent, and socially constructed meaning.

The ethical practice of art therapy services now demands that we consider the implications of social media and technology within our treatment. Identity, privacy, cyber violence, and confidentiality now carry a complex matrix of issues reflective of emerging technology. Screening and dialogue are essential to understanding the whole individual. Due to the nature of the emerging understanding and laws, it is essential that art therapists stay abreast of new developments to appropriately assist our clients.

In addition, the use of technology has embedded cultural implications regarding the communication of values and beliefs. Technology can be a powerful tool in breaking down cultural barriers, and this encourages discourse and mutual understanding. The absence of technology in the provision of services can create challenges to understanding the voice of the current generation. The global engagement with technology and its dominant role in communication is reflected in the identity of our clients. It is our ethical responsibility to both provide materials that honor and embrace the voice of our clients and find ways to engage the voice of the treatment-resistant client (Austin, 2011).

However, current immersion in technology and social media may blind individuals to the complex considerations of vulnerable populations (Orr, 2005). Ethical art therapists consider the use of technology as a medium and the complex neurobiological, social, and developmental lenses embedded in its use (Lusebrink, 2010; Orr, 2005; Seiden, 2001). As with any other media, art therapists must use careful, thoughtful consideration when making the choice of whether to include technology as an intervention, and special considerations will need to be clear in the informed consent.

This author (Lisa Manthe) works with a population of adolescents who have experienced extensive trauma and have voiced an internalized marginalization. They feel socially isolated, and many experience socioeconomic deprivation. They are often unable to access innovative technology, which is their preferred voice. I created an interdisciplinary project, 3D-ID, that addresses the neurobiological needs of adolescents who have experienced trauma through the use of technology, sculpture, and theatre. In group art therapy, students are invited to participate in a long-term assemblage, self-portrait sculpture project that engages a physical dimension of their self and the creation of an artist's statement. These pieces are also informed by two museum trips, which are utilized to help them reflect on self-portraiture in sculpture. The students take photographs of their sculpture pieces, and using an HP Sprout immersion computer, they create a collage of the photographs that reflects the group identity. This piece is then printed on a 3D printer. Students also create a 3D sculpture that reflects a core element of who they are in the group. The students then work with the facilitators and a theatre group to develop and put on one-act plays that reflect their personal and collective identities.

Long-term sculpture projects offer kinesthetic involvement; the whole body is immersed in the contemplation and resolution of the normative work of identity formation; it also provides the safety necessary for trauma work. Sculpture, in its inherent kinesthetic and somatic nature, addresses the neurobiological needs of the adolescent brain that has experienced trauma. The 3D-ID work is enhanced by the interdisciplinary collaboration and exposure to museum education. These experiences help the adolescent anchor a facet of their identity as artist and move away from the labels they feel define them. The Sprout technology and the 3D printer allow the adolescents to communicate in their cultural voice. The technology is a purposeful intervention that provides a unique way of engaging with their identities, while also providing an important and unique neurobiological engagement.

Careful consideration regarding the use of this technology with such a vulnerable population was essential and included a detailed informed consent and psychoeducation regarding the complexities of the use of technology. The adolescents voiced that they felt heard and celebrated through this process, and they mobilized to co-create other projects that utilize technology and art therapy for the future.

Technology, can create a bridge to understanding those whose primary means of relationships occurs within the context of social media and the internet. Sociopolitical and cultural evolution demands that the art therapist consider and engage with the social media identities of our clients. Technology can provide a mirroring and an engagement with the cultural voice of our clients. Intentional use of technology in clinical art therapy can enhance services if the ethical implications are thoroughly considered.

## Ethics of Evidence and Art

The ethical art therapist is required to practice evidence-based interventions in their work. In the interest of protecting the public and the profession, we must strive towards best practices and avoid procedures that are not grounded in evidence and that might put participants at risk. This imperative begins with having a clear definition of evidence. Staying within the parameters of the law, while incorporating our personal values and the wisdom of the profession, should serve as a critical monitor in determining what we trust as evidence.

The scientific approach to defining evidence can be seen in the medical model. The medical clinician determines evidence based on randomly controlled trials conducted in laboratory settings by researchers who are not necessarily clinicians. They prescribe medication and dosage based on the reports of these trials. Art therapy, from an ethical perspective, must determine whether this is the model that the profession should aspire towards. Each ethical art therapist must determine if he or she has trust in evidence that is generated from experiments in laboratory settings with emphasis on controlling all variables that might affect results. This type of evidence controls consistency in procedure and the dosage of art intervention. The preference in best practices of this type of evidence gathering is that the therapist is not the researcher; therefore, the therapist is not a person involved in the gathering of evidence.

Art therapists who follow ethical guidelines are accountable for their own evidence-defining practices and evidence-determining procedures. It is the ethical responsibility of the art therapist to inform the client of the procedures implemented in art therapy and the risks involved. Ethical art therapists must determine the definition of evidence that is the basis of their intervention strategies and their dosage. In cases in which that evidence is randomly controlled trials, then this should be understood and presented as the basis of the work. Ethical art therapists who have other forms of evidence, which is based on their own trials as clinicians, on their own experience in trainings and personal work, on their imaginative capacity emerging from clinical experience, and on their intuitive sense, tacit knowledge, and felt sense, have a responsibility to defend that as evidence. Ethical art therapists have confidence in their evidence; they

102 *Lisa Manthe and Richard Carolan*

can define it, and they can present it to the individuals with whom they work.

## Ethics of the Artist

By definition, art therapists embrace the art of therapy and the artist as therapist. Consequently, we have a responsibility to address the ethics related to the art of therapy, as well as our ethical responsibility as artists. It is not enough to have ethical standards that only concern the scientist as therapist. The function and process of art is not about predictability. The art therapist invites, supports, and facilitates the emergence of the artist as participant. Art therapists facilitate the process of trust that clients develop in creating the image. They facilitate the therapeutic process of the clients' developing a relationship with the image, which enables them to venture into uncharted territories of their own knowledge, emotions, imagination, and experience.

Many art therapists may identify that they, to an important degree, incorporate scientific procedures in their facilitation of this therapeutic process, and while this may be true of all art therapists to varying degrees, art therapists by definition use the artistic process, artistic procedures, and the engagement of the artist as therapist as a primary means of therapy.

Art involves the suspension of knowing (Hogan & Pink, 2010), which moves towards imagining and creating in the unknown. The art therapist elicits novel experiences in the participant. The process often involves interpretation and moving beyond what is observed or spoken to possible association with the unspoken and unobserved. The artist moves to the precipice of the known and leaps into the unknown. The art therapist facilitates this as the practice of therapy. We need to address the ethical considerations of the artist's side of the therapeutic process.

There are no specific laws that govern this process, and there are limited ethical guidelines other than those that fall under scope of practice and scope of competency. Art therapists are required to have taken a certain number of classes in studio art. Once they have met that criteria, they are no longer required to demonstrate any continuing relationship with art practice. The engagement with art is the primary distinguishing element of the art therapy practice. The ethics of art therapy requires that we address implications in terms of defining standards of practice and the protection of the public.

## Conclusion

Clear ethical standards and guidelines serve as a basis for defining our profession. It is not enough to allow our profession to more narrowly define ethics, which are modeled after the profession of psychology-based psychotherapy, with minimal attention paid to the unique qualities and possibilities of art therapy. We must take leadership in exploring and addressing ethical issues that are intrinsic to our work. This chapter adds to that conversation.

## References

Art Therapy Credentials Board. (2017). *Code of ethics, conduct, and disciplinary procedures*. Retrieved from www.atcb.org/Ethics/ATCBCode

Austin, B. (2011). Technology, art therapy, and psychodynamic theory. In Moon, C. H. (Ed.). *Materials & Media in Art Therapy: Critical Understandings of Diverse Artistic Vocabularies.*(p. 199). New York, NY: Routledge.

Berger, R., & Lahad, M. (2013). *The healing forest: Nature therapy and the expressive arts in post-crisis work with children*. London, UK: Jessica Kingsley.

Calisch, A., & Hiscox, A. (1998). *Tapestry of culture issues in art therapy*. London, UK: Jessica Kingsley.

Camus, A. (1956). *The rebel* (A. Bower, Trans.). New York, NY: Knopf.

Chapman, L. (2014). *Neurobiologically informed trauma therapy with children and adolescents: Understanding mechanisms of change (Norton Series on Interpersonal Neurobiology)*. New York, NY: Norton.

Culture. (n.d.). Retrieved from www.tamu.edu/faculty/choudhury/culture.html

Hogan, S., & Pink, S. (2010). Routes to interiorities: Art therapy and knowing in anthropology. *Visual Anthropology, 23*(2), 158–174. doi:10.1080/08949460903475625

Joseph, C. (2006). Creative alliance: The healing power of art therapy. *Art Therapy: Journal of the American Art Therapy Association, 23*(1), 30–33.

Knill, P., Levine, E., & Levine, S. (2005). *Principles and practice of expressive arts therapy toward a therapeutic aesthetics*. London, UK: Jessica Kingsley.

Lusebrink, V. B. (2010). Assessment and therapeutic application of the expressive therapies continuum: Implications for brain structures and functions. *Art Therapy, 27*(4), 168–177.

Moon, B. (2006). *Ethical issues in art therapy*. Springfield, IL: Charles C. Thomas.

Moon, C. H. (Ed.). (2011). *Materials and media in art therapy: Critical understandings of diverse artistic vocabularies*. New York, NY: Routledge.

Moore, T. (1994). *Care of the soul: A guide for cultivating depth and sacredness in everyday life*. New York, NY: Harper Perennial.

Orr, P. (2005). Technology media: An exploration for "inherent qualities." *The Arts in Psychotherapy, 32*(4), 191–196.

Partridge, E. (2016). *Amplified voices: Art based inquiry into elder communication* (Unpublished doctoral dissertation research). Notre Dame de Namur University, Belmont, CA.

Robbins, A. (2000). *The artist as therapist*. London, UK: Jessica Kingsley Publishers.

Seiden, D. (2001). *Mind over matter: The uses of materials in art, education and therapy*. Chicago, IL: Magnolia Street.

Springham, N. (2008). Through the eyes of the law: What is it about art that can harm people? *International Journal of Art Therapy, 13*(2), 65–73.

Stafford, K. (2016). *The art encounter for self-reflection: An art-based phenomenological inquiry* (Unpublished doctoral dissertation research). Notre Dame de Namur University, Belmont, CA.

Vick, R. M. (2003). A brief history of art therapy. *Handbook of art therapy,* 5–15.

Waller, D. (2013). *Becoming a profession (psychology revivals): The history of art therapy in Britain 1940–1982.* New York, NY: Routledge.

# 8 Wisdom Through Diversity in Art Therapy

*Louvenia Jackson, Claudia Mezzera, and Melissa Satterberg*

## Cultural Humility Through an Art Therapy Lens

The American Art Therapy Association Incorporation Membership Survey Report (2013) reported the following demographic data of its membership: In data collected in 2007, 2009, 2011, and 2013, Caucasian women comprised 86.6%, 91%, 89.1%, and 87.8% of the membership, respectively (Elkins & Deaver, 2015). Overall, women were reported to make up 93.4% of the membership in 2013 (Elkins & Deaver, 2015). Many of the theoretical underpinnings, philosophies, and ideologies represented in art therapy epistemology are those of the Western dominant group (Boston, 2014). Moreover, as indicated by the aforementioned membership survey, the field is predominantly practiced and developed by women of Anglo descent.

The field of art therapy has a strong scientific influence, with markedly less influence or wisdom from other cultures and ways of knowing. The following chapter examines perspectives from diverse populations through a paradigm of cultural humility and cultural competency. Art making and the creative process are recognized as ways of knowing oneself and of exploring other communities (Allen, 1995). Communities are encouraged to strive to understand each other's unique perspectives and to welcome emerging knowledge, particularly that which emerges from marginalized populations. In this way, the richness and splendor embodied in others which resides outside of the dominant culture can be met with cultural sensitivity, compassion, collective acceptance, and appreciation.

The field of art therapy would benefit from regularly implementing multicultural training that focuses on cultural humility and cultural competency, addresses diversity needs, and advocates for social justice. Areas of needed inquiry include ongoing personal reflection processes for art therapists, additional collaborative and cultural group studies to include cultural diversity and multicultural needs, and research focused on understanding human experiences from multicultural perspectives. The following sections provide examples of how these areas are currently being broadened and how differences that divide communities can be

## 106 Louvenia Jackson, et al.

examined. Furthermore, they explore how art therapy practices can be used to validate and integrate a greater appreciation of others' ways of knowing.

## Cultural Humility and Art Therapy in Practice

Developed on three core principles, cultural humility offers a continuous perspective to navigate through the diverse experience of life. Tervalon and Murray-Garcia (1998) outlined the core concepts as follows: (a) a philosophy that incorporates a commitment to engage in a lifelong process that individuals enter into on an ongoing basis with clients, constituents, and colleagues, as well as themselves; (b) it addresses power imbalances and sees individuals or communities as rich experts, or teachers, on the content of culture; (c) cultural humility is a process rather than an ultimate goal and is often developed in stages by building upon previous knowledge and experience. Cultural humility in art therapy becomes relevant through the deepening comprehension of how art plays a role in our self-reflective process and how that informs us about art. Art is a representation of our lived experience; therefore, the truth of an individual's experience lies in the art. Art can capture experiences that cannot be placed into language; thus, it creates its own language, lifting the limits of consciousness (Julliard, 1999).

In the practice and training of art therapists, cultural humility encourages the art therapist, student, or professional to know who they are, their history, their experience, and their worldview (Tervalon, 2015). This can be done through response art, investigating countertransference, and maintaining a personal art making practice. Practicing a culturally humble approach toward those with whom they work can reduce suffering; develop shared communication, trust, and mutual respect; and offer a collaboration of practice. It allows art therapists to view "the individual or community as a rich expert, teacher on the content of culture, 'isms,' and community life" (Tervalon, 2015, p. 33). The practitioner then becomes the student, partner, and facilitator with access to resources and knowledge.

Developed out of the need to address social unrest and as an elaboration to cultural competence training, cultural humility can broaden the practice and training of art therapists. Incorporating cultural humility into art therapy education encourages art therapists to view and encompass alternative ways of knowing outside of their own beliefs, assumptions, and biases. Challenging and expanding students' worldviews brings awareness that then transfers over into art therapy practice. The training of cultural humility encourages collaboration with individuals and communities to gain new knowledge, which is fostered by allowing others to be the experts of their experiences, while sharing one's own self-reflective experience. Promoting new epistemology through collaborative work and self-awareness can enhance cultural humility in art therapy. The practice of cultural humility, cultural competency, and empowerment will be demonstrated in the next section through research and the acknowledgement of art as a way of knowing within the Latina populations.

## Multicultural Perspectives: Latinas

The term *Hispanic* is used by the United States Census Bureau to classify persons originating or having ancestors from Spain and Latin American countries (Garcia & Marotta, 1997). In the United States, the Hispanic community is the most predominant minority group (Pew Hispanic Center, 2015). "United States Hispanic women, also known as Latinas, have recently and rapidly surfaced as prominent contributors to the educational, economic, and cultural well-being of not only their own ethnicity, but of American society and the consumer marketplace" (Nielsen, 2013, p. 1). The increase of Latina influence is connected to an expansion in population statistics, as well as an encompassing of Latina desire to maintain their ethnic and cultural mores while propitiously maneuvering through the world of technology and conventional American culture (Nielsen, 2013). Nielsen (2013) noted that Latinas endorse and encourage connectivity and "are adopting and adapting to all types of technology at a higher pace than United States females" (p. 1). Presently, Latinas are utilizing technology and social networking avenues to remain connected, express their identities, and communicate their cultural traditions and values (Nielsen, 2013).

### Prevailing Issues

Past experiences of trauma, socioeconomic challenges, acculturation, and assimilation concerns (National Council of La Raza, 2005), as well as roadblocks to mental health services, are prevalent issues for Latinas. Latinas' underutilization of therapeutic services is an increasing concern in clinical practice and in research(Kouyoudjian, Zamboanga, & Hansen, 2003). The considerable imparity amidst Latinas' need for, and use of, mental health services underscores the importance of understanding the mental health concerns of Latinas (Kouyoumdjian et.al., 2003). Latinas who openly express, explore, and find ways to commemorate their cultural roots in creative and conventional ways can employ art therapy to alleviate the aforementioned challenges and issues. Art therapy permits participants to create significance in ways that are cathartic and that encourage and support development and transformation (Pollanen, 2009). Therefore, art therapists attending to Latinas in a posture

## 108    *Louvenia Jackson, et al.*

of humility while respecting clients' social, ethical, and cultural customs, purposefully integrate cultural humility and competency.

### *Cultural Competency*

Cultural competency encompasses a set of conforming activities, outlooks, and policies that assist organizations in developing professionals who can function capably in cross-cultural situations (Cross, Bazron, Dennis, & Isaacs, 1989; Isaacs & Benjamin). Engebretson, Mahoney, and Carlson (2008) contended, "The development of cultural competence is a growth process rather than a static evaluative performance outcome" (p. 172). Smith and Montilla (2006) noted three key areas that support therapists in maintaining multicultural counseling aptitudes: (a) mindful awareness regarding the modes in which clinicians' cultural training has an impact on their comprehensive outlook and the ways in which they interact and consequently respond as a result; (b) grasping the meaning of various worldviews of multicultural clients; and (c) retaining the capabilities required to meritoriously provide therapeutic services with culturally and ethnically diverse clients (Corvin & Wiggins, 1989; D'Andrea, Daniels, & Heck, 1991; Holcomb-McCoy & Myers, 1999). There is an ever-increasing need for multiculturally competent research from the perspectives of Latina populations; this entails methods that are inclusive of their self-identified needs and their assessments of how effectively therapists meet their needs (Pope et al., 2002). Davis (1997) affirmed that systems that assimilate an understanding of various cultures also facilitate a higher quality of services and results.

### Empowering Latinas via Art Therapy

"Art (a category that includes works of design, architecture, and craft) is a therapeutic medium that can help guide, exhort, and console its viewers, enabling them to become better versions of themselves" (de Botton & Armstrong, 2013, p. 5). Art therapy can be a useful exploration tool for Latinas (Booker & Eastman, 2004) to examine their self-conception and cultural identity (Mauro, 1998). It befits art therapy practitioners to learn about and remain cognizant of Latina paradigms of thought and how Latinas develop self-esteem (Mezzera, 2016). The United States Census Bureau (2014) recognizes Latinos as the largest ethnic group in California, which numbers approximately 15,000,000 (Pew Hispanic Center, 2015). Comprehending elements that shape and inform Latinas' self-conceptions and self-esteem can prepare and inform the field of ways to effectually create programs that serve this rapidly growing populace (Mezzera, 2016). Utilizing art therapy with Latinas also offers the field the benefit of expanding global awareness around working with other cultures.

## Benefits of Art Therapy Work with Latinas

Art therapy can offer Latinas of all ages and capabilities the opportunity to genuinely connect, examine, and creatively express themselves. "Art therapists may have a particularly advantageous perspective from which to foster societal change in order to make a more humane and just world" (Junge & Asawa, 1994, p. 283). Art making can empower Latinas to convey their truth, and to assess and comprehend their experiences in relationship to others and to significant events in their lives. Dreikurs (1971) contended, "One event can be understood only when one sees the *whole field* in which the event takes place" (p. 171). Correspondingly, art making can provide Latinas with a multidimensional method to explore, analyze, and identify their hopes, desires, behaviors, and needs with the purpose of actively constructing positive results. Hence, art therapy can be a tool used to instruct Latinas to consider their realities as ever fluid and changing, versus fatalistic. In this way, art therapy can provide a mode through which Latinas may consider alternate ways of creating and shaping their desired outcomes. Dreikurs (1971) noted, "Things are no longer as simple as they once appeared. Interaction is constant; nothing is isolated. Cause and effect are not always certain. Truth and falsehood are relative to the situation. Everything is in change; nothing is definite" (p. 171). Latinas in treatment oftentimes contend with challenges resulting from unanticipated life developments that impinge on their sense of security and stability (Kouyoumdjian, Zamboanga, & Hansen, 2003). Art therapists working with Latinas must be attentive to their clients' cultural and personal histories, as well as the traditions, values, beliefs, and the imagery evident in Latina culture that influence their clients' views of the world and of themselves.

## Latinas, Stimulus Art, and Self-Esteem

Mezzera (2016) examined the result of employing stimulus art in the form of *universal survival archetypal* imagery to capture data related to understanding the influence of images on Latina women's self-esteem. Relationships between Latinas' universal survival archetypal image preferences, self-esteem, and demographic background were explored as a means of establishing art therapy as a "way of knowing" self, others, and community. This study established correlations between Latinas' image preferences of universal survival archetypes and their personal descriptions of how the images represented the self, their self-esteem, and their demographic context. Understanding prospective methods for using cultural imagery to collect data can provide the field of art therapy with important insights into working with Latina clients. Art therapy that invites Latinas to utilize culturally relevant imagery and traditional art making customs, symbols, patterns, and vivid colors may provide a strength-based approach to celebrating a self-discovery process that also honors and validates their cultural heritage.

110 *Louvenia Jackson, et al.*

## Traditional Art Making with Latinas

Traditional forms of art making can provide Latinas with a platform for actively authoring their dreams, desires, hopes, and realities, while validating their traditional values and acknowledging the richness and the healing available through their cultural heritage. Culturally competent approaches to treatment incorporate a posture of cultural humility, in which a therapist remains interested, curious, open to, and welcoming of clients in ways that both enrich the relationship and welcomes their clients' cultural values, principles, and beliefs. This can be done by actively exploring the use of creative processes that create safe spaces to validate and empower clients' cultural traditions, core values, and that utilize materials that are recognizable to the client.

Examples of Latin American conventional materials that can be incorporated into art directives may include: (a) *papel picado* (perforated paper), which can be used by clients to decorate and celebrate Latino festivities and holidays; (b) vividly colored yarns for weaving or creating braided bracelets that hold symbolic meaning to the clients; (c) *repujado* (embossed) cuffed bracelets can be made of cardboard and aluminum foil and invite discussions about significant cultural events or personal achievements; (d) *guiones gráficos* (personal storyboards) made with cardboard, paper or collage can be used to validate personal history, heroes, or events; (e) *luminarias de esperanza* (lanterns of hope), made with decorated perforated paper, tea lights, and simple glass jars, can be used to encourage clients to identify and examine their expectations and to optimistically reframe their challenges; (f) *instrumentos musicales* (musical instruments), such as castanets, made of bottle caps and poster board, or maracas created with the use of plastic eggs and spoons held together with colored tape can be used to highlight the beauty of Latino music and teach clients positive stress reduction techniques and tools; and finally (g) *muñecas quitapenas* (worry dolls), made with colored fabrics, wood, and yarn, can be used to teach anxiety reduction while celebrating Latino culture (see Plate 6).

All of these examples offer art making opportunities that can assist Latina clients in celebrating themes of growth, validating successful adaptations to life circumstances, and integrating their sense of empowerment. They allow for the building of strength-based bridges of trust, empathy, and insight between clients and therapists in ways that increase mindful engagement and enhance understanding of clients' cultures.

## Research, Current Challenges, and Further Inquiry: Latinas

Current art therapy literature apprises the field about non-vocal multiethnic approaches to the creative process (Linesch, Aceves, Quezada, Trochez, & Zuniga, 2012). However, art therapists must address the challenges that result from a lack of research focused on understanding Latinas' needs and their multifaceted culture: "In cross cultural research a fundamental taboo is the projection of a personal theory of behavior and values onto other cultural groups" (McNiff, 1984, p. 125). Proactive cross-cultural research can assist the field in establishing a consistent language and communal insight with respect to Latinas' strengths, values, traits, temperaments, and tendencies. Exploring and recognizing how imagery can be used to gather data can create new avenues of information about Latinas and their identities (Mezzera, 2016). Rethinking discordant distinctions in pathology and supporting an increased understanding of Latinas, as well as other cultures and their inimitable strengths, will empower art therapists to practice cultural humility and to continually actualize cultural competency, thereby building a more inclusive approach to other populations, such as the LGBT community.

## Lesbian, Gay, Bisexual, Transgender (LGBT) Community

### *Multicultural Assumptions*

Members of the LGBT community have been coming to treatment at higher rates to address mental health symptoms (Meyer, 2003). This increase in services gives art therapists opportunities to engage in art therapy practices that promote health and wellness specifically with this community. The American Art Therapy Association (AATA) recognizes that therapists who provide services to LGBT individuals require specific competencies. The AATA encourages a three-stage development sequence of awareness, knowledge, and skills required to provide competent treatment for the LGBT community (AATA, 2011).

Art therapists should be aware of existing assumptions regarding this community; the failure to do so can hinder growth and possibly cause emotional harm. First, the heterosexual assumption, identified by Dumontier (2000), is the presumption that each individual is heterosexual (attracted to the opposite gender) and that gender matches the individual's biological sex. This assumption reinforces the dominant cultures' dialectical oppositions of "preferred" or "not preferred" sexual identity and may be a contributing factor to the overall wellbeing of an LGBT-identified person (Burn, Kadlec, & Rexer, 2008). Dumontier (2000) stated that the heterosexual assumption plays a significant role in an individual's decision to come out as gay, lesbian, bisexual, or transgender identity, and which therefore keeps the individual "closeted" because he or she feels the necessity to be quiet about, or keep hidden, his or her sexual identity.

The second assumption is that "coming out" (sharing of one's sexual identity) is a one-time experience. Dumontier (2000) defined "coming

## 112  *Louvenia Jackson, et al.*

out" as a lifelong process, and Bacon (1998) described it as not just a simple statement, but rather a "shift in perspective" (Bacon, 1998, p. 251). Coming out to others occurs in the context of relationships (new and old) and environments (e.g., education, employment, geographic location), and it may evolve as people and situations change (Troiden, 1989). Bacon (1998) supported the notion that the coming out narrative is a freeing one, in that it allows one to come out from hiding under the "veil of heterosexual assumptions" (p. 251). Lastly, the assumption that LGBT-identified individuals seek mental health care because of their sexual identity is one that therapists should be mindful of (Israel, Gorcheva, Walther, Sulzner, & Cohen, 2008). Although in some cases this is a true assumption, LGBT-identified individuals experience mental health symptoms related to reasons outside of their sexual identity.

### Art Therapy, Wellness, and Identity in the LGBT Community

Observations from art therapists show that a pivotal factor that has an influence on the wellbeing of LGBT-identified individuals is their coming out narrative (Pelton-Sweet & Sherry, 2008). The use of art therapy is encouraged as a way to explore both physical and emotional health through the coming out process as a way to explore wellbeing (Pelton-Sweet & Sherry, 2008). Vaughn (1985) suggested that authenticity is birthed and shared from inner knowing and lends direction toward one's "real" or true self after one has examined existential ideals of freedom, isolation, and death. Living an authentic life and searching through the darkest of times can birth the advancement of the self, which then becomes realized (Vaughn, 1985).

Although this process is highly individualized, outcomes of coming out have resulted in higher rates of living honest lives and in turn forming an authentic life experience associated with health (Dumontier, 2000). Satterberg (2017a) identified themes and shared imagery within a small sample of lesbian-identified women. The women represented transitions and movements through line, shape, color, and form associated with a positive sense of self from the exploration of their sexuality identity formation. It was through the art process of exploring self and identity that new insights were born and a new way of seeing one's identity was realized (Satterberg, 2017a).

### Research and the LGBT Community

The art therapy community has begun to investigate the areas that continue to plague the LGBT community through education and research. The *kaleidoscope curriculum* (Satterberg, 2017b) was designed as part of a doctoral project investigating the efficacy of LGBT content in scholarly art therapy curricula. Core components include dialogues of LGBT research, discussions, written reflection, review of graduate art therapy course content in the United States, and art making as a reflection of personal values and judgments related to LGBT content. The targeted audience is art therapy graduate students and current practicing art therapists. Although the kaleidoscope curriculum is still in its infancy stage, the overall hope is that it will add to a new dialogue related to the inclusion of LGBT topics in multiple art therapy curricula.

Currently, published art therapy research specific to LGBT content consists of limited theories or small sample sizes, which means there are endless research opportunities (Joyce, 2008; Maher, 2011; Pelton-Sweet & Sherry, 2008; Schnebelt, 2015) available. In an effort to fill the gap in art therapy research within lesbian communities, Satterberg (2017a) investigated the role of sexuality and identity in lesbian-identified women through a phenomenological art therapy lens. The study investigated the role of art in knowing sexual identity formation and whether art making was preferred over the telling of one's story regarding sexual identity formation. Results of the study found that art was able to expose meaning otherwise unknown when compared to the telling of participants' sexual identity formation narrative. Shared themes of growth, transformation, emergence, and movement through both natural and whimsical imagery were also revealed (see Figure 8.1).

## Cultural Humility: New Paradigms of Thinking

Acquiring new knowledge through art can take scientific knowing from a place of situated knowing to one of experiential knowing (Dewey, 1934). Generating new knowledge requires a departure from stagnant ways of knowing toward knowledge that can be obtained through experiences similar to the approach of cultural humility in art therapy. Practicing and living the concepts of cultural humility encourages the art therapist to look beyond the dominant perspective, reflect on his or her own perspective, and move forward with an openness to others' ways of knowing. Outside of the cause-and-effect paradigm, which is formulated through the deductive reasoning of the dominant culture, other cultures' ways of knowing consist of feeling, lived experience, social engagement, spiritual influences, and ancestral guidance (Hiscox & Calisch, 1998). Cultural exploration of knowing, such as cultural immersion through humility, fosters an alternative ideology that can be adapted into art therapy training and practice. Cultural humility neither eliminates nor discredits cultural competence—it fosters the development and expansion of multiculturalism that transpires in all therapeutic practice.

*Figure 8.1* Transition.

## *Research Trends in Cultural Humility*

The concept of cultural humility has surfaced in various fields. These include counseling (Davis et al., 2016; Gallarado, 2014), medical practice (Foronda, Baptiste, Reinholdt, & Ousman, 2016; Isaacson, 2014;

## Wisdom Through Diversity in Art Therapy    115

Tervalon & Murray-Garcia, 1998), social work (Fisher-Borne, Montana Cain, & Martin, 2015), psychology (Hook, Davis, Owen, Worthington Jr, & Utsey, 2013), education (Brown, Vesely, & Dallman, 2016), anthropology (Farmer, 2016), theology (Owen et al., 2014), and occupational therapy (Hammell, 2013). However, in the field of art therapy, cultural humility has been minimally described in recent research (Har-Gil, 2010).

Principles of cultural humility have been, at times, referred to as *cultural sensitivity*, which is rooted in culturally based research in art therapy as early as Lucille Venture (1977), as well as other related works (Acton, 2001; Boston & Short, 1998; Joseph, 2006; Doby-Copeland, 2006; Hiscox & Calisch, 1998; Hocoy, 2002; Hogan & Pink, 2010; Kaplan, 2003; Lumpkin, 2006; McNiff, 1998; Potash, Doby-Copeland, & Stepney, 2015; Stepney, 2010; Talwar, 2015). Addressing alternative ways of knowing by expanding individualistic Western practice can be done using collective projects in art therapy. Group art therapy practice must broaden from one that involves solely group members and their facilitator to include therapists as collaborators and/or art therapists doing collaborative projects with each other. This experiential knowing process bolsters cultural humility and encourages identity development in art therapists, both as professionals and as individuals.

Self-identity exploration as a transformative learning process in counseling is demonstrated in Gallado's (2104) work, *Developing Cultural Humility*. Within its pages, counselors from different cultural backgrounds share their self-reflections as they relate to their lived experience. Similarly, self-exploration that encourages identity development through art can be illuminated by art therapists practicing from different cultural perspectives to depict cultural humility for training purposes and ethical growth.

### Application of Cultural Humility Principles in Art Therapy Research

Recent research in cultural humility and collective art in professional practice includes *Art Therapy Heuristic Study in Collaboration With a Collective Project to Help Promote New Epistemology, Self-Awareness, and Enhance Cultural Humility in Art Therapy* (Jackson, 2016). This research involved the collaboration of Black female art therapists and Black females from related fields of practice in a collective journal project. The results of the study displayed the significant ways the women collectively shared ways of knowing that encompassed core art symbols that reflected being culturally humble. The lived experiences of these women generated symbols, such as body, hands (touch), heart, eyes and

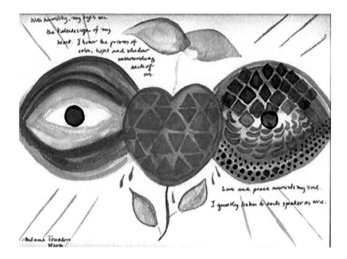

*Figure 8.2* A journal page from the collective journal research (Collaborator, Tervalon).

mandalas. The women also shared concepts of balance, social advocacy, and collective knowing (see Figure 8.2).

This research included a collective transformative learning experience through art, along with a self-reflective component, to demonstrate and elaborate cultural humility. When assembling all the components observed and analyzed in the above-mentioned collective journal research, significant constructs to policy, practice, and theory can be extracted.

### *Cultural Humility: Practice, Theory, and Policy*

The application of cultural humility can illumine art therapy practice through emphasizing the importance of collective learning and acknowledging non-Western ways of knowing and lived experience (tacit knowing). At the same time, it can encourage self-reflection as means of exploration and research in art therapy practice, as well as a way to recognize biases (both implicit and nonimplicit). In art therapy theory, cultural humility can be seen as: (a) fostering both collective and individualistic perspectives simultaneously; (b) underscoring interrelatedness through art in research; (c) increasing the acceptance of both Western and non-Western ways of knowing; and (d) recreating truth in art as wisdom. Within art therapy policy, conducting systematic evaluations of the field as well as the education of art therapists as it applies to diversity, social awareness, and justice structure will support the practice of cultural humility. Trainings and education on cultural humility through art offer visual outcomes, collaborative participation, and response.

## Future Vision Incorporating Cultural Humility and Cultural Competency

Cultural humility in art therapy practice can go beyond cultural competence, which avoids the checklist of "cultural traits." It can strengthen the practice of respectful, curious inquiry that encourages rather than obstructs the telling of the story. In effect, the training and practice of cultural humility in art therapy opens the window of curiosity, which sparks creativity, encourages art as an integrated experience, allows for the illumination of other ways of knowing, offers collective and transformative learning, and communicates human connectedness. The future vision of cultural humility in art therapy is to encourage growth in ways of knowing through making cultural considerations inclusive in treatment, not merely secondary. This can be done by including cultural aspects in all parts of art therapy training and education, more art self-reflection within education, and personally incorporating treatment models, methods, and materials developed by multicultural groups. Furthermore, it remains imperative that the art therapy field address the need for varying models in treatment across different cultural groups.

## Recommendations

In order to advance the continued practice of cultural humility and the development of cultural competency, ongoing research of other multicultural groups outside of the dominant culture must continue. Ongoing curriculum development geared toward the goal of increasing awareness about cultural diversity in the field is imperative. Ongoing multicultural research serves to equip the profession globally. Practitioners of art therapy who regularly practice a posture of curiosity, inquisitiveness, enthusiastic exploration, and acceptance of others help to move the field forward in positive ways. Thus, as the art therapy profession's therapeutic compass calibrates, it will also need to actively consider routes less traveled toward new journeys of self-reflection, diversity engagement, and serving multicultural communities. Further art therapy research on identity, self-esteem, and wellbeing within all diverse, unrepresented communities is critical to a community of individuals who have been stigmatized and marginalized due to their sexual identity, gender, ethnicity, religious affiliation, nationality, corporeality, language, age, and socioeconomic status, as well as to the art therapy professionals who serve them.

## References

Acton, D. (2001). The "color blind therapist." *Art Therapy: Journal of the American Art Therapy Association, 18*(2), 109–112.

Allen, P. (1995). *Art is a way of knowing.* Boston, MA: Shambhala.

American Art Therapy Association (2011). *Art therapy multicultural/diversity competencies.* Retrieved from www.arttherapy.org/upload/multicultural competencies2011.pdf

Bacon, J. (1998). Getting the story straight: Coming out narratives and the possibility of a cultural rhetoric. *World Englishes, 17*(2), 249–258.

Booker, M., & Eastman, S. (2004). *Art therapy with Latina battered women: Voices from the margin.* Paper presented at the Annual Conference of the American Art Therapy Association, San Diego, CA.

Boston, C. (2014). My identity: A mosaic design. In M. B. Junge (Ed.), *Identity and art therapy: Personal and professional perspectives* (pp. 58–72). Springfield, IL: Charles C. Thomas.

Boston, C., & Short, G. (1998). Afrocentric art therapy. In A. Hiscox & A. Calisch (Eds.), *Tapestry of cultural issues in art therapy* (pp. 36–48). London, UK: Jessica Kingsley.

Brown, E. L., Vesely, C. K., & Dallman, L. (2016). Unpacking biases: Developing cultural humility in early childhood and elementary teacher candidates. *Teacher Educators' Journal, 9*, 75–96.

Burn, S., Kadlec, K., & Rexer, R. (2008). Effects of subtle heterosexism on gays, lesbians, and bisexuals. *Journal of Homosexuality, 49*(2), 22–38.

Corvin, S. A., & Wiggins, F. (1989). An antiracism training model for White professionals. *Journal of Counseling and Development, 17*, 105–114.

Cross, T. L., Bazron, B. J., Dennis, K. W., & Isaacs, M. R. (1989). *Toward a culturally competent system of care: Vol. 1. A monograph on effective services for minority children who are severely emotionally disturbed.* Washington, DC: Georgetown University, Child Development Center, Child and Adolescent Service System Program, Technical Assistance Center.

D'Andrea, M., Daniels, J., & Heck, R. (1991). Evaluating the impact of multicultural Counseling training. *Journal of Counseling and Development, 70*, 143–150.

Davis, D. E., DeBlaere, C., Brubaker, K., Owen, J., Jordan, T. A., Hook, J. N., & Van Tongeren, D. R. (2016). Microaggressions and perceptions of cultural humility in counseling. *Journal of Counseling & Development, 94*(4), 483–493.

Davis, K. (1997). *Exploring the intersection between cultural competency and managed behavioral health care policy: Implications for state and county mental health agencies.* Alexandria, VA: National Technical Assistance Center for State Mental Health Planning.

de Botton, A., & Armstrong, J. (2013). *Art as therapy.* London, UK: Phaidon Press.

Dewey, J. (1934). *Art as experience.* New York, NY: Berkley.

Doby-Copeland, C. (2006). Cultural diversity curriculum design: An art therapist's perspective. *Art Therapy: Journal of the American Art Therapy Association, 23*(4), 172–180.

Dreikurs, R. (1971). *The Scientific Revolution. Social equality: The challenge of today.* (164–172). Chicago, IL: The Alfred Adler Institute.

DuMontier, V. L. (2000). Faith, the bible, and lesbians, gay men, and bisexuals. In V. A. Wall and N. J. Evans (Eds.), *Toward acceptance: Sexual orientation issues on campus* (pp. 321–341). Washington, DC: American College Personnel Association.

Elkins, D. E., & Deaver, S. P. (2013). American Art Therapy Association: 2011 Membership survey report. *Art Therapy: Journal of the American Art Therapy Association, 30*(1), 36–45.

Elkins, D. E., & Deaver, S. P. (2015). American Art Therapy Association: 2013 Membership survey report. *Art Therapy: Journal of the American Art Therapy Association, 32*(2), 60–69.

Engebretson, J., Carlson, E., & Mahoney, J. (2008). Cultural competence in the era of evidenced based practice. *Journal of Professional Nursing, 24*(3), 172–178.

Farmer, P. (2016). The second life of sickness: On structural violence and cultural humility. *Human Organization, 75*(4), 279–288.

Fisher-Borne, M., Montana Cain, J., & Martin, S. L. (2015). From mastery to accountability: Cultural humility as an alternative to cultural competence. *Social Work Education, 34*(2), 165–181.

Foronda, C., Baptiste, D., Reinholdt, M. M., & Ousman, K. (2016). Cultural humility. *Journal of Transcultural Nursing, 27*(3), 210.

Gallarado, M. (2014). *Developing cultural humility, embracing race, privilege and power.* Los Angeles, CA: Sage.

Garcia, J. G., & Marotta, S. (1997). Characterization of the Hispanic population. In J. G. Garcia & M. C. Zea (Eds.), *Psychological interventions and research with Hispanic populations* (pp. 1–14). Boston, MA: Allyn & Bacon.

Hammell, K. W. (2013). Occupation, well-being, and culture: Theory and cultural humility/Occupation, bien-être et culture: la théorie et l'humilité culturelle. *Canadian Journal of Occupational Therapy, 80*(4), 224–234.

Har-Gil, O. (2010). *Cultural humility in art therapy: An heuristic arts-based inquiry* (Unpublished Master's thesis). Concordia University, Montreal, Quebec, Canada.

Harper, G. W., & Schneider, M. (2003). Oppression and discrimination among lesbian, bisexual and transgendered people and communities: A challenge for community psychology. *American Journal of Community Psychology, 31*(3), 243–252.

Hiscox, A., & Calisch, A. (1998). *Tapestry of cultural issues in art therapy.* London, UK: Jessica Kingsley.

Hocoy, D. (2002). Cross-cultural issues in art therapy. *Art Therapy: Journal of the American Art Therapy Association, 19*(4), 141–145.

Holcomb-McCoy, C. C., & Myers, J. E. (1999). Multicultural competence and counselor training: A national survey. *Journal of Counseling & Development, 77,* 294–302.

Hook, J. N., Davis, D. E., Owen, J., Worthington Jr., E. L., & Utsey, S. O. (2013). Cultural humility: Measuring openness to culturally diverse clients. *Journal of Counseling Psychology, 60*(3), 353–366.

120  *Louvenia Jackson, et al.*

Hogan, S., & Pink, S. (2010). Routes to interiorities: Art therapy and knowing in anthropology. *Visual Anthropology, 23,* 158–174. doi:10.1080/08949460 903475625

Isaacs, M., & Benjamin, M. (1991). *Towards a culturally competent system of care programs, which utilize culturally competent principles.* Washington, DC: CASSP Technical Assistance Center, Georgetown University Development Center.

Isaacson, M. (2014). Original article: Clarifying concepts: Cultural humility or competency. *Journal of Professional Nursing, 30,* 251–258.

Israel, T., Gorcheva, R., Walther, W., Sulzner, J., & Cohen, J. (2008). Therapists' helpful and unhelpful situations with LGBT clients: An exploratory study. *Professional Psychology: Research and Practice, 39*(3), 361–368.

Jackson L. (2016). *Art therapy heuristic study in collaboration with a collective project to help promote new epistemology, self-awareness and enhance cultural humility in art therapy* (Unpublished doctoral dissertation). Notre Dame de Namur University, Belmont, CA.

Joseph, C. (2006). Creative alliance: The healing power of art therapy. *Art Therapy: Journal of the American Art Therapy Association, 23*(1), 30–33.

Joyce, S. (2008). *Picturing lesbian, informing art therapy: a postmodern feminist autobiographical investigation* (Unpublished doctoral dissertation). Southern Cross University, Lismore, NSW.

Julliard, K. N. (1999). Susan K. Langer and the foundations of art therapy. *Art Therapy: Journal of the American Art Therapy Association, 16*(3), 112–120.

Junge, M., & Asawa, P. (1994). *A history of art therapy in the United States.* Mundelein, IL: American Art Therapy Association.

Kaplan, F. F. (2003). The paradox of multiculturalism. *Art Therapy: Journal of the American Art Therapy Association, 20*(1), 2.

Kouyoumdjian, H., Zamboanga, B. L., & Hansen, D. J. (2003). Community mental health services for Latinos: Treatment considerations. *Clinical Psychology: Science and Practice, 10*(4), 394–422.

Linesch, D., Aceves, H. C., Quezada, P., Trochez, M., & Zuniga, E. (2012). An art therapy exploration of immigration with Latino families. *Journal of Art Therapy Association, 29*(3), 120–126.

Lumpkin, C. (2006). Relating Cultural Identity and Identity as Art Therapist. *Art Therapy: Journal of the American Art Therapy Association 23*(1), 34–38.

Maher, A. (2011). *The use of art and interview to explore the transgender person's experience of gender transition: A phenomenological study* (Unpublished Master's thesis). Drexel University, Philadelphia, PA.

Mauro, M. K. (1998). The use of art therapy in identity formation: A Hispanic case study. In A. R. Hiscox & A. C. Calish (Eds.), *Tapestry of cultural issues in art therapy* (pp. 134–153). Philadelphia, PA: Jessica Kingsley.

McNiff, S. (1984). Cross cultural psychotherapy and art. *Journal of Art Therapy Association, 1*(3), 125–131

McNiff, S. (1998). *Art based research.* Philadelphia, PA: Jessica Kingsley.

Meyer, I. H. (2003). Prejudice, social stress, and mental health in lesbian, gay and bisexual populations: Conceptual issues and research evidence. *Psychological Bulletin, 125*(5), 674–697.

Mezzera, C. (2016). *Archetypal imagery and self-esteem in Latinas* (Unpublished doctoral dissertation). Notre Dame de Namur University, Belmont, CA.

National Council of La Raza. (2005). *Critical disparities in Latino mental health: Transforming research into action.* Retrieved from www.nclr.org/index.php/publications/critical_disparities_in_latino_mental_health_transforming_research_into_action/.

Nielsen (2013, August). *Latina power shift.* Retrieved from www.nielsen.com/us/en/insights/reports/2013/latina-power-shift.html, accessed September, 2015.

Owen, J., Jordan II, T. A., Turner, D., Davis, D. E., Hook, J. N., & Leach, M. M. (2014). Therapists' multicultural orientation: Client perceptions of cultural humility, spiritual/religious commitment, and therapy outcomes. *Journal of Psychology & Theology, 42*(1), 91–98.

Pelton-Sweet, L. M., & Sherry, A. (2008). Coming out through art: A review of art therapy with LGBT clients. *Art Therapy: Journal of the American Art Therapy Association, 25*(4), 170–176.

Pew Hispanic Research Center. (2015, September). *Modern immigration wave brings 59 million to U.S., driving population growth and change through 2065: Views of immigration's impact on U.S. society mixed.* Washington, DC: Pew Research Center.

Pollanen, S. (2009). Craft as context for therapeutic change. *Indian Journal of Occupational Therapy, 41*(2), 43–47.

Pope-Davis, D. B., Toporek, R. L., Ortega-Villalobos, L., Ligie´ro, D. P., Brittan-Powell, Smith, R. L., & Montilla, R. E. (2006). *Counseling and family therapy with Latino populations: Strategies that work.* New York, NY: Routledge.

Potash, J.S., Doby-Copeland, C., Stepney, S. A., Washington, B.N., Vance, L.D., Short, G.M., Boston, C.G. & Ballbé ter Maat, M. (2015). Advancing multicultural and diversity competence in art therapy: American Art Therapy Association Multicultural Committee 1990–2015. *Art Therapy: Journal of the American Art Therapy Association, 32* (3), 146–150. doi: 10.1080/07421656.2015.1060837

Satterberg, M. A. (2017a). Perspectives through art: *Exploration of art sexual identity formation with lesbian-identified women.* Unpublished manuscript.

Satterberg, M. A. (2017b). *Kaleidoscope curriculum.* Unpublished manuscript.

Schnebelt, B. A. (2015). *Art therapy considerations with transgender individuals* (Unpublished Master's thesis). Loyola Marymount University, Los Angeles, CA.

Smith, R. L., & Montilla, R. E. (2006). *Counseling and family therapy with Latino populations: Strategies that work.* New York, NY: Routledge.

Stepney, S. (2010). *Art therapy with students at risk: Fostering resilience and growth through self-expression.* Chicago, IL: Charles Thomas.

Talwar, S. (2015). Culture, diversity, and identity: From margins to center. *Art Therapy, 32*(3), 100–103.

Tervalon, M. (2015). *Cultural humility training.* Paper presented for Working in Partnership with individuals, Families and Communities October in Daly City, Serramonte del Rey.

Tervalon, M., & Murray-Garcia, J. (1998). Cultural humility versus cultural competence: A critical distinction in defining physician training outcomes in multicultural education. *Journal of Health Care for the Poor and Underserved, 9*(2), 117–125.

Troiden, R. R. (1989). The formation of homosexual identities. *Journal of Homosexuality, 17*(1–2), 43–73.

## 122  *Louvenia Jackson, et al.*

United States Census Bureau. (2014). Retrieved October 1, 2014 from www.census.gov/population/projections/data/national/2014.html

Vaughn, F. (1985). Discovering transpersonal identity. *Journal of Humanistic Psychology, 25*, 13–38.

Venture, L. (1977). *The Black beat in art therapy experiences* (Unpublished doctoral dissertation). Union Institute (formally Union Graduate School), Cincinnati, OH.

# 9 Art Therapy and Social Change

*By Jennifer Harrison*

## Promoting Dialogue

In my office, I am working with a 14-year-old adolescent who identifies as polyamorous. We talk about the current political climate, and she has a lot to say on the subject. In therapy, she can vocalize her anger and disappointment about the hate and rage that she has seen expressed around the world. She talks about her disgust for individuals who speak negatively about marginalized and oppressed persons. She also recognizes that she lives in what she calls "a bubble." She has decided to publicly express her pain and frustration. To that end, she has a Tumblr page—multiple pages, in fact. She uses them to express, through art images, words, and other creative content, her deeply felt thoughts and emotions. Her social action takes the form of reaching others and initiating conversations among individuals with similar viewpoints who desire to address the issues she finds compelling.

Art therapy creates a space for a dialogue that is designed to encourage relationship formation, activism, and social change. Art therapists have defined frameworks for viewing, experiencing, and creating art that are aimed at promoting connection with the world and its people (Potash, 2011). Through viewing the art makers' perspective, people may better understand their own biases or political views—realizations that may engender greater empathy towards the artist's situation or experience (Kaiser & Deaver, 2013). If a sense of perspective and empathy towards others are to act as driving forces for social change, artistic expression must be nurtured and protected.

Art can be utilized to provide solutions for dialoguing; it can also act as a connector. As it helps to eradicate the social distances frequently perceived as primary causes of misunderstandings, it empowers clients and communities to end injustice and discrimination. When applied consistently to addressing specific societal wants and needs, art therapy, too, possesses great potential for social change. Art therapy creates a space to build empathy and initiate dialogue with client-artists whose voices may not be heard and whose faces are, in most cases, hidden. Through the use

## 124  *Jennifer Harrison*

of various skills unique to their field, art therapists can advance the ideals of equality and justice through art and relationship building. New methods continually emerge by which art therapists can make contributions to society beyond familial and individual healing.

Art therapy facilitates opportunities in communication, expression, and understanding through its role, image, and the creative process that serve as the central meeting ground for participants. For example, art therapy promotes the development of art-based perspectives, which practitioners can apply to bridge the social empathy gap between healthy people and those living with mental illnesses. The process of viewing and making artwork enhances individuals' understanding of mental illness because art permits viewers to connect with the art and its maker in different ways. Art has the potential to evoke a greater consciousness in the viewers, of their own subjective biases, as well as an enhanced understanding of others; these realizations in turn deepen their connection to the artist's plight (Kaiser & Deaver, 2013). The outcome allows participants to experience a relationship with the art and its maker, which could arouse an increase in empathy and initiate a desire to provide assistance to people living with mental illnesses.

When art therapy incorporates responsive art making, reflective tools, and other related strategies, it attains the ability to facilitate social change. It is not easy to produce or identify art therapy pieces that create emotional engagements with both the viewers and the artists (Gipson, 2015). By providing viewers with a platform for experiencing art in supportive surroundings, art therapy creates a structure for viewing art in a manner that allows the art to function as a major driving force for sustainable social change.

## Feminist Approaches

It is important that practitioners of art therapy maintain a culture of awareness, which is necessary for maintaining a critical stance in the field of psychology. Such a stance allows the art therapist to use the practices and theories associated with art therapy to avoid the oppression of women that has at certain points been associated with traditional psychotherapeutic approaches (Stoppard, 2014). Art therapy should, therefore, be social in nature and extend beyond the narrow boundaries of individual psychopathology. Hogan (2012) saw art therapy as an activist process by which the hegemonic structures associated with traditional therapies could be undercut: "in order to avoid oppressing women with misogynistic discourses that are embedded in theories and practice" (p. xx).

Talwar (2010) called for an intersectional framework in the field of art therapy. She proposed that such a framework is essential to the field of research and scholarship. "Feminist scholars—especially women of color, gay men, and lesbians—have called for an examination of identity construction and have critiqued the biased nature of social science research" (Talwar, 2010, pp. 11–12). McCall (2005) emphasized that intersectionality may be "the most important theoretical contribution" (p. 1771) that feminist researchers have made thus far.

Women still experience oppression and discrimination. Discrimination against women has, in some cases, become so prevalent that it can go unnoticed. Women who have been marginalized seem to want a way to speak out and tell society about their suffering. On January 21, 2017, intersectional feminism was on display in an event known as the Women's March when an estimated 2,600,000 individuals worldwide marched to advocate for the protection of human rights. This display of unity was communicated by not only the presence of protestors, but also the signs. This creative expression provided an outlet for the marchers to express their thoughts and feelings about their (mis) treatment, as well as a way to communicate the problem to others effectively. "Art made in the service of social protest is a piece of the whole in helping women to change their lives and change their world" (Wadeson, 2000, p. 312).

As the field of art therapy continues to evolve, we can see macro trends emerging that enable the expression of one's own identity development via art. However, just as in traditional psychotherapy, in which therapists help individuals pursue a process of uncovering parts of the self that are raw, messy, and in conflict, art therapists use a type of aesthetic pun referred to as a *messthetic* (Terms, 2017) to denote a framework in which an individual can explore themes that transgress and threaten one's sense of cleanliness and propriety. Within art therapy, the presence of a *messthetic* provides a safe place to be awkward and vulgar—to confront the messy parts of our lives in order to elevate ourselves.

Art therapists are in a position to champion justice because their profession provides a platform for client-artists to tap into their creative tendencies and achieve greater understanding through the creative process. Because art therapists sit with other individuals in their raw states, these practitioners also need to explore their own *messthetics*. Art therapists must engage in their own artistic self-discovery to be facilitators of change (Figure 9.1).

## Art Therapists as Social Change Agents

With its emphasize on providing service to others, art therapy is deeply rooted in social justice principles; thus, art therapy lays a foundation for providing opportunities to take part in community building (Landgarten, 1981). Social change can be achieved through various platforms, ranging from advocating for policy change to attitude change. As mentioned previously, art therapists are provided with wonderful opportunities to build empathy and initiate dialogue with client-artists whose voices may not otherwise be heard. It

*Figure 9.1* Darkness matters.

is through such opportunities that art therapists can advance the ideals of equality and justice through art and relationship building.

Alfred Adler developed community psychology by articulating the constructs of *gemeinschaftsgefühl*: social interest, or the connection between individual and community wellbeing, and systemic/structural community intervention, such as that manifested in preventative public health measures. He believed that socially responsible practitioners are educated to be effective personal and social change agents in the pursuit of justice. Individual and social change can lead to increased mental health (Adler & Ansbacher, 1999).

Artists play a key role in effecting social change; art therapists have their part to play in these changes as well. New methods are continuously emerging through which art therapists can make contributions to society beyond individual and familial healing. From a clinical perspective, opportunities to contribute to the social fabric have been focused primarily on healthcare professionals; this limitation restricts art therapists to prioritizing individual clients with emotional, mental, or neurological problems (Haley, 2013). Placing the focus solely on the individual stymies access to professional and personal resources that can provide a platform for healing societal ills, such as injustices.

Art therapists equip artists with opportunities to use their art to evoke environmental changes that foster relations and sustain empathy. Despite the fact that the majority of art therapists are agents of social justice, in that they represent clients who might be underserved, art therapists can underestimate their power to spur social change in the community (Gipson, 2015). Art therapists' skills can effectively aid the addressing of societal ills such as inequality and discrimination.

A long-standing connection exists between poverty and increased symptoms of mental illness (Joseph, 2006). Growing numbers of populations are exposed to the negative effects of stressors that accompany economic marginalization, such as homelessness, hunger, familial instability, crime, substance abuse, and domestic violence. Poverty has been shown to increase depression, anxiety, and hopelessness (Kuruvilla & Jacob, 2007). Neurobiologically speaking, the chronic stress associated with such conditions has extremely debilitating effects on individuals, such as fatigue, loss of control, impairment of the body's ability to fight infections, and impairments in memory. We now know that the body responds to extreme stress by shutting down in self-preservation (Van der Kolk, 2015). Art therapy can effectively address the stress response (Hass-Cohen & Findlay, 2015) and help clients develop creative stress-management options (Joseph, 2006). Art therapy can illuminate new ways of knowing that create solutions to social issues and reposition individuals via empowering options.

Change through art happens through the use of meaningful messages. Soul searching and contemplation are key elements in this art therapy trend, as evidenced by the integrity and authenticity with which individuals communicate their perceptions of self through art. Culture affects how the self is perceived. This is a phenomenon that in turn prompts questions on the part of both artist and art therapist: What are self and identity, and what is the relationship between them? What is the relationship between consciousness and the unconscious? What is the relationship between knowledge and wisdom? And what is the relationship between the body, the mind, and the world? See Figure 9.2.

Technology is changing the way we live our lives, share our experiences, make our art, and experience our surroundings. It also challenges our idea of what it means to be human. Through technology, we are gaining a better understanding of humanity's quintessence. Our experiences and perceptions of the world are translated through the artist's lens, and these can reach the larger global community. Technology, in its apparent perfection, conversely emphasizes the beauty of being flawed. Spinning off of the transformations wrought by technology and the new perceptions that result from them, art therapists can, through art, offer clients the tools needed to rebuild their lives and rise up against the oppression and self-negation they encounter in society. A unique power of art is its

*Figure 9.2* Outside myself.

ability to uncover the deception of social forces (Joseph, 2006), which constitutes a foundation for social change if ever one existed.

Art therapists may encourage the general populace to effect change through their work with clients. They may help clients reevaluate the influence of discrimination and stigma on their identity by helping them reframe and broaden their self-understanding beyond the self-negating

## Art Therapy and Social Change 129

perception that because they are affected by societal elements, they are therefore subjected to them. These new self-understandings that clients express may prompt other individuals to rectify imbalances that cause inequality. People in attendance at an art exhibit may receive an opportunity to effect change through advocating, lobbying, and voting; art therapists can, therefore, have an impact on social change by linking creative ideas for activist artists with acceptable mental health interventions for their clients (Waller, 2014). Art therapists can also invite members of the public into social change efforts by helping them to understand their role in sustaining client-artists and inspiring members of the general public to minimize discrimination. Lastly, art therapists should have a platform for exhibiting their clients' work to the community. Through all these avenues, art therapists can adapt their skills to encourage social change, broadening their focus from the individual level to the social-healing level.

## Art as a Means of Promoting Change

Art is an element of human development and social cohesion. Social change is both the process and product of efforts aimed at positively altering societal conditions. It encompasses a range of outcomes—healing, increased awareness, attitudinal change, more diverse and increased civic participation, movement building, and policy change. Art and creativity facilitate social synergy, in which different components of the community function in concert as a whole greater than the sum of its parts. Art triggers innovation and solution crafting, helping to simplify societal problems and encouraging the development of realistic and achievable solutions (Rosenthal & Flacks, 2015). Through art, people acquire the ability to conceptualize visions and communicate those visions to others who may improve on them or help actualize the initial ideas. Similar problems affect different individuals in different ways; therefore, finding effective and responsive collective solutions to these problems becomes a combined effort.

Wadeson (2000) described the work of Jean Durkin, ATR-BC, as "art therapy as social action" (p. 285). Durkin has worked with homeless persons since 1987, when she established art therapy at a shelter's various locations in the Chicago area. One public art project that she organized was a mural painted by the shelter's female clients on the exterior of the agency's building. She described it as "making a mark on an outside wall, making a public, self-determining, willful, self-identifiable image that will last a very long time" (Wadeson, 2000, p. 276). From Durkin's perspective, her work as an art therapist extended beyond her own clients. She stated her belief that her work could extend out into a neighborhood, a city, and hopefully the world. Women could, through the public mural, tell the community who they were and that they were there. Their

## 130 Jennifer Harrison

public artwork served as social action by giving a voice to these forgotten women in the community.

Pat B. Allen (Kaplan, 2007) described a project involving art therapy and social action with the homeless. Entitled "Facing Homelessness," the project was a yearlong mask-making project, the goals of which were to "raise awareness about issues of homelessness, to break down stereotypes about who is homeless, and to experiment with art-based social action as a means of creating community and exploring a social problem" (Kaplan, 2007, p. 59). This project involved not only the homeless but also other members of the community who volunteered their faces for the masks. Their participation in mask-making supports the idea that art therapy and social action offers an attractive combination for the homeless population and African American women—two groups of individuals desperately in need of a voice in society.

Art involves people from all walks of life. To unleash its full potential, art needs to become a more understandable and tangible tool for the whole population. To achieve this, public forces must come together to form one holistic component. Art is a never-ending improvement process that moves society forward and engenders innovation through encouragement. Innovation, in turn, comes from reorganizing, reshaping, and rearranging what is already there. Every individual is unique within his or her distinctive organization and situation. The experiences that an individual encounters determine how that individual views the world—that is, what the person stands for, the person's character, and who that person is (Figure 9.3).

Art is an element of human development and social cohesion. As I discussed above, art and its creative expression create opportunities for different components of the community to function as one. The tactics and philosophy of nonviolence—an approach designed to bring different, often disparate, parties into a state of equality by reconstructing their dynamic relation and promoting the growth of empathy (Rubin, 2016)—can be utilized through art. Because "Art is the most effective mode of communication that exists" (Dewey, 2005 p. 286), and art triggers innovation that helps simplify societal problems, which results in realistic and achievable solutions (Rosenthal & Flacks, 2015); enacting these solutions necessarily becomes a holistic community effort. Art therapy can, therefore, contribute to social change by facilitating the activation of imagination and creativity and allowing participants (including both viewers and artists) to "step beyond" oppressive paradigms.

We art therapists have the opportunity to unite societies through the "holy fires" of individual and communal passion, empathy, creativity, and truth, while simultaneously extinguishing the "unholy fires" of violence, self-interest, and conformity, which are destroying a generation's cooperative possibilities. Through the conscious mirroring of "held truth" in art, individuals can reconnect to hope and health. Art, in its inception, depends upon introspection, but once externalized, art becomes a plea

*Figure 9.3* Ambiguity.

for empathy. Through the art or images they create, previously overlooked populations are now allowed not only to be seen, but also heard.

## References

Adler, A., & Ansbacher, R. R. (1999). *The individual psychology of Alfred Adler: A systematic presentation in selections from his writings*. New York, NY: Harper Collins.

## 132  Jennifer Harrison

Dewey, J. (2005). *Art as experience.* New York, NY: Penguin.

Gipson, L. R. (2015). Is cultural competence enough? Deepening social justice pedagogy in art therapy. *Art Therapy, 32*(3), 142–145.

Haley, J. (2013). *Leaving home: The therapy of disturbed young people.* New York, NY: Routledge.

Hass-Cohen, N., & Findlay, J. C. (2015). *Art therapy and the neuroscience of relationships, creativity, and resiliency: Skills and practices.* New York, NY: Norton.

Hogan, S. (2012). *Revisiting feminist approaches to art therapy.* Retrieved from www.amazon.com/Revisiting-Feminist-Approaches-Art-Therapy/dp/0857453491

Joseph, C. (2006). Creative alliance: The healing power of art therapy. *Art Therapy, 23*(1), 30–33. https://doi.org/10.1080/07421656.2006.10129531

Kaiser, D., & Deaver, S. (2013). Establishing a research agenda for art therapy: A Delphi study. *Art Therapy, 30*(3), 114–121.

Kapitan, L. (2015). Social action in practice: Shifting the ethnocentric lens in cross-cultural art therapy encounters. *Art Therapy, 32*(3), 104–111. https://doi.org/10.1080/07421656.2015.1060403

Kapitan, L., Litell, M., & Torres, A. (2011). Creative art therapy in a community's participatory research and social transformation. *Art Therapy, 28*(2), 64–73. https://doi.org/10.1080/07421656.2011.578238

Kaplan, F. F. (2007). *Art therapy and social action.* London, UK: Jessica Kingsley.

Kuruvilla, A., & Jacob, K. S. (2007). Poverty, social stress & mental health. *The Indian Journal of Medical Research, 126*(4), 273–8. Retrieved from www.ncbi.nlm.nih.gov/pubmed/18032802

Landgarten, H. B. (1981). *Clinical art therapy: A comprehensive guide.* New York, NY: Routledge.

McCall, L. (2005). The complexity of intersectionality. *Signs, 30*(3), 1771–1800. doi:10.1086/426800

Munson, C., & Saulnier, C. F. (2014). *Feminist theories and social work: Approaches and applications.* New York, NY: Routledge.

Potash, J., & Ho, R. T. H. (2011). Drawing involves caring: Fostering relationship building through art therapy for social change. *Art Therapy, 28*(2), 74–81. https://doi.org/10.1080/07421656.2011.578040

Rosenthal, R., & Flacks, R. (2015). *Playing for change: Music and musicians in the service of social movements.* New York, NY: Routledge.

Rubin, J. A. (Ed.). (2016). *Approaches to art therapy: Theory and technique.* New York, NY: Routledge.

Stoppard, J. M. (2014). *Understanding depression: Feminist social constructionist approaches.* New York, NY: Routledge.

Talwar, S. (2010). An intersectional framework for race, class, gender, and sexuality in art therapy. *Art Therapy, 27*(1), 11–17. https://doi.org/10.1080/07421656.2010.10129567

Terms. (2017, February 24). *The six visual trends that will define 2016.* Retrieved from www.campaignlive.com/article/six-visual-trends-will-define-2016/1377971

Van der Kolk, B.(2015). *The body keeps the score: brain, mind, and body in the healing of trauma.* New York, NY: Penguin Books.

Wadeson, H. (2000). *Art therapy practice: Innovative approaches with diverse populations*. New York, NY: Wiley.

Waller, D. (2014). *Group interactive art therapy: Its use in training and treatment*. New York, NY: Routledge.

# 10 Global Art Therapy

*Arnell Etherington Reader*

*In all the arts there is a physical component which can no longer be considered or treated as it used to be. . . . For the last twenty years neither matter nor space nor time has been what it was from time immemorial. We must expect great innovations to transform the entire technique of the arts.*
(Valéry,1931 as cited in "New articulations in the art therapies", para.1).

The continuous growth in the understanding, acceptance, and uses of art therapy currently provides a clear profile that is global. That profile has many facets that together make up *art therapy*. The definitions of art therapy are multilingual, the orientations constitute a multiplicity of theoretical reasoning, the practice is multi-purposed, and still the thread of art therapy has not been broken in its outcome. This may indicate that the breadth and width of the field of art therapy has stretched around the world, touching people who may benefit from art therapy and providing another impetus to develop and change as a profession. "In the global village, the idea of the integration of art and therapy has taken hold" (Junge, 2016, p. 15). The innovative and creative approaches, the research findings, and the scientific underpinnings hold together the dynamic blossoming of the ideas that art brings to psychology and that psychology brings to art.

Beginning in antiquity, with the history of using art for solace, understanding, and communication, we know, at times without explicitness, the depth and richness with which art speaks about life. Ancient art, such as the beauty of the bulls in the Lascaux caves or the remarkable spotted horses of Peche Merle, reflect a community, a culture, and a value for our environment. With art, ritual, movement, and music, a culture and a community may be held together with its most meaningful traditions. Artistic expressions can be found in every culture.

## Development of a Successful Discipline

As Achterberg (1985) implied, the engagement with all art and imagination historically involves healing and ritual. Peoples around the world

## Global Art Therapy    135

have used art in differing ways for distinctive reasons. That people respond, and in cases respond well, to art became the art therapist's bailiwick. By submitting the notion that using art helps individuals in need, early professionals working primarily in "education, rehabilitation, and psychotherapy" (Ulman, 1961, p. 10) began to illuminate the therapeutic aspects therein. From the moment in which early art therapists began crafting and articulating clinical examples, *art as therapy* began to flood the field of psychotherapy and other adjoining fields, such as psychology, psychiatry, and social work.

"The art in art therapy is not just the expression of our psychological world, but also reflects the social, cultural, and political realities of everyday lived experiences" (Talwar, 2016, p. 117). Within this everyday lived reality, the clinical art therapist's experiences and ideas have been clarified into theories on how art therapy may function; writings began to spring from education and psychology per se, although they were grounded in a variety of therapeutic settings. Therapeutic approaches have been nuanced for certain populations; educational programs opened and criteria were articulated. Credentialing, licensing, and certification have put ethics and rigor behind the art therapist. Professional journals and educational texts on art therapy are now published, and professionals attend national conferences developed to exchange ideas and methods.

In global originations of art therapy, we have added to our vision and have a plethora of partnerships (Cruz, 2005). The trend is not only the articulation of partnerships but the integration of previously undeclared specific information as new words and ideas are born. We have grown into other fields and other fields have grown into us. Bucciarelli (2016) suggested that art therapy needs to be reconceptualized as a *transdiciplinary* rather than an interdisciplinary field. The current changes require bringing together differing concepts and so transcending the boundaries of each that the result is "a more nuanced field that moves beyond yet builds upon its foundational values" (p. 152).

Art therapists are conducting qualitative and quantitative research to support the evidence of art therapy. To be on this edge of research is to be on the edge of new knowledge and understanding. These paths have led art therapy to the boundary edges of countries and domains that are now disappearing.

The call to humanitarian need has been a call to service for many individuals. The oldest and most well-known organization is the International Committee of the Red Cross, which began in 1863 to provide humanitarian services, as well as protection and neutrality for wounded soldiers (International Red Cross, 2017). Currently, human innovations and technological progress have ushered in an era of increased trade and financial flow globally. There has also been a vast movement of people and knowledge crossing international borders, which brings cultural, political, and environmental dimensions to global attention (International Money Fund staff, 2000, para. 6–7). The individual is more fully

## 136  *Arnell Etherington Reader*

aware of the needs of disadvantaged peoples, natural disasters, and political unrest.

Médecins Sans Frontières (MSF)—Doctors Without Borders—is an international, independent, medical humanitarian organization that delivers emergency aid to people who are affected by armed conflict, epidemics, natural disasters, and exclusion from healthcare. This organization was started in 1971 by a group of French doctors who "believe all people have a right to receive medical care no matter who they are or what they believe in" (Doctors Without Borders, n.d., para. 1). Other partnership fields are responding to this globalization with a call to let go of professional debate that may have hindered service. In a review of global needs for training psychiatrists, Holmes, Mizen, and Jacobs (2007) reported the following:

> Cartesian dualism (amongst psychoanalysis, neurobiology and psychopharmacology) is passé: [T]he relational context of neurological development is coming to be widely recognized. The interaction between environmental triggers for genetic susceptibility and their potential reversal through psychotherapy is another current growth point. Neuroimaging studies are beginning to illustrate the impact of psychotherapy on the brain (Spence, 2006). Understanding and exploiting these interactions will come to dominate worthwhile psychiatric curricula.
>
> (p. 93).

### Education

The international art therapy practiced today consists of two aspects. The first involves formalizing the globalization of the field of art therapy with educational specifications and standards of practice within professional organizations on six continents. The second concerns the practice of art therapists working in international sites around the world in "cross-cultural contexts by international practitioners" (Bordonaro, 2016, p. 676). These two aspects begin to work hand-in-hand as the development of art therapy within a region reaches beyond distinct borders.

What may be critical to the globalization of art therapy is the education of an art therapist. We can challenge old approaches that may not be bringing results, and we can encourage ourselves, colleagues, and students to come forward with different ways of observing, with new paradigms of working, and with unique thinking and feeling about art therapy. Our educational institutions have taken up the task of supporting the move into the global art therapy world of uncharted pathways:

> Assuring that art therapy education accentuates adaptability (Wadeson, 2002) may require educational standards that emphasize diverse

theoretical perspectives, comfort with all health delivery services, internships in general health settings, and knowledge of both mental and physical health.

(Glueck as cited in Potash, Mann, Martinez, Roach & Wallace, 2016, p. 124).

The expansion of education in art therapy's global application may be twofold: first is acknowledging that the vision of the art therapist has expanded to include globalization, and second is considering the ways in which globalization could, and perhaps ought to, be included in education. This may include art therapists reading across continents in professional art therapy and allied fields' journals and texts and attending art therapy conferences in another country or region before graduating. It also may include regularly inviting international art therapists to present at home campuses, engaging in art therapy international online discussions and debates, and presenting lectures, workshops, and panels on art therapy topics in other countries. Publishing in other disciplines, having exchange student trips from one university program to another in a different environment could be another way globalization could manifest in educational pursuits. Finally, art therapists may want to consider requiring academic, cultural diversity, and/or service units as part of degree programs, rather than solely having these units be optional.

From this it follows that the education requirements of the art therapist may expand to encompass and validate opportunities for experiences in globalization. There are many institutions that provide rich and diverse global educational opportunities for art therapists in training. Often, due to governing body restraints or the cost of additional educational requirements, these opportunities remain tangential. Too often these options lag due to funding. Perhaps when these opportunities are truly a priority, we may find creative ways to subsidize them; perhaps monies need to be delegated to sustain the international flow of information, experience, and journeys. Studying abroad or outside of one's comfort zone would then regularly be funded and supported as a practice.

Encounters with difference grow art therapists in both their personal and professional dimensions. Just as art therapy within one environment is a language unto itself, that language is expanded in dialogue with other regions, other peoples, other problems, other approaches, and other successes in the field. The globalization of education pushes educational models into new realms where students and professionals alike may add unique ways of studying and understanding the art therapy platform. Likewise, new outcomes and discoveries may ensue.

## Notes from the Field

The development of art therapy programs across various cultural fabrics begins with the work of understanding a land and a culture, its needs, and

138    *Arnell Etherington Reader*

its limitations. Bringing art therapists to settings where art therapy is then offered, whether it be setting up a new academic degree or whether it be a gesture of service, is a journey of great complexity. We must acknowledge this complexity if we are to reach or continue to strive for success. The following are conversations with five art therapists/psychotherapists who have engaged in these endeavors. Each was asked to speak about their experiences and ideas about global art therapy as well as consider the future in these terms.

### *The Birthing Process of Art Therapy Into a Culture*

The following is derived from a conversation with Ron Lay, MA, ATR-BC, AThR, that took place on December 10, 2016. Ron is a doctoral candidate, School of Creative Industries, a faculty member of the Fine Arts, Media, and Creative Industries in LASALLE College of Arts in Singapore. The Masters in Art Therapy training at LASALLE College of Arts in Singapore is 12 years old and is considered a new program. New programs must take strategic steps to build a new mental health modality, to have it accessed within the existing mental health landscape, and to provide a full range of options. In this cultural region, especially, the traditions are rich, complex, and not to be minimized. Art therapy, having been developed in the West, needs a regional context to be effective. Student pioneers, having a deep understanding of their own cultural referents, have been re-interpreters of art therapy in this global context (see Figure 10.1).

Here, the culture of therapy is not intended to be weekly. This has an impact on the students' personal therapies, which is an important part of their overall training, and it also has an impact on services that can reflect results. This culture may not realize that certain problems could be dealt with through the introduction of therapy of any kind. Through securing access to situations of need and providing positive results, clinical placement settings have begun. Increasingly, a range of settings for clinical placements have opened, many of which have become important and sustaining industry partners with the MA art therapy training program. Jobs for the students and funding to support their training has been a result of these partnerships (R. Lay, personal communication, December 10, 2016).

In the Singaporean culture, families and communities are vitally important. One foray into the community has been to have the LASALLE training program host a variety of significant collaborative community programs. For example, the "Art of Autism" was opened to the community at large at the college as well as in the local domain. The community was invited to see the art and hear a lecture on autism to see how the art reflects the lives of those with autism and how art therapy was utilized in treatment (R. Lay, personal communication, December 10, 2016).

*Figure 10.1* Mentor doll.

Culturally, in this region, discussion of death and dying is a taboo. LASALLE College engaged with a local hospice to host a program called "Hospice is ___." This helped make information available on what hospice does, and it invited students, faculty, and the community to participate in

## 140  *Arnell Etherington Reader*

painting doves, which were later curated in a show, raising money for charity while raising a voice about hospice services and their use of art therapy. Another program, entitled "Let's Talk about Addiction," helped give voice to issues that were not being openly discussed in the culture, given the reality of local laws and the complexities around this topic; it presented the work done in this area in an effort to respectfully educate the public and to reinforce the recovery of those involved in this process. The discussion of issues that may be considered unacceptable also brings in government monitoring. The movement into mental health areas of taboo needs to be very carefully achieved (R. Lay, personal communication, December 10, 2016).

New art therapy educational training programs may reside within a local art therapy professional's organizational region. The credentialing of art therapists locally, such as LASALLE's program through ANZATA, allows art therapy to show mastery in the field, be valued, and provide leadership roles that move global art therapy forward (R. Lay, personal communication, December 10, 2016).

The Red Pencil, an art therapy children's humanitarian foundation developed in Singapore, utilizes creative arts therapy locally and internationally to respond to natural disasters. This foundation has quickly expanded to 20 countries and now includes psychosocial services for adults. The Red Pencil promotes expression, healing, and wellbeing through the creative process of art making, and LASALLE is their educational partner. Art therapy students from LASALLE can receive scholarships for their educational training, and many opt to volunteer for local and overseas missions or projects. All work is cultural and region specific, and they are linked to the Red Cross (R. Lay, personal communication, December 10, 2016).

Another global situation that is reflected in Southeast Asian region is that in many instances the development of art therapy may go through a period in which there are no regulators or ethics boards: no voice of authority. Thus, many people without sufficient training may begin to call themselves art therapists. There may be no title protection for art therapists. These situations with non-art therapists can confuse potential funding sources or mental health providers, who are just coming to understand the graduate level work involved in art therapy. In the meantime, it is up to the art(s) therapy organizations, such as ANZATA and Art Therapists' Association Singapore (ATAS), to assert internationally accepted best practices, ethics, and educational standards, in addition to their integral role in monitoring and developing the discipline and credentialing those who are trained accordingly (R. Lay, personal communication, December 10, 2016).

### *Entering the Third World with Paint, Paper, and Brushes*

The following section is based on conversations I had with Gwen Sanders, Ph.D., LMFT, ATR-B.C, on January 20, 2017. Gwen is director of the practicum program of the Graduate Art Therapy Psychology Department at Notre Dame de Namur University in Belmont, California. The Graduate Art Therapy Psychology Department of Notre Dame de Namur University (NDNU) has travelled to Nicaragua four times over the past five years, and Gwen has been a co-leader on these trips. Entering a third world country as art therapists can mean that everything feels uncertain, for the intent of volunteering services begins with the need to submerge oneself into the fact that all is relative. The art therapy students and teachers who provide art therapy internationally need to give up their expectations of certainty and predictability on such a journey. Leaders in art therapy who have made these journeys with students set the tone of respectful curiosity, cultural humility, and openness. A journeying group may often work simply to make a connection, promote opportunity for art, and model flexibility in creativity.

Viva-Nicaragua! is a nongovernmental organization (NGO) in Granada, Nicaragua, that partners with community members, educators, and social service agencies. They provide mentorship opportunities and college scholarships for young people in communities. Viva-Nicaragua! works with international colleges and organizations who want to offer their services with the goal of empowering women and children. Sociologist and founder of Viva-Nicaragua!, Carrie McCracken, has provided NDNU art therapists with the opportunity to work with disenfranchised or underserved groups of people, including members of a small community, elder women in a government-run nursing home, elementary school teachers at a public school, and women and children at a food kitchen housed in a Catholic church. The vision of Viva-Nicaragua! is consistent with the NDNU mission in calling for service activities that empower and strengthen communities, increase social justice by actively partnering with international organizations, and fostering a peaceful collaborative partnership (G. Sanders, personal communication, January 20, 2017).

Nicaragua has a culture of war and political unrest. Gwen Sanders (personal communication, January 20, 2017) stated that as American visitors, the NDNU art therapists had to prepare for their trip by educating themselves about the culture and history of Granada, as well as engaging in activities to promoted their own cultural awareness and humility. Viva-Nicaragua! leaders educated the students and teachers about how the United States government participated actively in war in Nicaragua. As such, those in the art therapy community who want to engage in this work must begin to understand and take responsibility for what Americans may represent to those in communities with whom they will be working. She added that art therapists must understand and work within the privileged and oppressive status that they as Americans represent. Acknowledging this with humility is part of the process of being allowed to enter their world, to find a ground from which to bring forth art therapy. At the end of each trip, the work ends with a community-based art show. This offers opportunities for the participants and for the

142 *Arnell Etherington Reader*

whole community to view their artwork (G. Sanders, personal communication, January 20, 2017). NDNU reciprocated in the cultural exchange by providing a training for the Viva-Nicaragua! mentors using art to foster awareness of their growth through mentoring, and assisting them in their quest to be conscious of the vast cultural differences and the possibilities of collective empowerment.

The NDNU art therapists worked collaboratively with leaders in the NGO to develop culturally appropriate and relevant art therapy interventions. Some of the art therapy projects included creating a shield, a mask, and a cultural doll. In another visit, the art therapy students devised the art experientials, which included a community mural, sensory and tactile art for the elderly, and shared scribble drawings for the youth and elderly. In the teacher training, materials found in nature were used to create *mandalas* in partnership with the art therapy students. Here they could find beauty and meaning at home in their own environment, without the use of any formal art materials. Using natural resources that are readily available helps students develop humility and appreciation, allowing them to avoid the exploitative colonizing that takes place when we in the West believe someone "needs" what we have. Using natural elements of the Nicaraguan environment further assists the Nicaraguan trainers in absorbing art therapy methods and ideas within this particular cultural, social, psychological, and spiritual context. (G. Sanders, personal communication, January 20, 2017).

People often want to "travel" on these global journeys rather than do the internal and external work required to make a meaningful connection and build lasting relationships before, during, and after a trip. Sanders (G. Sanders, personal communication, January 20, 2017) stated she hopes that in the next 20 years, there will be more emphasis in global art therapy to train the trainers with respectful cultural humility and collaboration, with more grassroots organizations receptive to art therapy. She further hopes that more scholarships will be developed for native peoples to be able to move beyond their present circumstances with art training and to further potential artists who would bring financial support back to these groups (G. Sanders, personal communication, January 20, 2017).

## Art Therapy Trainee Voice in Nicaragua

Amy Hill, Ph.D., MFT, ATR-BC, is an adjunct faculty member of the Graduate Art Therapy Psychology Department at Notre Dame de Namur University in Belmont, California. This section is the result of conversations I had with Amy Hill about her experience in Nicaragua. Amy Hill, as a trainee, participated in two trips to Nicaragua. Both trips differed, but being able to participate twice as a trainee gave her a sense of what global art therapy can be, the value it holds as a training experience, and

*Global Art Therapy* 143

the experience of a living context in which she could observe the ways in which art therapy is valued by the Nicaraguan participants.

On reflection, she stated that she continues to be curious about who benefits and to what extent (A Hill, personal conversation, January 13, 2017) and this is reflected in her response in Plate 7. She related that holding trainings for paraprofessional art therapists and other trainers is a powerful experience. There was the further question of leaving home and traveling to do art therapy versus working in one's own community with persons in need. In the future, she believes it would be important to have increased dialog with art therapists from differing countries and those working in various contexts, where there is a value for art therapists as culturally humble lifelong learners (Tervalon & Murray-Garcia, 1998). Avenues for sharing international development projects would connect global art therapists. Having the ability to bring real opportunities for the people to whom one is reaching out could be even more significant; this could occur through the development of mutually respectful and dynamic partnerships with communities. Finally, seeing more value given to what art therapists can bring to a community would be extremely helpful (A Hill, personal conversation, January 13, 2017).

### Creative Arts Therapy Doors into East Africa

Catherine Moon is professor and chair of the Art Therapy Department at the School of the Art Institute of Chicago, in Chicago, IL. The following emerges from a conversation I had with her on January 27, 2017. She related that she was making her 11th trip to East Africa; previous to this one, she had taken two as a co-leader of study trips and the other nine as a collaborative facilitator of paraprofessional therapeutic arts trainings. She stated that the work she did in Africa was associated with Global Alliance for Africa (2016), a nonprofit organization whose mission is to transform "the lives of orphans and vulnerable children affected by the AIDS pandemic in sub-Saharan Africa by partnering with grassroots organizations to design and implement innovative economic development programs that enable families and communities to become self-sufficient" (para 1). The therapeutic arts program (TAP) is one facet of the work the organization does. TAP addresses a variety of circumstances within which the children are situated, including domestic violence, child abuse, grief/loss, or the impact of child labor. The Global Alliance for Africa also provides small loans to women developing businesses so that they can financially sustain their families, and it also assists in building and supporting community libraries.

Catherine Moon (personal conversation, January 27, 2017) stated that before she became involved, the Global Alliance for Africa (2016) had organized and provided annual arts enrichment camps for children organized by artists Penny Burns and Judy Sullivan, but it was interested

144 *Arnell Etherington Reader*

in developing a sustainable program of psychosocial support through the arts. She had been invited to travel to East Africa to assist them in developing this aspect of the work. She collaborated in the first couple of years with American art therapist Angela Lyonsmith. Their approach was, and has continued to be, highly collaborative in nature.

The Alliance had the idea of building an arts therapy center in Tanzania, but after talking about this idea with local artists, school personnel, social workers, and therapists, they realized their focus ought to be not on a "place" but on "people." The Director of Programs for Global Alliance for Africa, Linda Stolz, travels frequently to East Africa, and she began to identify artists and other human service workers who demonstrated a commitment to assisting vulnerable children through the arts and who expressed interest in learning about art therapy. So began the influx of dance, drama, music, and visual arts therapists into Tanzania and Kenya to share their skills and knowledge and to learn from the East Africans. This past year they had 13 visiting arts therapists, three new East African trainees, and nine East African training partners with whom they had previously worked, some for as long as 10 years (C. Moon, personal conversation, January 27, 2017).

Moon (personal conversation, January 27, 2017) stated that she learns something new every year and is inspired by the work. Initially, the alliance-sponsored trips had multiple agendas, including providing educational, tourist, and service opportunities for the visitors. Over time, the agenda became much more focused on the development of the TAP through a collaborative exchange model. Now arts therapist participants need to explicitly agree to share their knowledge and skills as a part of this exchange. In this way, art therapists are training future trainers, people who come from varied geographic and sociocultural contexts, such as artists from the Kibera slum in Nairobi and middle-class Africans from elsewhere in East Africa.

Moon stated that the way in which training the trainers has occurred grows and changes as "we learn and develop together" (C. Moon, personal conversation, January 27, 2017). She stated that this year she did not attend the full training due to other commitments and believes that her absence more readily allowed for the transfer of leadership from herself to others. They implemented a leadership team model this year, with the team consisting of five seasoned therapeutic artist trainees from Kenya and Tanzania and American art therapist Tally Tripp. They are currently developing a tiered model for the paraprofessional trainings because the participants range from those who are brand new and have had no exposure to the arts therapies to those who are in their 10th year of being part of the TAP training. With multiple training levels, clearly articulated content for each level, and certificates that document multilevel achievements, long-term committed participants can be recognized as the leaders they are (C. Moon, personal conversation, January 27, 2017).

# Global Art Therapy   145

One important aspect of this global work is to actively engage visiting participants in relinquishing their roles as "experts" by decentering their participation within the training process. Visiting participants are asked to privilege the East Africans' needs, agendas, and voices. Each training series begins by identifying what the East Africans want to learn and what skills and knowledge each participant can contribute to the learning environment (C. Moon, personal conversation, January 27, 2017).

In terms of global art therapy per se, there are problems with some of the work being undertaken through study trips, service work, and *voluntourism*. Some individuals who have participated globally in art therapy focus on how great it was for them, but they do not consider the positive or negative impact they may have had on the people, organizations, and communities with which they have worked. Sometimes both adequate preparation and responsible follow-up are missing from experiences of global art therapy. Preparation, which includes education about the sociocultural and historical context of the host country, enhances the potential for ethical, responsible, and relevant cross-cultural exchanges. Follow-up gives those in the visiting group a chance to critically consider what they think and feel about the cross-cultural experience. Follow-up with participants from the host country is part of respectful and responsible exchange and provides opportunities for critical feedback and ongoing learning, support, and supervision. Another problem occurs when art therapists "parachute" into and out of people's lives, providing brief therapy or other services without concern for what happens when those services disappear (C. Moon, personal conversation, January 27, 2017).

Ideally, cross-cultural international work is not undertaken without first considering the question of sustainability. It has been important to make a long-term commitment to working in Tanzania and Kenya. Doing so has allowed adequate time for students and trainers to negotiate the significant learning curve involved in working cross-culturally and cross-continentally. It has also allowed for the development of trust between the collaborating partners, which has been crucial to developing arts therapies applications that are context specific and culturally relevant. Moon (personal conversation, January 27, 2017) stated that given the brief nature of her visits, which are typically two to three weeks in duration, a long-term commitment has been necessary for both providing in-depth trainings and evolving the program over time. At the same time, the *train the trainers model* helps establish a plan for how the work will continue once foreign art therapists are no longer involved (C. Moon, personal conversation, January 27, 2017).

The development of art therapy in different countries seems to follow a similar pattern. Initially there may be little knowledge about the field of art therapy in the country, although there is typically a long history of the arts having been used for therapeutic or healing purposes. Art therapy then begins to be introduced as a professional field and then expands to

## 146  *Arnell Etherington Reader*

reach a larger population in need. Frequently, divergent ideas about the nature of art therapy leads to competing professional organizations. As the field begins to settle and become established, it takes on a character that is unique to the country's context. It is important to be humble with the offer of international art therapy services or training and to subsequently move out of the way to allow for development (C. Moon, personal conversation, January 27, 2017).

### Art Therapy in Ethiopia

Claudia Mezzera, Ph.D., MFT ATR-B.C, is a faculty member of the Graduate Art Therapy Psychology Department of Notre Dame de Namur University in Belmont, California. I spoke with her on January 25, 2017, about her work in Ethiopia. In 2007, she took a two-week art therapy trip to Addis Ababa, Ethiopia, in conjunction with the Menlo Park Presbyterian Church to provide art therapy to women in need. The group consisted of four art therapy NDNU graduates, faculty member Doris Arrington, and four volunteers. Prior to journeying, training occurred in language, food, music, customs, and supportive participation, as well as the country's topography. Mezzera (personal conversation, January 25, 2017) stated that upon arrival she was impressed with the diametrical change in cultures from her day-to-day reality. It was painful to see the poverty, the heartbreak, and the suffering evident in Ethiopia. Self-care became very important.

The trip involved making contact with five different institutions and providing service when it was appropriate. The team visited Hope Enterprises to volunteer in their program serving food to homeless children and adults. Hope Enterprises operates throughout Ethiopia with food programs and has seven elementary schools, five high schools, and a variety of vocational programs, in particular Hope College of Business, Science and Technology. These resources strive to empower children and adults in becoming self-sufficient and overcoming poverty.

The team visited Hamlin Fistula Hospital to learn more about their work, which strives to prevent and to treat childbirth injuries called *obstetric fistulas*. A fistula is a rupture, which creates incontinence. Because of these injuries, these women are often abandoned by their husbands, families, and they are banished by their communities. The team then visited the Trampled Rose, which is an organization focused on three goals: (a) providing presurgery fistula care; (b) providing postsurgery rehabilitation for women already suffering from a fistula; and (c) prevention of new fistula cases. The team offered art therapy, but due to a lack of interest from participants, they instead facilitated a celebration of dance and music, which was created together with the women being served. Plastic garbage containers became drums, wooden spoons became musical sticks, and everyone began to clap and dance, exchanging dance moves, smiles, and unconditional acceptance. It was a shift of energy, and dancing became art in motion.

The team also visited the Sisters of Charity, founded by Mother Teresa; the sisters provide love, care, food, and medical services for the destitute and dying. All ages are welcome and treated with dignity and love. The team went on to Ellilta International, a nonprofit organization that provides services to women escaping from sex trafficking; the services involve individual and group counseling, Christian discipleship, financial support for school-aged children of women in the program, daycare services, skills training and job placement, nutritional and monthly living support for basic needs, full medical support for all of the women and their children, prevention education about the risks of prostitution in the communities, as well as methods that may prevent sexual exploitation. Mezzera (personal conversation, January 25, 2017) stated that the team provided art therapy training to counselors working with Ellilta clients, and they facilitated art directives with their clients. The primary focus was to address trauma and the resulting symptoms and challenges using Doris Arrington's instinctual trauma response protocol. Additional art directives included compassion cards, grief and loss bags, bridge drawings, batiking fabric, personal portraits, and scribble chase.

Discussions were held about team members' feelings, fears, and obstacles to encourage resiliency, reduce fear, and inspire trust and collaboration. The discussions were helpful in providing ongoing support between team members. Art crossed the language barriers. The experiences these women and girls had was beyond words in many instances; thus, the art gave nuance to the unexplainable. Giving voice to the pain and creating a place of hope appeared to be healing; this indicated that what was most needed was to allow these women and children to be heard, for their voices to be sounded through their own art (C. Mezzera, personal conversation, January 25, 2017).

Women in Ethiopia often face economic and sociocultural discrimination that consequently limits their access to education, employment, health care, personal development, and in some ethnic groups, ownership rights to property. Traditional cultural practices, such as female genital mutilation, early marriage, childbearing, and gender-based violence, not only create adverse effects on Ethiopian women, but they also may trigger strong feelings in team members working to serve them, especially those coming from another domain where women's rights are celebrated. Women who have been trafficked are additionally cast out, and to begin to understand what it means to them to be cast aside forever is critical (C. Mezzera, personal conversation, January 25, 2017).

Bringing art materials into this country was challenging because some of the supplies (i.e., color printer) were confiscated upon arrival by customs. Other supplies, like crayons and craypas, photo film, and color paper/card stock were allowed. Despite the loss of the photo printer, with ingenuity, photographs of the individual women and girls could be processed. Seeing themselves for the first time was a profound experience (C. Mezzera, personal conversation, January 25, 2017). They could see themselves in a completely different light. Many surprises occurred on this journey, such as witnessing a traditional *coffee ceremony* and exchanging choreography with the women who performed spontaneous traditional dances; learning ethnic customs and crafting was also enriching (C. Mezzera, personal conversation, January 25, 2017). This was a gift exchange. In another context, spontaneous drumming and singing played a role in lifting the mood of the women. A short period of joy and normalcy seemed to ensue for the women and girls as they immersed (if briefly) in their traditions of music and dance (C. Mezzera, personal conversation, January 25, 2017).

Mezzera (personal conversation, January 25, 2017) stated that the biggest mistake is to enter the context of another country and culture with a rigid agenda. Often participants do not see they are entering with an agenda. She advised others to go equipped with possibilities and assume a flexible stance. The experience of this journey to Ethiopia, from the beginning to end, was to live in the unexpected, and in that there was a miraculous side to the experience. She stated that they began to learn a way to join. It was important to remember that we may have tools, materials, training, and experience to which they may not have access (C. Mezzera, personal conversation, January 25, 2017). It is not helpful to create a longing for something (art materials) they have no means to purchase. It is important to celebrate what is available (such as materials from their natural environment or traditional craft making) so they can continue to use art if they desire.

Mezzera (personal conversation, January 25, 2017) stated that what is important in any global art therapy is to "always remember that to enter another culture is a privilege and one must arrive in a posture of humility and be prepared to look inside oneself to make room for the other culture." She added the following:

> to observe, to respect the other's perspective, and to mindfully remember that we are not the experts of their life experiences regardless of our training and skill. To strive to be open to the people in front of you in order to share in some format from the heart and mind what they might want and need from us, the art therapist. Otherwise we are just voyeurs. We should not approach these sacred encounters as if we are in charge and instead we must strive to go humbly and to be open to receive their gifts of creativity and to make room for others' ways of knowing and for the magic that can be created together with art.
>
> (C. Mezzera, personal conversation,
> January 25, 2017)

The global art therapist has a privileged opportunity to learn what art is to individuals who have other ways of knowing and who have much to offer.

### Living Art Crosses the Pond

Arnell Etherington Reader, Ph.D., MFT, ATR-B.C, is a clinical psychologist and professor emeritus at the Art Therapy Psychology Department NDNU in Belmont, California. Her international class, "Art as a Way of Knowing: International Ancient Sites and Living Art," brings NDNU art therapy psychology graduate students and art therapists from various global cities to Britain for a week. This in itself enables a cross-cultural interaction of art therapists. The class is based on two points of inquiry: Pat Allen's *Art as a Way of Knowing*, an authentic mindful approach to psychological insight using art, and Lady Jane Corey Wright, British art therapist's *Living Art Painting Process*, a method for self-reflection within small group settings. Living art therapy is based on retreats Arnell Etherington-Reader (personal conversation, January 18, 2017) has given to explore self and culture in Sedona, Arizona, Hawaii, and Kuala Lumpur.

Many individuals who come to the UK class believe that because English is spoken in Britain there is a great similarity in cultures; however, firstly, the words and accents used to describe most things are quite different. Secondly, the cultural history and remaining sites of antiquity are remarkable. Present-day British culture—its people, politics, social and psychological expressions, and religion—are quite distinct from that of the US, and participants encounter a bit of personal culture shock, mostly because they come with false expectations.

The course involves travel to ancient British sites, such as Stonehenge, as well as travel to London's British Museum and the Tate museums. Participants live, travel, and interact with the British people and their cultures—all to enhance an understanding of art and culture as a way of knowing. A service day is offered at a local primary school, in which participants work with children from a variety of backgrounds. The art therapist participants engage in an art-day project with 40 children. Participants spend time in the art studio following these experiential days, which allows an integration of the experience through art. The practice of response art within these two points of inquiry is done to increase insight, expand one's vision, and encourage working and interacting mindfully. This practice in another country's context appears to sharpen the nuances of that learning and application (A. Etherington-Reader, personal conversation, January 18, 2017).

Participants' pre-departure assessment dialogs help set the parameters for the class (e.g., staying with the group, long days, safety issues, flexibility, and respect for others). Participants summate their

150  *Arnell Etherington Reader*

experiences in a final art project that serves to help them reflect on and integrate their experiences (see Figure 10.2). Reentry debriefings occur on the last day and several months later to review and integrate material. Overall, the class provides an academic format for learning new approaches to art, culture, and people, and simultaneously applying these approaches while immersing oneself in a new culture. These types of entries into global art therapy can enhance the knowledge

*Figure 10.2* Grounded feet but wandering heart.

and practical experience of different peoples' cultures. Classes evolving from university settings allow art therapists to begin their global experiences in art therapy in an unfamiliar, though somewhat protected, environment. It begins to broaden their thoughts and feelings of what and where art therapy might find itself helpful and how it can be used sensibly (A. Etherington-Reader, personal conversation, January 18, 2017).

### Various Considerations on Global Art Therapy

Jill Westwood, MA, is a program convener for the Master's in Art Psychotherapy program in the Department of Social, Therapeutic and Community Studies Goldsmiths, University of London. My conversation with Westwood took place on January 20, 2017. She (personal conversation, January 20, 2017) stated, "Global art therapy makes me think about how differently art therapy is practiced or is emerging in different parts of the world." She said she thought that the various contexts have lent nuances to the field of art therapy. It is constructive and realistic to allow for these global differences and to respect the variations that reflect the contextual understanding of place. Some of these distinctions follow. For example, a determining factor is whether there is a National Health System or a Department of Mental Health or some other regulating body that sets the standards for what an art therapist can do. These regulatory bodies both structure and influence the ways the profession develops or in some instances delineates and curbs the art therapist's work boundaries. Another factor that may vary is the relationship with and to the art tradition: is the art in the therapy or is the therapy in the art? Further, in defining what constitutes a professional art therapist, contexts vary in how much emphasis is placed on art therapists continuing to work in art themselves. Naturally, the economic, social, and political arenas in which the art therapy is practiced affect what it will look like. How art therapy evolves in an area takes its position in defining the particularities in the region. The manner in which the system of care delivers its services influences the relationship between art therapy providers and patients. The stakeholders that have an investment in providing services may cast shadows on the work of the art therapist. Small but often fierce battles might ensue concerning ownership and professional territory, for example between psychiatrists and art therapists or other closely related professions. These battles fragment the subgroups and can be detrimental to what is offered to the patients (J. Westwood, personal conversation, January 20, 2017).

The development of professional organizations with employment systems and regulatory systems in place may restrict or expand a framework in which the art therapist practices. For example, Australian art therapists do not have an overarching regulatory body that imposes professional sanctions, aside from professional organizations, and as a result,

## 152 *Arnell Etherington Reader*

the art therapy practiced there may be evolving with more varied and creative approaches. By comparison, in the U.S. there is both a national art therapy regulatory body and each state carries its own regulatory framework, which allows or disallows aspects of practice (J. Westwood, personal conversation, January 20, 2017).

There are different clinical challenges in different places. Reaching into the context of the people, the work springs from a particular therapeutic training, but it is then greatly shaped by the present clinical challenges, such as addressing the welfare of migratory influences. Language and how art therapy tenets are interpreted also may limit the educational knowledge available to a student. For example, many countries' excellent writings in art therapy may not be translated into the spoken language of the art therapy reader. We do not know what we do not know (J. Westwood, personal conversation, January 20, 2017).

Social justice art therapy occupies what might be a space that creates clashes between cultures yet is driven by a hierarchy of human needs. Recently, we have witnessed the largest migration of peoples around the world since World War II. The combination of political unrest and the kind of "missionary zeal" in response to it takes art therapists to places of need where art therapy may be adapted in practice (J. Westwood, personal conversation, January 20, 2017). Still, the art therapy work in these circumstances will be shaped by the hierarchy of needs, community interventions, and the social, philosophical, psychological, and spiritual needs of that community. This work requires flexibility in thinking and practice to meet these needs. With this in mind, art therapy is recognized in its creative evolution and must not be overly rigid. Its boundaries and edges could be slightly blurred, although not blunted. This is required to allow for multiple exploration in the global context (J. Westwood, personal conversation, January 20, 2017).

## Conclusion

In a variety of ways, some clarity is always found through experience. Providing global art therapy as a direct service, a developing intervention, and the *training the trainers* model works alongside artists and other service providers. These services are provided as a one-time intervention with a disadvantaged group in a respectful manner, as part of an international group of art therapists immersing into another culture to learn an art therapy skill, or as a sustained commitment with partner organizations. Each of these contexts can be of considerable value for art therapists and the communities they are working within.

Journeys across the globe may involve the realization that art therapy, having been developed in the West, does not fit neatly with other cultures and that rich, complex traditions cannot be minimized. In addition, those journeys involve the recognition that there are many steps to building a new modality in a mental health landscape (R. Lay, personal communication, December 10, 2016). In addition, the journey may involve giving up expectations while entering a land one has never seen. The new setting necessitates adopting a tone of respectful curiosity, cultural humility, and openness. These are journeys that are made in an attempt to make a connection and promote opportunities, and they require the art therapist to be flexible (G. Sanders, personal communication, January 20, 2017). The focus needs to remain on people rather than a place (C. Moon, personal conversation, January 27, 2017), trusting that art therapy will be nuanced by context (J. Westwood, personal conversation, January 20, 2017).

Whatever the journey, the focus of art therapy is that art is the language spoken and a way of meeting the needs of a community (A Hill, personal conversation, January 13, 2017). If art therapists have opportunities to train the trainers, they realize they must give up their "expert" position (C. Moon, personal conversation, January 27, 2017), as well as any rigid agenda (C. Mezzera, personal conversation, January 25, 2017). When one enters into participatory learning, one makes a commitment to share one's skills within a value-based relationship oftentimes established within a host country and culture. Taking cross-cultural learning and cultural humility into consideration enables greater understanding of art therapy and its application in context (J. Westwood, personal conversation, January 20, 2017). Through a constructive and realistic view, and an openness to differences, thoughtful global art therapy concepts and experiences can continue to emerge.

## References

Achterberg, J. (1985). *Imagery in healing: Shamanism and modern medicine.* Boston, MA: Shambhala.

Bucciarelli, A. (2016). Art therapy: A transdisciplinary approach. *Art Therapy: Journal of the American Art Therapy Association, 33*(3), 151–155.

Cruz, R. F. (2005). Introduction to special issues: The international scope of art therapists. *The Arts in Psychotherapy, 32,* 167–169.

Doctors Without Borders. (n. d.). *The purpose and mission.* Retrieved from http://sites.google.com/site/doctorsborders/project-definition

Gleuck, B. P. (2015). Roles, attitudes, and training needs of behavioral health clinicians in integrated primary care. *Journal of Mental Health Counseling, 37*(2), 175–188.

Global Alliance for Africa. (2016). *Our mission.* Retrieved from www.global allianceafrica.org/mission/

Holmes, J., Mizen, S., & Jacobs, C. (2007). Psychotherapy training for psychiatrists. *UK and Global Perspectives, 19*(1), 93–100.

International Monetary Fund Staff. (2000, April 1). *Globalization: Threat or opportunity?* [Online forum comment] Retrieved from www.imf.org/external/np/exr/ib/2000/041200to.htm#II)

## 154  *Arnell Etherington Reader*

International Committee of the Red Cross. (2017). Retrieved from https://en.wikipedia.org/wiki/International_Committee_of_the_Red_Cross

Junge, M. (2016). History of art therapy. In D. Gussak & M. Rosal (Eds.), *Wiley handbook of art therapy* (p. 15). West Sussex, UK: Wiley.

Potash, J., Mann, S., Martinez, J., Roach, A., and Wallace, N. (2016). Spectrum of art therapy practice: Systematic literature review of art therapy, 1983–2014. *Art Therapy: Journal of the American Art Therapy Association, 33*(3), 119–127.

New articulations in the art therapies. (2017). *European Consortium for the Arts Therapies Education.* Retrieved from  http://www.ecarte.info/conference/conference-theme.htm

Spence, S. (2006). All in the Mind? The neural correlates of unexplained physical symptoms. *Advances in Psychiatric Treatment, 12,* 349–358.

Sperry, L. (2013). Integrated behavioral health: Implications for individual and family counseling practice. *The Family Journal: Counseling and Therapy for Couples and Families, 21*(3), 347–350.

The Red Pencil. (2015). *Who we are.* Retrieved from www.redpencil.org/red-pencil-singapore

Talwar, S. (2016). Is there a need to redefine art therapy? *Art Therapy: Journal of the American Art Therapy Association, 33*(3), 116–118.

Tervalon, M., & Murray-Garcia, J. (1998, May). Cultural humility versus cultural competence: A critical distinction in defining physician training outcomes in multicutural education. *Journal of Health Care for the Poor and Underserved, 9*(2), 117–125.

Ulman, E. (1961). Art therapy: Problems of definitions. *Bulletin of Art Therapy, 1*(2), 10–20.

Wadeson, H. (2002). Art therapy: Problems of definitions. *Bulletin of Art Therapy, 1*(2), 10–20.

Wolf Bordonaro, G. (2016). International art therapy. In D. Gussak & M. Rosal (Eds.), *Wiley handbook of art therapy*. West Sussex, UK: Wiley.

# 11 Emerging Paradigms in Art Therapy Supervision

## The Use of Response Art

*Gwen Sanders*

This chapter informs art therapist students, supervisors, and educators about the emerging transformative formats that can be used in supervision to enhance the field of art therapy. Response art is created as a visual reflection of developing art therapists' unconscious reactions to their clinical work. The experience of reflecting on one's art work, especially in a group setting with the support of a supervisor, encourages developing art therapists to take risks, to be vulnerable as they evolve, to be aware of their biases, to admit mistakes, and to identify their defenses, as well as their emotional reactions to their clients. Such a process surrounding response art can foster a greater willingness in trainees to embrace the unknown and be open to novel experiences. It instills in art therapist trainees both curiosity and psychological mindedness. These attributes, especially when cultivated in the novice therapist, encourage interest in self and in the differences between self and others.

Recognizing one's emotional reactions to clients is the hallmark of utilizing countertransference to inform therapy. Countertransference, in which a clinician's emotional response to their clients serves as an important indicator of the dynamics at play in therapy, is an important tool that is utilized in many psychotherapeutic approaches (Colli & Ferri, 2015). However, novice therapists may interpret these emotional responses as deficits in themselves.

The art therapy supervisor can serve as an auxiliary ego in this path towards the unknown, providing a safe place to explore aspects of the self, while using art as the vessel. The primary task of the supervisor is to foster the student therapist's professional development, including the student's awareness of self and others, capacity for presence, responsiveness, and resilience in relationships with clients (Brown, 2010). The relational dynamics that occur between supervisor and developing therapist often mirror the unconscious dynamics that are salient in the students' therapeutic relationships with their clients, in what is referred to as *parallel process* (Navarro, 2003; Frawley-O'Dea & Sarnat, 2001).

Supervisors can intensify the parallel process experience in several ways. Through their engagement with the supervisee, they can help

## 156 Gwen Sanders

supervisees focus on their subjective impressions regarding their client (Brown, 1996). They can also create art in response to their supervisory experience. In the latter case, response art can be used by the supervisor as a means of enhancing the insight gained through the supervisees' processing of the clinical dynamics. The supervisor's artwork can help the supervisee increase his or her understanding by deepening the process and shedding light on the parallel process that emerges in supervision.

In supervision within graduate art therapy schools (Franklin et al., 2000), groups provide a container in which all the members play a role in processing therapy-client relationships. Groups provide a present focus, and as students develop trusting relationships with group members, students begin to learn that their risk-taking is honored. Best practices in the graduate art therapy supervision group format have developed in which the students and supervisors are engaged in a process of stretching to become present with the range of feelings that are elicited in the clinical situation; an environment is created in which all group members feel it is safe to self-disclose through visual means and self-reflection.

In the group supervision, art made in response to clients is reflected on by the group and serves to increase the developing therapist's awareness (Fish, 1989, 2005, 2008). Thus, with the support of the supervisor, these images help students access unconscious responses to the client. Kielo (1991) asked art therapists to reflect on an uncomfortable affective response after a session with a client. They were then asked to create art in response; students who did response art were able to access knowledge about important aspects of the treatment process. The techniques Kielo created during supervision appeared to help supervisees articulate new thoughts about the clinical situation. They also helped them to develop empathy for the client and clarify their confusion concerning their countertransference reaction. Thus, the process encouraged deeper levels of reflection, which emphasized introspection and exploration.

Art as a response to uncomfortable therapeutic reactions creates a type of bonding experience for the group members. Group supervision provides an interpersonal relational learning experience that amplifies the subjectivity of each supervisee in the microcosm of the group process. This group learning experience is witnessed by all members, and each of these individual, solitary experiences can be mirrored in the collective community to hopefully create a cohesive collaborative learning experience. The many benefits of group processes, such as emotional release, catharsis, and increased self-awareness, provide individuals with opportunities to develop new inner strength to confront and resolve barriers (Gladding, 2005).

When members express strong emotions, whether positive or negative, the most meaningful group interactions occur (Yalom, 2005). The expression of these powerful emotions often recapitulates the largest emotional life experiences for group members. Group members' powerful

## The Use of Response Art    157

emotional responses to input from other group members tends to stimulate the group (Waller, 2014) and bring its members closer together. Thus, sharing art during group helps members uncover and work with the important issues and experiences that influence their clinical work (Fish, 2005). The groups' experiential commonality can in turn support group members' active engagement in the art process as a means of exploration.

## Related Research on the Topic

The therapist uses the self as an instrument, and this self is a vessel of embodied know-how, which is developed through learning by doing (Bugental, 1987). Developing therapists need to be aware of their own experiences as they develop professionally. The self-awareness they cultivate through their own introspection informs them about the experience of others.

A key aspect of the learning process for a developing art therapist is understanding that the clinical process is filled with uncertainty and that the experience of not knowing may be difficult to understand and verbalize. New therapists must undergo personal and professional changes, and often emotional healing. Only in this way do they become reliable containers for their clients' cognitions and emotions. Developing this capacity as therapists involves having a curiosity and willingness to explore, inquire, and observe, which then yields insights (Conte, Ratto, & Karasu, 1996; Kashdan, et al., 2009).

Group supervision is enhanced by a supervisor's capacity to develop an environment of safety. Qualities associated with good supervisors include demonstrating flexibility about theory, having knowledge of principles, skills and techniques, a respectful attitude towards the trainee, an ability to be supportive and nonjudgmental. Other attributes include humility, curiosity, a relaxed and patient manner, thoughtfulness, and the ability to communicate clearly (Boulware, 2010). Additionally, it is important that supervisors have the capacity for self-reflection and that they be vigilant in monitoring their own emotional responses in order to follow the interpersonal processes in the supervisor/supervisee dyad. Practicing regular, direct, and truthful communication, and honoring personal disclosure relevant to students' growth capacities, can enhance trust in students and help create an environment in which they are willing to take risks and be vulnerable. This mentoring includes teaching and modeling relationship skills, whereby therapists develop senses of curiosity, openness, and trust, and the ability to communicate and collaborate.

In trainings taught within graduate schools (Franklin et al., 2000), groups provide a present focus. Students learn to trust, and they begin to learn that their risk-taking is honored. Best practices in the graduate art therapy training group format utilize a process whereby stretching to become honestly present with a range of feelings is encouraged and

## 158 Gwen Sanders

honored, so that group members will feel safe to self-disclose through visual reflection.

## Challenges for the Future and Areas of Needed Inquiry

The field of art therapy has few outcome studies on the efficacy of group art therapy supervision. Sanders' (2016) research on group art therapy supervision was aimed to build on the work of Fish (2005, 2008), who examined the effects of art as a response to strong emotions of uncertainty to deal with countertransference, as well as Kielo's (1991) approach of asking art therapy students to retrospectively reflect on an uncomfortable affective response during a clinical session and then create art. Sanders (2016) asked students to create art at home in response to the emotions that are typically elicited in the therapy situation. They were asked to make art in response to confusion, uncertainty, and curiosity, and to share their art during group art therapy supervision. Creating art at home allowed for time and self-reflection in an environment that would be free from the pressures of the group experience. However, unlike Fish's research, the group supervisor did not create art in relation to the students' art.

Sanders (2016) gathered data from 40 student participants who were attending five art therapy graduate education programs; the purpose was to examine how levels of curiosity and psychological mindedness might increase when using art as a vehicle to processing emotions in supervision. Students completed two instruments before and during the group supervision process: The *Curiosity and Exploration Inventory-II* (CEI-II) and the *Balanced Index of Psychological Mindedness* (BIPM). The CEI-II assesses curiosity, including the motivation to seek out knowledge and new experiences (i.e., stretching) and the willingness to embrace the novel, uncertain, and unpredictable nature of everyday life (i.e., embracing; Kashdan et al., 2009). The BIPM measures psychological mindedness, which refers to an interest in, and the ability to extract, psychological information (e.g., thoughts, feelings, and behaviors) from a scenario to gain insight (Nyclicek & Denollet, 2009).

Curiosity and psychological mindedness are fundamental psychological traits for therapists to have (Conte et al., 1996; Hall, 1992). When individuals have the attributes of curiosity and exploration, they are more apt to tolerate distress and uncertainty in the process of exploring (Kashdan et al., 2009; Loewenstein, 1994). These qualities enable individuals to view difficulties more as challenges than as threats. Although findings were limited due to the small sample size, nonparametric measures, and confounding variables, the study confirmed that students do show significant increases in stretching and interest over the course of a group supervisory experience when utilizing response art. These findings suggest that through the process of exploring response art and reflecting on it during the group supervision experience, students showed curiosity and tended to stretch towards the unknown. Curiosity and awareness, in turn, help to increase insight (Kashdan et al., 2009), as well as lead to a greater interest in exploring.

While students' insights were expected to significantly increase as well, there was a surprising finding. Students who had more semesters of supervision tended to endorse less insight. One possible interpretation for students showing more insight early in the course, relative to the end, is that as students develop more clinical experience, they may develop more humility regarding what they do not know. Other findings showed that students in smaller groups (i.e., group sizes of four or less) had greater increases in insight relative to students in larger groups. These results suggest that group members may feel greater levels of safety in smaller groups compared to larger ones; they also emphasize the need for ongoing research to shed light on how insight is developed in group supervision. This study highlighted a way to collaborate with educators in AATA-approved graduate programs to conduct research on the efficacy of group art therapy supervision practices; this aspect of the study is in keeping with recommendations from the Carnegie Foundation for the Advancement of Teaching (2015).

In line with the scholar-practitioner model of education, learning, and research, current best practices will move the field towards more evidence-based treatments with new art mediums that use contemporary technologies. Training that utilizes art as a vehicle sparks a process whereby the countertransference reactions of art therapist trainees can be processed and understood in a safe environment. This process is enhanced when the supervisor helps to foster a safe cohesive group that provides a healthy framework for the collective. When the supervisor engages in art in response to the dynamics emerging in group supervision, the art lends further insight into the processes at play in the therapy room. Group dynamics can enhance the learning in which art therapy students are encouraged to use their art to seek internal answers and share them with other art therapy group supervision members. These emerging paradigms can become methodologies that evolve to provide contemporary evidence for the efficacy in the field of art therapy supervision.

## Proposed Models of Art Therapy Group Supervision

This author believes that the field of art therapy would benefit from the following emerging trends that utilize art as a response and as a visual reflection to encourage the beginners' minds (Gordon-Graham, 2014). She believes that these practices will further the developing therapist's capacity to garner insight and clinical competence. The three main future trends within this model that are emphasized here are: (a) the importance of vulnerability and facing the unknown; (b) the importance of

## 160  Gwen Sanders

repurposing art as a reflection of the work of therapy; and (c) the importance of supervisors practicing their own art and response art. These practices will help trainees develop strength and resilience in the face of inevitable personal chaos, which is stimulated in clinical practice, and to build a capacity for honest reflection of oneself and one's reactions. They will also help create an environment for trusting the self while being immersed in the present. Group supervision can provide a container for this experience so that when feelings of vulnerability are explored, the group supervisor and the group members all collaboratively gain through reflecting upon and witnessing each other's changes.

### Importance of Vulnerability and Going into the Unknown

During their training, developing art therapists often experience emotional reactions to novel situations. These emotional reactions may or may not prove to be distressing. Among the possibilities mentioned previously is that they may contribute to an increased interest in exploration. Heightened curiosity can increase awareness and bring about insight and optimal experiences, which leads to a deeper understanding of others (Chilton, 2013b). Porges (2011) found that when individuals experience curiosity and social bonding, and self-disclose their emotions, the hormone oxytocin is released. Highly curious people are more readily able to tolerate anxiety and to continue in the direction of their desired explorations (Deci, 1975). These findings have implications for emerging trends of art therapy supervision; they suggest group engagement through use of response art may stimulate heightened creativity.

Further, by engaging in response art, students cultivate an acceptance of not knowing and a greater openness to welcoming the unknown; these are important factors in lifelong learning especially in therapists (Gordon-Graham, 2014). When experiencing strong emotions in reaction to clients, developing art therapists' best practice is to create response art to process these emotions using any art medium, while taking as much time as necessary to express these emotions. By then sharing in group art therapy supervision the art they create, they are able to be present with others who honor the process of sharing, and in turn, they are able to witness others' sharing art in response to strong emotions; this process, which is facilitated by an adept supervisor, increases group cohesion and the willingness to venture deeper into unknown territory. As group members discover the benefits of self-disclosure in the group process, group members have the sense that it is safe to be vulnerable.

This regular practice can benefit art therapists and the collective as they witness the creative process as a tool of self-care. Self-exploration has been found to increase the brain's flexibility and accommodation to the unknown during the process of learning by doing (Hass-Cohen, 2008). The action of therapy is not didactic but experiential and can be

The Use of Response Art    161

reflected upon through art expression, which is visually and verbally witnessed (Deaver & McAuliffe, 2009).

Fish reported that art-based supervision encourages students to use their images—the tools of the art therapist—to contain, explore, and express clinical information, as well as to give and accept feedback in the group as they examine themselves in their development. Response art "is fundamentally the therapist's work" (Fish, 2008, p. 70), and the clarity that a therapist experiences as a result of response art will ultimately benefit clients.

### Importance of Repurposing Art as a Reflection of the Work of Therapy

Response art can be utilized during art therapy supervision to encourage new insight in many ways. There are many transformational experiences that occur through engaging in response art. One way to do response art is through recycled art: the repurposing of material objects. Examples include altering books, which can be deconstructed and infused with a new meaning.

Altering books involves altering the shape, appearance, and content within the book to create a new art piece that reflects personal power and the recasting of experience. In the process of working with clients, therapists encounter aspects of themselves that they may find disturbing. These could be parts of their past that are being reawakened through doing therapy with a client. In the process of repurposing books, students find a book with a synchronistic or relevant title to encourage the act of re-authoring their stories symbolically; these can show how knowledge from old stories can be embraced to bring clarity to the path of becoming a therapist. During group art therapy supervision, the altered books are shared to identify a story that shows how the past can be incorporated and transformed into a therapist's new reality.

In these green times, environmentally sensitive practices that use fewer consumer products encourage the incorporation of recycled materials as art. Repurposing materials and objects scavenged and transformed from the recycled waste of one's life brings new meaning to life experiences. Previously utilized "old stuff," like old habits, can be re-authored and transmuted to encourage an openness to change, a reframing of old idioms which give new meaning and life to old objects.

This transformative quality of repurposing of art could mirror the process of change. It can show how one can let go of beliefs and behaviors that are no longer relevant, while simultaneously understanding their usefulness for the time in which they were formed and used; this process encourages acceptance and understanding that a residue from the previous archives of life informs the next steps toward change. Pieces and parts of one's recycled waste, such as shredded documents,

## 162  Gwen Sanders

papers, and ripped clothing, can be embedded sculpturally into three-dimensional art pieces; these items are then integrated and imbued with new meaning, thus replicating the process of change over time. Transformative learning experiences are cathartic; they replicate this recapitulation through recycled parts of the student's life to encapsulate new knowledge. This would be an assignment that entails finding some objects of significance, shredding, breaking down, and transforming them so that they can be absorbed into a new contemporary configuration (Plate 8).

The supervisees may also shape images of themselves and their unconscious responses through self-portraits that evolve over time; in this way, their art can mirror changes emerging through their psychological growth and immersion into the unknown. Materials for these portraits could include clay, which has representational mutability and can be a powerful kinesthetic action when facing the unknown in responses to clients.

At the beginning of art therapy supervision, the initial directive might be to create a self-portrait weekly using clay. In subsequent weeks during group supervision, the supervisee could continue to change and remold the self-portrait in clay in ways that coincide with their new psychologically minded self. Thus, the project assists learning by doing by capturing the emotional resonance that reflects the therapist's kaleidoscope of feelings. Meanwhile the students could write weekly about the clay metaphor and address how the clay self-portrait mirrors their internal stage of psychological development. The process might include time lapse evolution of the clay self-portrait in a PowerPoint or a video to comprehend and mirror these internal changes (Figure 11.1).

A similar art experiential is already being used in art therapy supervision. In a process referred to as *El Duende*, acrylic paint is added to and built upon weekly through a process of layering during a semester of practicum. Abbenante (2011) presented the paper "*El Duende* Process Painting" during the 2011 AATA conference in Washington, DC. Robb and Miller (2016) later presented the paper, "Layering as a Mechanism of Change in *El Duende* One-Canvas Process Painting" to show how this technique can serve as a mechanism of change through the layering of paint. In the supervision experience, art therapists would be given a canvas in which to paint weekly throughout the practicum experience. Changes they experienced during the semester, which would be reflected in their piece, could be processed in the group. Interestingly, one of my practicum supervisor colleagues offered her supervisees large, extra heavy watercolor paper to paint on weekly throughout the semester. She had never heard that this had been introduced elsewhere; nor that there had been several presentations. She was doing what art therapists do, creating art making experientials derived both from her own interests and experiences and her yearning to expand the use of art for her students in learning.

*The Use of Response Art* 163

*Figure 11.1* Emerging transcendence.

Another way to create response art through the repurposing of materials is to create puppets, or dolls, from old clothing, found objects, buttons, beads, and string during the course of the semester. These puppets could change shapes and shift over the course of the semester. Art therapists would be asked to reflect on their weekly work with clients using cloth in this

164   *Gwen Sanders*

transformative experience, and they would write about this process during the weeks of supervision. This process would provide primitive, tactile, sensory modalities akin to attachment and attunement memories that originate from the past (Findlay, Lathan & Hass-Cohen, 2008), thus bringing to life in the present a response to clinical work and to professional and emotional development. These soft mediums provide a kinesthetic evolution that parallels the novice therapist's emotional experience to promote processes unearthed in this primary process medium. The goal is to integrate these reflective practices during the uncertainty of experiential learning.

These past few art experientials all demonstrate an evolution over time, which engages the process of art making to parallel the art therapist's psychological growth. Digital visual media can be used to record this process, as these shapes made through these materials are recorded week after week. All of these can be combined into a book, a film, or a video, with words embedded or a voiceover that can be exhibited as a group process of transformation. This project can be offered as a legacy for those who follow. These objects could be useful for other clinical trainees to witness as well. New students could witness the work of others who have preceded them, whose willingness to disclose, divulge, and honor their valuable experiences can be informative to those who follow. These works could serve as testaments to an important transformative process. They would validate students' vulnerabilities in face of experiences of uncertainty and the unknown when engaging in the therapeutic journey with others. All the art experientials discussed can be digitized in some archival fashion.

Timelines are cognitive due to a linear-time focus; thus, the art medium continuum often consists of paper, pencil, markers, paint, and collage. Incorporating multiple timelines into scrolls shapes how curiosity longitudinally changes over time. Beginning with a weekly timeline, significant events of each art therapist's psychological experience are created on separate pieces of paper using art. The timeline builds on previous weeks to create themes that reflect the creativity infused in each therapist's unique life events. At the end of the timeline, the pieces are taped or glued down as a collage onto a scroll that contains the emotions, words, events, and symbols of their unfolding stories. Metaphorically this scroll remains as a stable product that can be a reminder to upcoming students that disclosure and biases are normal during personal development. Voice memos can capture the poetry of words, language, and culturally rich explorations from each unique student perspective. These scrolls can be exhibited or reproduced as a training guide for upcoming students to enhance longevity in the field.

### Importance of Supervisor Doing Their Own Art and Response Art

The art therapy supervisor would benefit from engaging in some of these experientials as a solitary experience or as part of a group that reflects the

The Use of Response Art   165

work of the supervisees and their clients. A supervisor's response art may highlight the dynamics that the developing therapists are attempting to grapple with. Supervisors' willingness to engage in this type of work represents a nonhierarchical exploration of self in order to reach understanding and can serve as a model for students. This clinical work through the arts emulates how learning is experiential, embodied, and lived in the present.

As mentioned previously, the dynamics between the art therapist student and the client are often played out in the supervisee-supervisor relationship, which can then be identified or clarified by the dyad of therapist and supervisor art. These synchronistic expressions may allow more opportunities for understanding what the client elicits in others as well as in the art therapist and supervisor, informing more clarity of countertransference issues.

Examples of how the parallel process can inform therapy though response art includes the repurposing of books. Either one or two books would be altered separately by each clinical trainee and supervisor, taking turns over time. Each book may then hold a specific intention and focus that is decided on initially and then is kept in mind during the process. The books would be altered to enhance the clinical work and treatment by adapting text and images; they would be used to provide individual understanding as well as a joint understanding of the clinical work; they could provide a view of the dynamics the client may bring out in both supervisee and supervisor.

Supervisors can create their own art and story about their experiences of being a supervisor. The supervisor can create response art to group dynamics and group interactions, and these images, stories, and words may be incorporated into the group collaboration during their time together. Creating collaborative environments from found objects can replicate how the repurposing of previously used items into new functions parallels the stages of growth (Figure 11.2).

An example of repurposing is captured in the art therapy magazine, *Art Therapy: Journal of the American Art Therapy Association*, with a cover photograph entitled *Rose Garden* created by a community of older adults in a memory care unit with art therapist collaborator, Kiehn (2016). Moving from the beginning stages of a group piece provides the group members with a collective voice in final decisions. The family systems perspective can be a template for group interactions that evolve and transform during group decisions. Egalitarian group interactions include the supervisor as participant and could be videotaped so the group can retrospectively identify the moving parts of the system as it changes. Each member, through written and spoken word, can offer their unique perspective to the learning community as a means of systemic self-understanding applied collectively about participatory action in group and in the practicum experience.

All of these ideas are adaptable in response art depending on time and interest; they may last a month, a semester, or a year, depending on the

*Figure 11.2* Are words art? From the heart or the head?

practicum experience, but they should include the ritual of documenting the process of change over time by visual means and in words. Additionally, capturing the metaphors and the essence reflected when feeling curious, vulnerable, and open to novel experiences, while taking risks into the future unknown, transmutes and reconfigures life like alchemy. Finally, sharing the art and writing may occur weekly, but it is very useful to do so at the end when there is a formal presentation of the transformational experiences to help group members find the key elements of growth while being submerged in the present and not knowing the future.

Art therapists experience a variety of emotional responses to clients, and they utilize art mediums and group collaborations to align themselves with their experiences to deepen their ability to be authentic in their work as therapists. Finding new materials, and repurposing used material captured in a digital form, while encompassing all members, contains and emulates the ever-changing landscape of a relational feminist framework, which deconstructs hierarchical supervision and emphasizes egalitarian power-sharing and mentoring during learning. Collaboration in art production can serve as a catharsis to the group members who undergo transformative experiences as they develop from novice clinician to professionals who know themselves well enough to do the difficult work of helping others transform. In essence, the therapist can use the self as an instrument, a vessel of embodied know-how, which is developed through learning by doing (Bugental, 1987). The goal is to seek new perspectives and opportunities to creatively expand the triadic parallel process of the supervisor-supervisee-client relationship. The supervisor willingly exhibits flexibility and resilience and mentors these skills and attributes in art therapy supervision; thus, the student witnesses, adopts, and learns through example.

## References

Abbenante, J. (2011). *El Duende process painting*. Paper presentation at American Art Therapy Association Conference, Washington, DC.

Boulware, S. (2010). The interactional nature of supervision: A psychodynamic perspective. In *Practical applications in supervision*. Los Angeles, CA: California Association of Marriage and Family Therapists.

Brown, J. R. (1996). *The I in science: Training to utilize subjectivity in research*. Oslo, NO: Scandinavian University Press.

Brown, J. R. (2010). Relationship and subjectivity. *Practical applications in supervision*. Los Angeles, CA: California Association of Marriage and Family Therapists.

Bugental, J. F. (1987). *The art of the psychotherapist*. New York, NY: Norton.

Carnegie Foundation for the Advancement of Teaching (2015). *The Carnegie classification of institutions of higher education*. Retrieved from http://carnegiefoundation.org

Chilton, G. (2013b). Art therapy and flow: A review of the literature and applications, art therapy. *Art Therapy: Journal of the American Art Therapy Association, 30*(2), 64–70.

Colli, A., & Ferri, M. (2015). Patient personality and therapist countertransference. *Current Opinion in Psychiatry, 28*(1), 46–56. doi:10.1097/YCO.0000000000000119

Conte, H. R., Ratto, R., & Karasu, T. B. (1996). The Psychological Mindedness Scale: Factor structure and relationship to outcome of psychotherapy. *Journal of Psychotherapy Practice and Research, 5*(3), 250–259.

Deaver, S., & McAuliffe, G. (2009). Reflective visual journaling during art therapy and counseling internships: A qualitative study. *Reflective Practice, 10*(5), 615–632.

Deci, E. (1975). *Intrinsic motivation*. New York, NY: Plenum.

Findlay, J. C., Lathan, M. E., & Hass-Cohen, N. (2008). Circles of attachment: Art therapy albums. In N. Hass-Cohen & R. Carr (Eds.), *Art therapy and clinical neuroscience* (pp. 191–206). London, UK: Kingsley.

Fish, B. (1989). Addressing countertransference through image making. In H. Wadeson, J. Durkin, & D. Perach (Eds.), *Advances in art therapy* (pp. 376–389). New York, NY: Wiley.

Fish, B. (2005). *Image-based narrative inquiry of response art in art therapy* (Unpublished doctoral dissertation). Union Institute & University, Cincinnati, OH.

Fish, B. (2008). Formative evaluation research of art-based supervision in art therapy training. *Art Therapy: Journal of the American Art Therapy Association, 25*(2), 70–77.

Franklin, M., Farrelly-Hansen, M., Marek, B., Swan-Foster, N., & Wallingford, S. (2000). Transpersonal art therapy education. *Art Therapy: Journal of the American Art Therapy Association, 17*(2), 101–110.

Frawley-O'Dea, M. G., & Sarnat, J. E. (2001). *The supervisory relationship.* New York, NY: Guildford Press.

Gladding, S. T. (2005). *Counseling as an art: The creative arts in counseling.* Upper Saddle River, NJ: Pearson Education.

Gordon-Graham, C. (2014). Beginner's mind. *Therapy Today, 25*(5), 22–25.

Hall, J. A. (1992). Psychological-mindedness: A conceptual model. *American Journal of Psychotherapy, 46*, 131–140.

Hass-Cohen, N. (2008). Partnering of art therapy and clinical neuroscience. In N. Hass-Cohen & R. Carr (Eds.), *Art therapy and clinical neuroscience* (pp. 21–42). London, UK: Kingsley.

Kashdan, T. B., Gallagher, M. W., Silvia, P. J., Winterstein, B. P., Breen, W. E., Terhar, D., & Steger, M. F. (2009). The Curiosity and Exploration Inventory-II: Development, factor structure, and psychometrics. *Journal of Research in Personality, 43*(6), 987–998.

Kiehn, K. (2016). Rose Garden [Monograph]. *Art Therapy: Journal of the American Art Therapy Association, 33*(3), cover.

Kielo, J. (1991). Art therapists' countertransference and post-session therapy imagery. *Art Therapy: Journal of the American Art Therapy Association, 8*(2), 14–19.

Loewenstein, G. (1994). The psychology of curiosity: A review and reinterpretation. *Psychological Bulletin, 116*(1), 75–98.

Navarro, T. (2003). *The use of art making to recount parallel process* (Unpublished thesis). Drexel University, Philadelphia, PA.

Nyclicek, I., & Denollet, J. (2009). Development and evaluation of the Balanced Index of Psychological Mindedness (BIPM). *Psychological Assessment, 21*(1), 32–44. doi: 0. 1037/a0014418

Porges, S. W. (2011). *The polyvagal theory: Neurophysiological foundations of emotions, attachment, communication, and self- regulation.* New York, NY: W. W. Norton.

Robb, M., & Miller, A. (2016). *Layering as a mechanism of change in El Duende one-canvas process painting.* Paper presentation at American Art Therapy Association Conference, Baltimore, MD.

Sanders, G. J. (2016). *Art response to confusion, uncertainty, and curiosity during group art therapy supervision.* ProQuest Dissertations and Theses database.

Waller, D. (2014). *Group interactive art therapy: Its use in training and treatment.* London, UK: Routledge.

Yalom, I. D. (2005). *The theory and practice of group psychotherapy* (5th ed.). New York, NY: Basic Books.

# Index

Achterberg, J. 134
action potentials 42
aesthetic responsibility 95
aesthetics 6–7
Allen, Pat B. 130, 149
altmetric score 61
American Art Therapy Association
  (AATA) 53, 59–60, 66, 67, 105,
  111, 159
Arnheim, R. 21, 22
Arrington, D. B. 18, 50, 147
art: as active, creative means of
  balance and experience 24–25;
  definition of 7; ethics of evidence
  and 101–102; facilitating holism
  in knowing 22–24; facilitating
  self-reflection 28–29; as form for
  holding and emergence 25–27;
  inviting the artist 27–28; as means
  of promoting change 129–131;
  models informed by neuroscience
  and 33–34; as a response 156–157;
  as therapy 62, 135; understanding
  the landscape of neurobiology and
  40–42
*Art as a Way of Knowing* 149
*art brut* 7–8
artist(s): art inviting the 27–28; art
  therapy role of 3, 6–10; ethics of
  102; as scientist researcher 42–44
art psychotherapy 62
*Art/Research International:
  A Transdisciplinary Journal* 60
*Arts and Health* 60, 61
*Arts in Psychotherapy* 60, 61
art therapists: artist role of 3,
  6–10; healer role of 3, 4–6;
  psychotherapist role of 3, 10–13; as
  social change agents 125–129

Art Therapists' Association Singapore
  (ATAS) 140
art therapy: artist role in 3, 6–10;
  digital media in (*see* digital media);
  diversity in 68, 105–117; education
  in 48–51; emerging paradigms in
  supervision of 155–167; ethics
  in 93–103; facilitating holism in
  knowing 22–24; foundational
  pillars of 3–13; global 134–153;
  healer role in 4–6; interdisciplinary
  teams 68–69; Latinas and 107–111;
  LGBT community and 111–113;
  neuropsychology and 33–44;
  pedagogy of 48–56; program
  evaluations 67–68; promoting
  dialogue 123–124; psychotherapist
  role in 3, 10–13; research in 58–69;
  scholarship on technology in 77;
  social change and 123–131; social
  justice 152; theory in 17–29;
  wisdom through diversity in
  105–117
*Art Therapy* 60
*Art Therapy: Journal of the American
  Art Therapy Association* 165
Art Therapy Alliance 61
Art Therapy Credentials Board 53, 55
*Art Therapy Heuristic Study in
  Collaboration With a Collective
  Project to Help Promote New
  Epistemology, Self-Awareness, and
  Enhance Cultural Humility in Art
  Therapy* 115
*Art Therapy Journal* 33
art therapy relational neuroscience
  (ATR-N) 34, 35
artwork as data 64–65
attachment theory 38

# 170  Index

Ault, Robert 6
authenticity 112
autism 60
avatars 76

Bacon, J. 112
beauty, perception of 7
Belkofer, C. M. 38, 42
biomarkers 65
blogs 79, 81
Bloom's Taxonomy of Learning 50, 55
brain measurements 39–40
Bruner, J. S. 49
Bucciarelli, A. 13
Budd, M. 8
Burnham, D. 9
Burns, Penny 143–146

Camus, A. 95
*Canadian Journal of Art Therapy* 60
Carlson, E. 108
Cartesian dualism 136
Cartesian methods of analysis 19
Chapman, L. 35
Chapman art therapy treatment
  intervention (CAATI) 36
Clinton, R. 86
collectivism 11
computed tomography (CT) 39–40
consciousness 26, 124
countertransference 155
craft 8
creative arts therapies (CATs) 65–66
creative embodiment, relational
  resonating, expressive
  communicating, adaptive
  responding, empathizing, and
  compassion (CREATE) 34
Csikszentmihalyi, M. 23–24
cultural competence 108; future vision
  incorporating cultural humility
  and 117
cultural humility: art therapy in
  practice and 106–107; future vision
  incorporating cultural competency
  and 117; new paradigms of
  thinking and 113–117; through art
  therapy lens 105–106
cultural sensitivity 115
cultural traits 117
culture and ethics 94–95

data, artwork as 64–65
Davis, D. E. 108

Defense Advanced Research Projects
  Agency (DARPA) 62
*Developing Cultural Humility* 115
Dewey, John 20–21, 22
diffusion tensor imaging (DTI) 40
digital media 74–77; computer
  applications and materials for
  78–81; integrations in art therapy
  85–87; mixed with tangible media
  as transcending media 75–76;
  varieties of 74; *video appropriation*
  81–83; virtual reality 83–85
digital social responsibility 79
Dissanayake, E. 6, 20, 24
diversity in art therapy 105–117;
  cultural humility and art therapy in
  practice and 106–107; and cultural
  humility through art therapy lens
  105–106; innovation in methods
  and 68; Latinas and 107–111;
  LGBT community and 111–113
Doctors without Borders 136
Dreikurs, R. 109
DuMontier, V. L. 111
Durkin, Jean 129

East Africa, creative arts therapy in
  143–146
education, art therapy 48–51; content
  in 53; future directions in 56; global
  136–137; professionals as lifelong
  learners and 55–56; students in
  54–55; teachers in 51–54
*Eight Steps of Women* 50
*El Duende* 162
electroencephalograms (EEG) 39
Ellilta International 147
Elo, M. 86
empathy 127
Engebretson, J. 108
Etherington-Reader, Arnell 149–151
ethics: of the artist 102; culture
  and 94–95; of evidence and art
  101–102; general ground 93–94;
  of materials 97–99; of place 96–97;
  social responsibility and 95–96;
  technology and 99–101
Ethiopia, art therapy in 146–149
evidence and art, ethics of 101–102
expressive therapies continuum (ETC)
  33–34, 36
externalized dialogue (ED) 38
eye movement desensitization and
  reprocessing (EMDR) 39

## Index   171

"Facing Homelessness" 130
fan labor 75
Fellmann, F. 20
feminist approaches 124–125
Fish, B. 158, 161
Five Standards of Effective
  Pedagogy 50
flow 23–24, 34
foundational pillars of art therapy
  3–13; artist 3, 6–10; healer 3, 4–6;
  psychotherapy 3, 10–13
Fregeau, Joelle 10
Freire, Paulo 52
Freud, Sigmund 9, 10, 12

Gagne, Robert 49
Gallardo, M. 115
Gantt, Linda 37, 41
Gee's Bend, Alabama 8
gemeinschaftsgefühl 126
Gerber, N. 49
Gestalt Institute 51
Global Alliance for Africa 143–146
global art therapy 134, 152–153; art
  therapy trainee voice in Nicaragua
  142–143; birthing process of art
  therapy into a culture 138–140;
  creative arts therapy doors into
  East Africa 143–146; development
  into a successful discipline
  134–137; education 136–137;
  entering the Third World with
  paint, paper, and brushes 140–142;
  in Ethiopia 146–149; living art
  in the UK 149–151; notes from
  the field 137–152; trainee voice
  in Nicaragua 142–143; various
  considerations on 151–152
graphic narrative (GN) 38
Greer, Mandy 8

Hagman, G. 28
Hamlin Fistula Hospital 146
Harel, D. 65
Hass-Cohen, N. 34, 35
healer role 3, 4–6
Hegel, Georg 7
Herring, M. P. 65
Hilgenheger, N. 48
Hill, Amy 142–143
Hinz, L. D. 34
historical perspective of theory in art
  therapy 17–20
Hogan, S. 124

holding and emergence, art as a form
  for 25–27
holism 19, 22–24
Holmes, J. 136
homeostasis 24–25
Hope Enterprises 146
HP Sprout 76–77
Human Connectome Project 42
human experience and art: and art as
  active, creative means of balance
  and experience 24; Dewey on
  20–21
Huss, E. 65
Husserl, Edmund 19

I Ching 4
impact factors 61
instinctual trauma response (ITR)
  37–38
integration phase in NDAT 37
intensive trauma therapy (ITT) 37
interdisciplinary teams 68–69
International Committee of the Red
  Cross 135
International Journal of Art
  Therapy 60
International Journal of Education
  and the Arts 60
intuition 21, 22

Jacobs, C. 136
Jones, Don 6
Joseph, Cliff 95
Journal of Allied Arts and
  Health 60
Journal of Clinical Art Therapy 60
Jung, Carl 9, 23, 27

Kagin, S. L. 34
Kaiser, D. H. 60
kaleidoscope curriculum 112–113
Kandel, Eric 9, 19, 21
Kant, Immanuel 7, 8, 9
Kapitan, Lynn 6
Kiehn, K. 165
Kielo, J. 156, 158
King, J. L. 43
Klimt, Gustov 9
Knill, P. 95
knowledge and new paradigms of
  thinking 113–117
Kokschka, Oskar 9
Kopp, S. B. 4
Kramer, E. 18, 24

## 172  Index

Langer, Susan 19, 21–22, 23, 49
LASALLE College 138–140
Latinas: empowered via art therapy
108–111; perspective 107–108;
stimulus art, and self-esteem 109;
traditional art making with 110
Lay, Ron 138–140
Leonard, Ashley 12
Levine, E. 95
Levine, S. 95
LGBT community: art therapy,
wellness and identity in 112;
multicultural assumptions regarding
111–112; research and 112–113
*Living Art Painting Process* 149
lobotomies 43
Lòpez, A. 86
Lusebrink, V. B. 33, 34, 36, 41
Lyonsmith, Angela 144

MacAdam, Toshiko Horiuchi 8
magnetic resonance imaging (MRI) 40
Mahoney, J. 108
Mann, S. 137
Martinez, J. 137
materials, ethics of 97–99
McCall, L. 125
McGilchrist, I. 23, 41
McNiff, S. 4
measurements, brain 39–40
Médicins Sans Frontières (MSF) 136
messthetics 125
Mezzera, Claudia 109, 146–149
Miller, A. 162
Miller, Gretchen 79
mind-body connectivity 34
Mizen, S. 136
Moniz, Egas 43
Montessori, Maria 53
Montilla, R. E. 108
Moon, Bruce 6
Moon, Catherine 6, 143–146
Morley, C. A. 65
MRI-spectroscopy (MRS) 40
Murray-Garcia, J. 106

National Endowment for the Arts 62
National Institutes of Health 62
National Institutes of Mental
Health 67
Naumburg, M. 18, 26
neurobiology and art, understanding
the landscape of 40–42

neurodevelopmental model of art
therapy (NDAT) 35–37
neuroscience/neuropsychology 13,
19, 33; artist-scientist researcher
in 42–44; measuring the brain and
39–40; models for healing trauma
35–39; models informed by art and
33–34
new media 64–66
Nicaragua, art therapy in 140–143
Nielsen 107
Nolan, E. 38, 42
nongovernmental organization
(NGOs) 141–142
Notre Dame de Namur University
(NDNU) 141–142

online-source video collage (OSVC)
81–83
outcome studies 65–66

Partridge, Erin 5, 76–77
pedagogy, art therapy *see* education,
art therapy
*Pedagogy of the Oppressed* 52
*Philosophy in a New Key* 19
Piaget, Jean 49
place, ethics of 96–97
Plato 54
Porges, S. W. 160
positron emission tomography
(PET) 40
Potash, J. 137
poverty and mental illness 127
problem phase in NDAT 36–37
program evaluations 67–68
psychotherapist role 3, 10–13
psychotherapy: role in art therapy 3,
10–13; "talking cure" in 18
Puetz, T. W. 65

quilting 8

rationality 22–23
reductionism 18–19
repurposing of art 161–164
research, art therapy: aligning
individual research interests with
research paradigms outside the
field 64; applications of cultural
humility principles in 115–116;
approaches to 59; current
dissemination options 60–61;

emergent funding opportunities for 62; emergent within-field researcher capacity 61; influences of other disciplines in 58–59; and the LGBT community 112–113; new areas of clinical practice and 62–64; new media, artwork and research tools in 64–66; objective measures including biomarkers 65; ongoing dissemination and education of peers 66–67; outcomes 65–66; preparing for the future of 62–67; preparing the next generation of professionals for 67–69; as a priority for the field 59–60; response art 157–158; today 58–61; trends in cultural humility 114–116

response art 155–157; challenges for the future and areas of needed inquiry 158–159; proposed models of art therapy group supervision and 159–167; related research on 157–158; repurposing art as reflection of the work of therapy and 161–164; supervisor doing their own art and 164–167; vulnerability in 160–161

Riegl, Alois 9
Roach, A. 137
Robb, M. 162
Roshi, Suzuki 52–53
Rubin, J. A. 18

Sandak, B. 65
Sanders, Gwen 11, 140–142, 158
Sarid, O. 65
Satterberg, Melissa 112, 113
Schiele, Egon 9
Schore, Allan 37, 41
scientific process 19
scientist researcher, artist as 42–44
Second Life 76
self-expression through art 11
self-identity exploration 115
self-phase in NDAT 36
self-reflection 28–29
sense-based data and experience 21–22
*Shutter to Think* 79
Siegel, Daniel 37
Singapore, art therapy in 138–140

single photon computed tomography (SPECT) 40
Sisters of Charity 147
Skinner, B. F. 51
Smith, Patti 12
Smith, R. L. 108
social change: art as means of promoting 129–131; art therapists as agents of 125–129; feminist approaches in 124–125; promoting dialogue and 123–124
social justice art therapy 152
social media 74, 78–79; photography-driven 81
social responsibility and ethics 95–96
Stafford, K. 26
Stolz, Linda 144
Sullivan, Judy 143–146
Sundararajan, L. 75
supervision, art therapy 155–157; challenges for the future and areas of needed inquiry 158–159; proposed models of group 159–167; related research on 157–158; and supervisors doing their own art and response art 164–167

"talking cure" 18
Tallis, R. 9
Talwar, S. 3, 9, 62, 124
tangible media 75–76
technology: ethics and 99–101; social change and 127–128
Teresa, Mother 147
Tervalon, M. 106
textile crafts 8
theory and art therapy 17, 29; Arnheim on 21; art as active, creative means of balance and experience and 24–25; art as a form for holding and emergence and 25–27; art facilitating self-reflection and 28–29; Dewey on 20–21; historical perspective on 17–20; key figures in 20–22; Langer on 21–22
therapeutic attunement 39
Tilt Brush software 83–85
Tinnin, L. 37
train the trainers model 145
Trampled Rose 146–147
transcending media 75–76
transcultural insight 95

174  *Index*

transformation phase in NDAT 37
trauma, models for healing 35–39, 41
Tripp, T. 39, 41

United Kingdom, art therapy in the 149–151
United States Census Bureau 108
universal survival archetypal imagery 109

Vaughn, F. 112
Veterans' Affairs Medical Center 12
*video appropriation* 81–83
Vienna School of Art History 9

Vienna School of Medicine 9
virtual communities 75
virtual reality 83–85
Viva-Nicaragua! 141–142
voluntourism 145
vulnerability, importance of 160–161
Vygotsky, L. 49

Wadeson, H. 18, 129
Wallace, N. 137
Walsh, R. 20
wellbeing 34
Westwood, Jill 151
Wright, Jane Corey 149

PGSTL 01/09/2018